The Making
of Second Life

The Making of
Second Life

NOTES FROM THE NEW WORLD

Wagner James Au

An Imprint of HarperCollinsPublishers

HarperCollins books may be purchased for educational, business, or sales promotional use. For information, please write: Special Markets Department, HarperCollins Publishers, 10 East 53rd Street, New York, NY 10022.

FIRST EDITION

Library of Congress Cataloging-in-Publication Data

Au, Wagner James.
   The Making of Second Life : notes from the new world /
      Wagner James Au. — 1st ed. p. cm.
   Includes index.
   ISBN: 978-0-06-135320-8
   1. Second Life (Game) 2. Shared virtual environments. I. Title
GV1469.25.S425A9 2008
794.8—dc22

                                                    2007028684

08 09 10 11 12 OV/RRD 10 9 8 7 6 5 4 3 2 1

For all those who strive for a life enriched by ideas and imagination—and all those who create the tools to make them real.

Contents

Preface

This is the epic story of an empire that exists inside a metal box.

It is not about a game, because while the inhabitants of this empire are playful, to be sure, they are citizens of this place for a wealth of reasons besides whimsy. (It's just that whimsy usually imbues everything they do.) It is not about a utopian escape, because while the empire is, on balance, a better place than the world that exists outside, the populace who came here brought their troubles with them.

It is not a story about computers or software programs defined by the torrential flickering of ones and zeroes. The world that comes into being through that process is, in every meaningful sense, a part of the one we already know. And even if you have no home inside it now, odds are that you eventually will. (Or at the very least, find yourself becoming an occasional visitor.) For that reason it is, above all, not a story about a fantasy world totally cut off from what we call real.

Those who've already made a place for themselves in this empire might prefer to forge on ahead to the first chapter. Those who haven't—who have heard only vague or half-formed rumors of Second Life—might prefer to stay awhile to get a better sense of what it is, and to find a reason for pressing on.

Second Life is an immersive, user-created online world. By explaining this sentence in full, the reasons for this book's existence will, I hope, become plain.

So:

By "world," I mean just that: a place with earth and sky, rivers and trees, deserts and meadows, with a sun that makes regular trips across the horizon, a moon that crests in its passing, and most of all the natural elements that quietly comprise a place: gravity and wind, and an ocean that responds to both. All of this, depicted on the computer monitor before you. There are people there, too. By and large, they refer to themselves in one of two ways: as Residents, a title the company that made the world gave them (not "subscribers" or "users," or similar commercial designations, for reasons we'll come to later). Or as avatars, a designation with a deeper history, taken from the Sanskrit word for "godly incarnation." The word has a contemporary history as well because it's the term used to describe the alter ego, person, or character you control when you're in an online game world.

Residents are avatars, but unlike their predecessors, they are avatars with differences that should become obvious in a moment. Avatars are controlled with a keyboard and mouse, as you would a character in most any computer game. Hit the right key, and your avatar lurches forward; tap another, and the avatar begins to fly, as if pulled by heavenly puppet strings. Like the world, the Residents within it are depicted on your computer with graphics resembling a movie animated with 3-D computer imagery.

By "online," we mean on the Internet—and more precisely, on

the quicksilver streams of broadband. To say "online" is also to imply community, in the sense of a group inhabiting the same place—and an awareness that they do, in some socially crucial way, share it.

"Immersive" is a more elusive term, but it roughly means this: Since the world of Second Life and the Residents in it are described by your computer in three-dimensional graphics, with mass, texture, and the dynamic interplay of light and shadow, and since the sounds within that world are stereophonic—when a Resident comes up behind you, you'll hear his muffled footsteps as if they were behind you—the experience is realistic enough to make you feel a sense of physical embodiment. This stems from a clever trick of the mind and its need to bring context to our perceptions. It seems related to the same phenomenon that makes us see distance and perspective within a painting or a moving image in a strip of film. To be immersed in an online world is to be helped into a similar illusion, but also to feel *enveloped* within it, as a bodily sensation. So if your computer depicts a roaring waterfall, and your avatar is inside it, you will, with enough concentration, feel the overhanging rock behind you, feel a sense of vertigo, even feel a chill from the thundering flume nearby. And if you run *through* that waterfall, your stomach will lurch in the moment you leap and see the sharp rocks rushing up at you from below.

This is a subjective sensation, of course, but recently, two scientists working separately reproduced variations of the phenomenon in controlled experiments. As reported in the August 2007 issue of *Science*, Henrik Ehrsson of the Karolinska Institute in Stockholm and Olaf Blanke of Geneva University Hospital depicted avatars on a virtual reality display. On the screen, these simulated persons had their backs turned to Ehrsson and Blanke's volunteers, who saw them as if they were looking over the avatars' shoulders. (As it happens, this is the default view for Second Life and most other worlds.) After focusing their attention on them awhile, Blanke's volunteers came to associate the avatar's physical location with their own. Ehrsson went a step farther, by pretending to swing a hammer at his avatar; when he did, his volunteers actually broke out in a sweat, as if they themselves were being attacked.

Finally, by "user-created," we mean that everything within Second Life is given form and substance by its Residents. And this is where the SL avatar is unique, for in most online worlds, reality is part and parcel a conception of the company that created it. The world is a theme park, and a tightly regulated one at that. The avatars inside it are called players, or subscribers, and they are there to enjoy it—but for the most part, only in company-approved ways.

The physical world of Second Life, by contrast, is a kind of 3-D palette for the avatars within it. Standing on a hill like a demi-urge, a Resident can wave her hand and cause the ground to swell, expand, or even collapse into the sea. Moving her palm above the ground, she can make wooden shapes emerge from thin air (there is a deep rumble as these objects take on substance), and once there, her hands can mold and transmute their shape, even their substance—stretching a cube into a flat sheet, twirling a sphere into a torus made of shimmering silver, and so on.

The technology that makes this possible will be explored later, but for now, the distinction you need to make is this: With a few early exceptions, everything described in this book, all the homes and vehicles and fashion and marvelous devices, are the creation of Residents. And when those objects have special attributes—when they interact with the environment, when they move through the air, or when they whirl off on their own as self-powered robots or clownfish schooling along the shore—these characteristics are also endowed by the Residents who gave them form, through a special programming language.

I need to unpack all these attributes, because when you are able to look at their discrete parts, you can see how they might merge with trends that are applicable to more than just this one place. While this story is mainly about Second Life, much of it will also apply to all the other online worlds spinning out there.

Which is fortunate, for in recent years, the cost of computers capable of running 3-D graphics has plummeted low enough to turn the medium into a mainstream activity. World of Warcraft, an online world from the Vivendi media conglomerate, has, as of this writing in mid-2007, some nine million subscribers around the globe—some 4.5 million in China alone. (It will likely be larger by the time you read these words.) To be in World of Warcraft is to share the same virtual space with thousands of people from more than a dozen countries living a lucid dream of adventure and hero-ism. But as the Chinese tally hints, Warcraft is only the most popu-lar online world that's also popular in the West. In Asia, a number of home-grown worlds claim several million more citizens.

Fantasy role-playing games like World of Warcraft and her Asian cousins are but the most recognized examples of a far larger phenomenon, for if you were to expand the definition of online worlds to include *any* simulated physical space that two or more Internet users can share, the census count would geometrically expand. You would have to include Web-based chat rooms such as CyWorld of South Korea, which has transformed the social net-working site into a simulated space. It now boasts fifteen million members—a breathtaking one in three of the entire South Korean population. The Swedish Habbo Hotel has eight million regular users; Club Penguin, recently bought by Disney, some five mil-lion avid members. All three of the above worlds, it should be noted, are dominated by teens and pre-adolescents. (Ninety per-cent of all South Koreans under thirty have a CyWorld account.) Joined to these in coming years will be a veritable galaxy of new worlds, and for this reason, some experts are even more bullish on the near future: In May 2007, for example, renowned technology analyst firm Gartner, Inc. projected that 80 percent of all active Internet users "would have a second life (though not necessarily a Second Life)" by 2011.

If we were to expand the definition of online worlds even further to include worlds that are simulations of abstract space, you would bring social networks like Facebook or YouTube and its many successors into this fold. (Some have observed, for all their apparent dissimilarity, that social networks are in essence fantasy role-playing games, in which individuals create a stylized and enhanced version of themselves on their pages, collecting friendships and other tokens of success as if they were gold coins and magical totems.)

At this point, you are describing at least 100 million people globally with some affiliation to an online world. There are many reasons that this book dwells on Second Life alone, but I suspect readers familiar with other worlds and systems will recognize patterns in the conflicts that emerge, the communities that form, and the identities that are chosen.

This is why, as I said at the start, this book isn't really about a fantasy world cut off from reality. Even so far along into the Internet age, some insist on making distinctions between the digital and the material, as if we were still able to cleanly demarcate the two, and this is a strange thing to do. Most of us get into passionate discussions in e-mail and blogs, outrageously flirt on instant messaging systems, share our personal photos on world-accessible Web sites, buy our consumer goods online, watch videos made on webcams by a thousand anonymous people, create an ideal image for ourselves on social networks, and conduct much of our work, recreation, and cultural engagement through the Internet, and even when we walk away from our desks, we maintain a tether to the world's datastream via cell phone—this, today, is what generally counts as living in the real world. No matter how cartoonish or gamelike they appear at a superficial glance, these virtual worlds are becoming just another Net-driven channel of experience and interactivity. And for many people, especially the young, they're becoming the most essential one.

And since it's a user-created world, the development of Second Life runs roughly parallel to what is happening now throughout the Internet at large. Sometimes known as the read-write Net, or Web 2.0, it broadly describes the software-driven tools for common users to create new content on the Internet, be that blogs and social network pages or sites that upload and display their videos and photos. As with social networks, the legacy media companies are still struggling to get a handle on the phenomenon—the paradox, really—of all this user-generated content, generally made without expectation of compensation and eagerly consumed by viewerships that rival their own. This, they fear, is the future, and they are right. And so they wonder whether they can co-opt or absorb these ecologies of grassroots creativity without losing their own rapacious character. (And they are wrong.)

But if assimilation isn't entirely possible, some kind of alliance may be. That's the détente companies have been trying to secure, in recent years—be it News Corp in its purchase of MySpace, Google in its acquisition of YouTube (and the buy-in by media conglomerates that will entail), or all the other partnerships that will probably reach fruition by the time you read this preface. Odds are that user-created virtual worlds like Second Life will soon be the targets of financial mergers (and again, as this book reaches press, you may have already read about such plans on business news sites).

But user-created communities are fragile, fractious, and capricious, prone to wither away if the wrong outside force intrudes—

or just as often, when a more attractive realm beckons. This is true of user-created social networks—by my count, at least four, Friendster, Orkut, MySpace, and Facebook, have temporarily dominated, then declined, after a mass exodus to the next promised land. This phenomenon is even more prevalent in online worlds, where there's a deeper sense of ownership and habitation. (And often, it's caused when influential individuals in the community decide that the holding company has broken the social contract that makes their place worthwhile.)

So this book is also meant as an allegorical reference guide to that tension between the democratic, grassroots Internet and the many industries struggling to understand it. At the same time, I want to write about how a world like Second Life is already transforming the industries with which it comes in contact. In essence, any real-world business or enterprise that can be enhanced or leveraged by a 3-D world has a future at stake here.

In a sense, this book is written by two authors. In the spring of 2003, Linden Lab, the creators of Second Life, offered me the oddest assignment in all my years as a freelance writer. Ordinarily, their world was the kind of thing I'd cover for magazines like *Wired* and *Salon*, in my passion to translate this new medium of gaming and online worlds for a mainstream audience. But during the software demonstration about which they had first meant for me to write, Linden vice president Robin Harper suggested something else. They didn't want me to write about their world so much as to write *within* it, as a journalist—an embedded journalist, as it were. (Since Kevlar-clad reporters were riding in the hulls of armored Humvees toward Baghdad at the time, it was a term that came quickly to mind.) Only in my case, I wouldn't be inserted with an invading army but on an expanding continent that was literally growing outward, extending its shores on a near-daily basis.

So Linden Lab contracted me to cover this place, my role a cross between historian, ethnographer, and sole reporter of a frontier-town newspaper. And in my capacity as "Hamlet Linden"—my alter ego's chosen name—I began reporting inside Second Life, for a blog I dubbed New World Notes. I created an avatar, a somewhat stylized variation of myself, dressed in a crisp white suit, in tribute to Tom Wolfe. In the combat-allowed war zones—and from the beginning, those were raging—I had an avatar made to look like Hunter S. Thompson, with aviator sunglasses, a Colt .45, and an open bottle of Jim Beam. With rare exceptions, the company left me free to report and generate stories on my own. At the same time, they fully intended my work as a kind of indirect marketing—for how else do you tell people about a service that is literally being created every moment of the day? But then, a funny thing occurred: The stories I wrote that had the most chaos and social upheaval had the most readers.

I left Linden in early 2006 to write this book but retained my Hamlet avatar, rechristened "Hamlet Au" (only company staff have the Linden surname), and continued the ground-level story of Second Life's continuing evolution as an independent writer.

So the first author observes Second Life from the inside and at its grassroots, as an avatar interviewing other avatars, chronicling their conflicts and aspirations in person, with reportage taken from copious instant messages and chat logs. Hamlet saw wars fought, saw marriages and betrayals, saw ancient evils revived in new forms, saw entrepreneurial tycoons arise from nothing to millionaire status. And saw himself, to his owner's surprise, get far more emotionally invested in the virtual than he'd ever planned.

The second author, less dreamlike and more sober, takes those avatar-based chronicles, illustrative vignettes primarily taken from New World Notes, and explains why they are meaningful to the wider world. This author will propose a road map of where the world is headed, as it becomes integral (in his humble opinion) to the Internet's future.

Looking back on my near five-year survey of the world, I see three essential elements to the Second Life experience, qualities that make the world unique, enable it to thrive, and will determine how it grows (or doesn't) in the next several years. As I'll try to delineate in the earliest chapters, which track the development of SL as a platform, these weren't consciously implemented by Linden Lab. Nor were they codified by the Residents, as will become evident in the later chapters, which track the often fractious evolution of SL as a culture. Rather, they emerged from the interplay between company and community, and over its history, have been quietly transcribed into the world's social DNA. I hope these concepts will become clearer through repeated illustration (and pay close attention, for they often come up in the most unlikely places). But to define them here in brief:

Bebop Reality: My term to describe a universe in which the fundamental laws of physics and identity are open to constant improvisation by its inhabitants, who instantly modify and embellish it to a positive effect without breaking the world's underlying structure. Think of Second Life Residents as members of a worldwide, wildly informal improv group, playing out thematic variations in 3-D; think of things like gravity and environment and other avatars as the underlying harmony, elements to riff on.

Impression Society: Societies are often defined by their most cherished or powerful principle; for this reason, we call one society materialistic, another hedonistic. Among Second Life citizenry, by contrast, any cultural, economic, or social contribution is judged and valued in direct proportion to its organic creative flair and sustained effect. By organic, I mean that it must be made from the internal content creation tools and be a grassroots effort by members of the community. (Established painters and photographers have uploaded their work into SL, but with few exceptions, these meet less acclaim than sculptures and other artwork built *within* Second Life.) "Impression" is meant in several senses of the word: as a deep and lasting impact, and as a heightened response to excellence, innovation, and to what is, for lack of a better word, cool.

Mirrored Flourishing: The belief that positive contributions to Second Life can and should have a positive impact on Residents in their real lives, and vice versa. This quickly became the underlying principle by which Linden Lab crafted its user policies and a fundamental expectation to which Residents would hold the company. It is also a recurring theme in the stories that SL users tell each other, a shared mythology that strengthens their bonds to the community and an anthem that inspires them to expand it. What constitutes "positive," of course, is often left to conflicting personal interpretation, and when the benefit is most dubious, controversy and strife often follow.

With these compass points laid down, here is the route to come:

The Introduction is a brief primer for those whose experience with online worlds is selective or nonexistent; it takes readers from online worlds' early days in the seventies to now, and explains how Second Life emerged in that evolution. (Longtime gamers may do fine to lightly glide over these pages.)

The following chapters, from "Touching Knowledge" through "The Unwisdom of Crowds," follow the creation of Second Life itself from its origins as a virtual reality test bed. Much of this plays out from a gods'-eye view—that is, from the perspective of Linden Lab developers who began forming, often with cumbersome, intrusive, or unexpectedly successful hands, a living world.

The next chapters, from "Self-Made Mankind" through "Burning Down the House," are largely told from Hamlet's point of view, based on first-hand accounts of the world inside, as a society emerges—fighting, loving, creating, and collaborating, and in that churn, developing rules and mores of its own. This is also where the people in Linden's world defy their creators, to demand a greater share of autonomy.

The remaining chapters, from "Avatar as Entrepreneur" through "Convergence," merge the pursuits within Second Life with the real world, as its inhabitants learn to turn their passions into commerce, culture, and practical applications with consequence in both realities. That final chapter speculates how the world will evolve in the next few years and decades, from the Net's next generation and beyond.

The Afterword contains the most recent updates to the world of Second Life, especially as its vision of a future Internet are matched by competing companies with worlds of their own. As you read it, bear in mind several months will have passed from its writing to its printing, and if it's true that the Internet develops at sonic speed, that is so far doubly, even triply true of Second Life.

Finally, the Glossary presents a compendium of otherwise obscure lingua franca that the inhabitants of this empire have

made their own, and a couple Appendixes offer pointers on what
to do next.

A full disclosure before going any further: I have no financial
stake in Linden Lab, and this book is tied to no contractual agreement with the company. At the end of our business relationship,
Linden transferred to me the intellectual property rights to all I
had written in New World Notes while on their payroll as a contractor, with no existing obligations. That said, my personal and
professional investment in Second Life is still considerable. Much
like many developers of the original Internet, who left government and academic posts to launch private ventures, my blog is a
kind of commercial spinoff of Linden Lab—one of many, for other
Linden staffers have moved on to start their own SL-based businesses. I sometimes consult with corporate and nonprofit groups
interested in creating a space in SL. (It was a surreal milestone
when I added, without irony, the title "Metaverse Consultant"
to my business card.) I remain friends with several staffers and
managers of Linden Lab, and in the time I spent with the company came to admire, and in the broadest sense support, their
ultimate aim—to create an immersive Internet in which all the
world's knowledge and perceptions will be embodied in a single,
unified reality all can share. As a technology writer, I see this as
an inevitability that transcends any one company, and in the end,
there is a high probability (and in my view, high desirability) that
no one corporation will own the 3-D Web.

A final qualifier: My observations of Linden's inner office work-
ings are based on interviews with staff and management (past and
present), and on scattered occasions, my own experience there as

a part-time contractor. As with my reporting in-world, my observations should not be construed as a definitive judgment of the
company's policies then or now, and instead be read as my own
personal interpretations, and mine alone.

To begin, however, we need to go back several decades, when
the metal box was accessible to only a few, and the empire inside
existed as merely lines of flickering words.

The Making
of Second Life

Introduction:
From Old World to New World

A Brief History of the Metaverse

He was tall, stern, and statesmanlike, and on September 2006, he strode with purpose through a cavernous auditorium. Then considered a leading candidate to be the next president of the United States, he was awaited by a capacity crowd of voters and members of the press. He waved and continued walking, and as he neared the stage, he vaulted thirty feet into the air, diving into his seat in a manner less suggestive of a politician than the hero of a kung fu film. And that's where he spoke on the most fractious issues of the day—Iraq, abortion rights, the war on terrorism—to a constituency that included a gnome wizard, a busty supermodel, and a cluster of sentient PVC pipes. (The latter was a sly joke at the expense of befuddled old Senator Ted Stevens, who memorably described the Internet as "a series of tubes." Avatar, in other words, as political satire.)

At the time, former Virginia governor Mark Warner was considered second only to Hillary Clinton as the most viable Democratic candidate for president in 2008. And to help boost his ascent to the

White House, he visited the online world of Second Life. When he subsequently dropped out of that race, some were inclined to dismiss the appearance as an ineffectual gimmick; only months later, however, Federal Judge Richard Posner of the U.S. Seventh Circuit took on avatar form, lecturing in a Roman coliseum to a crowd of avatars about law in the post–9/11 era, intellectual property, and the jurisprudence of online worlds. The monumentally influential jurist didn't consider his appearance a gimmick at all, but part of his research on the future of law: "MMORPG (if that's the correct acronym) are an enormously important development," he told an audience that included a six-foot raccoon and a woman with black angel wings. "[W]ith real money being invested in virtual worlds, there needs to be law-like rules to resolve disputes, protect property rights, enforce contracts, protect intellectual property and so forth."

In the several dozen weeks after this, more would follow these figures into Second Life, from a Democratic congressman, to several Dutch parliamentarians, to an official Swedish embassy and the sanctioned headquarters of France's two leading political parties (though their arrival, as I'll come to later on, would be marked by war).

Governor Warner's appearance signaled the moment when the term "avatar" entered the lexicon of contemporary American politics, as the latest lever of influence in Net-driven political campaigning. The 2004 election was fueled by blogs and meet-ups conceived and arranged on the Web; in the next election, some now thought, avatars might help drive a nominee's rise to power.

But the governor's virtual whistle stop was just one of many recent footnotes to a story that has been unfolding over the past thirty years. Months before Warner's arrival in Second Life, U.S. Homeland Security was already there, financing biochemical terrorist attack simulations; Harvard's Berkman Center was well ensconced, too, offering lectures on law and society to humans and flying robots alike; the venerable BBC was hosting live music concerts; NBC was launching their annual Christmas lighting ceremony virtually, while CBS was busy creating a metaverse version of *Star Trek*. Warner Brothers was promoting its latest artist with listening kiosks that resembled a New York loft; a research team from IBM was prototyping next-generation Internet technology; and Cisco, Dell, and Microsoft had virtual islands and schemes of their own.

Projects like these suggest milestones of a medium that has finally left most of its origins from computer gaming far behind, merging with everything else essential to modern life in the digital age.

This book is about that evolutionary leap, and what it means for our future.

Its particular ascent starts in 2002 or thereabouts, but the germination process began decades earlier, in the late seventies. And though it may seem strange to revisit these arcane beginnings, it's worth knowing the history in brief to roughly know how the medium began—and where, in retrospect, it has always been heading.

Even before the Internet's wide adoption, there were online virtual worlds, the simulation of a contiguous reality in which multiple users could interact at the same time. But with computing power so modest and graphics all but nonexistent, these worlds first evidenced as text churning across the blinking screen:

> *You are in a small cottage.*
> *There is an oak tree to the northwest.*

There is a stream to the west.
There is a road to the north.
There is pasture to the east.

... and so on. Purists argue this was the online world at its most ideal, fantastic realities evoked purely through imaginative words. At any rate, these worlds were known by the charming acronyms MUD and MUSH—the former, for Multi-User Dungeon; the latter, for Multi-User Shared Hallucination. Eventually, their successors would be integrated into the international, multibillion-dollar game industry, with several major media corporations holding stakes in the largest worlds, and finally would reach a point where potential U.S. presidents visited them. But throughout the late seventies and early eighties, they were largely the playthings of those with the means and wherewithal to access them on the university mainframes where they first existed. Obscure and occasionally secretive portals (often hidden away from frowning system administrators), they had quirky names like Avatar (1977), Moria (1978), and of course, MUD (1978), from two Essex University developers who coined the term for their game world.

The terse words and sparse graphics were more than enough to create a picture in your mind and give you enough context to interact within the place it described. And there was something more tangible going on, for if there were additional users in that same area of the world, you could chat and interact with them. Maybe they were actually sitting at another terminal across campus; maybe they were in a computer lab in another college. Or maybe—even back in the mid-eighties, when I myself discovered worlds like these, this struck me as extraordinary—they were on the other side of the planet.

Looking back, I see this as a realization that was also being made by thousands of other college students, especially programmers and computer users with a creative bent. Many of them would go on to code the backbone of the first Internet revolution or become Web developers who'd shape its appearance. More often then not, they were the people who made it possible for tens of millions others to move, by steady incremental steps, into the commercial Net's first generation. And while they did their daily work in Silicon Valley and other technology hubs, jury-rigging the Web in its awkward early years, they kept their citizenship in these virtual worlds—or at least retained a nostalgia for this other way of interacting online.

Because when you are in a virtual world engaging with someone else inside it, two realities exist in tandem. You are aware of your hands on the keyboard, the twinkling words and moving images on the screen; you are also aware that other avatars in the same space are puppeteered by other people. And you know that the people who control them have, more or less, a similar image on their own screens. This made it like an act of collectively experienced literature, or the freeform pretend games of childhood, conducted through code online. But it was a deeper kind of play because it was play that sometimes resembled culture, romance, commerce, and all the other aspects of our offline lives.

Early on, as their acronyms suggest, there was a fork in the development of the MUDs and the MUSHes. Broadly speaking, if you played in a multi-user dungeon, you were there to be in a world that resembled an abstract version of Tolkien's *Lord of the Rings*, as codified by the rules for Dungeons & Dragons (1974), the eternally geeky role-playing game that employed pointy metal figurines and ornately shaped dice. In a MUD, the world was static, for the most part, created by a team of volunteer developers who would painstakingly erect whole towns and monster-stocked caverns by entering line after line of text into the network database. (Sometimes players had the means to add castles and cities of their own, but most of them were there primarily to battle and explore.) In a MUSH, by contrast, players would pay more attention to their home (which they were constructing) and the city (which they were also building, with many others). It's why the MUSH was more likely to be the exploratory space of educators toying with the possibility of collaborative creation online. And since most of these MUSHes came without dungeons to explore for gold and glory, the emphasis was on building and socialization.

Habitat (1987), from LucasArts, was among the first commercial incarnations of online worlds, with players connected to each other by the smoke-signal slowness of dial-up modems. Under the guidance of Randy Farmer and Chip Morningstar, Habitat established much of the sociopolitical framework from which successive online worlds would draw. (Farmer and Morningstar once polled subscribers to find out whether they considered "killing" other avatars immoral, or just fun.) It wasn't even 3-D, and playing in it seemed more like participating in a low-budget cartoon; you communicated with other players (called avatars, the first known use of the term in this context) through dialog bubbles that popped up above your pixilated heads. Also worth noting is its provenance as a product from George Lucas's media conglomerate. In the mid-eighties, for-profit media corporations were already beginning to see virtual worlds as a revenue source with a potential mass market.

Running parallel to this technological evolution was a growing cultural awareness of the medium, evoked most vividly by Neal Stephenson's novel *Snow Crash* (1992). It had predecessors, of course, as virtual worlds (of a kind) made their way into William Gibson's "cyberpunk" novels of the eighties (most notably the now-classic *Neuromancer*) and Vernor Vinge's *True Names* (1981), among others. But it was *Snow Crash* that made a virtual world (there called the Metaverse) an accessible, fully formed concept to a wider readership, weaving into it the martial arts action and hacker sabotage that subsequently inspired the *Matrix* films. Stephenson also emphasized that this 3-D virtual world of cityscapes and foreboding neon bars, accessed through head-mounted high-resolution displays, was not just a fantasy world but also a portal for interacting within the Internet datascape itself. (In the novel, the hero meets a man who, though physically nonfunctional in real life, runs a successful business from *within* the Metaverse.)

At the same time, this vision of a future Net was converging with an intense (if blessedly brief) vogue for virtual reality and initial experimentation with headset monitors, force-feedback gloves, and treadmills that eventually would—it was claimed—become an entrance into a digital alternate world just as tangible and tactile as our own. (It's here, as well, that the term "immersive" enters the high-tech lexicon, as the standard by which to judge how realistically a virtual world could engage the user's senses.)

This became part of a grander techno-utopianism emanating from California visionaries like Howard Rheingold and John Perry Barlow, who often evoked, of all people, a Jesuit priest from the early twentieth century: Father Pierre Teilhard de Chardin, who foresaw a time when mass communication technology would yield a noosphere, an aggregate of all human intellect, united electronically into a global mind. It was Teilhard's vision of this world soul we were moving toward, these new utopians insisted (despite the bulky equipment, the blobby graphics, and the high cost required to achieve even those pokey results).

Practical shortcomings deflated the hype, and frankly, so did an underlying creepiness to the whole enterprise. Why exactly, many wondered, were these technologists so interested in cutting themselves off from the outside world? And when the mainstream media did turn its brief, easily distracted attention to virtual reality and virtual worlds, the immediate (often only) pressing question they had was, "Can people have sex in there?"

Undeterred by (and often unaware of) the failure of these theories to take on practical form, the computer and video game industry pressed on. Who had time to read some French priest when there were Orcs to kill?

Electronic Arts' Ultima Online (1997) was more graphically rich than anything that came before it, although it only had limited dimensionality, since you were looking at the world from a bird's-eye view. Your character had a recognizable form and personality (you could alter his clothes, size, hairstyle, and so on) and it seemed that you were floating about twenty feet above him, looking over his shoulder like a godlike puppeteer. Ultima Online also introduced to a large audience the concept of a virtual home you could own (or if you were lucky, a whole castle). For the most part, however, your main interest as a UO player was not in the markets or cities, but in the wilds. That's where Ultima's creators had put the dungeons with treasures to loot and beasts to slay, on a karmic treadmill of self-improvement. (The more monsters you slayed, the better you were able to slay other, larger monsters.)

Implementing the latest in 3-D graphics to put you even deeper into their world, Sony's Everquest (1999) was Ultima Online's undisputed successor. And it's around here that the painfully unwieldy term MMORPG, for massively multiplayer online role-playing game (or MMO for short) entered common usage, and inexplicably became the universal term for this new genre. MMOs are a subgenre of virtual worlds, however, and while most of these games clung closely to the sword-and-sorcery fantasy template of the MUD, at least two high-profile worlds in the mid-nineties revived the non-genre MUSH model: Active Worlds (1995) and There (1998), both of which allowed some limited user-created content. If the role-playing worlds were fixated on adventure and combat in the wilderness, these places were situated in civilized, habitable spaces suited for socialization—even if, in practice, that really just meant nightclubs and beach parties.

Around then, academia began to perceive MMOs as a petri dish for socioeconomic and legal analysis. This was fueled in large part by CSU-Fullerton professor Ed Castronova's 2001 paper "Virtual Worlds: A First-Hand Account of Market and Society on the Cyberian Frontier," an analysis of Everquest's economy, which famously placed the GDP of its internal currency and goods above those of Russia and Bulgaria. This was the genesis of a multidisciplinary field that brought together economists, law professors, sociologists, and other academics interested in a sustained analysis of virtual worlds.

As their popularity grew, so, too, did a concern that MMOs were causing negative social behavior. In a study by Stanford online world expert Nick Yee, 50 percent of his respondents described themselves as "addicted" to an MMORPG—that is, said it caused them to lose sleep, spend less time with offline loved ones, and so on. Many researchers attribute this to the goal-and-treadmill structure of traditional fantasy role-playing games, which generally require players to devote increasing amounts of time online accomplishing quests and improving their characters. As with any powerful, enveloping experience, this is a legitimate concern (the number of "Warcraft widow" support groups testifies to that), but Second Life's absence of a gamelike structure or time commitments seems to diminish this downside. In an extensive 2007 survey of several hundred SL users conducted by Global Market Insite, some negative consequences were evident, but significantly attenuated in comparison: Only 16 percent of respondents said they now spent less time with loved ones, while 14 percent of them said they got less exercise. On the ledger's other side, 13 percent reported now shopping less, while a notable 54 percent said that they watched less television. It's important to note personal risks like social detachment and sloth, but then, it's also worth acknowledging apparent, culturally positive effects, too, such as a lessening of consumerism or reliance on passive entertainment.

Ivory tower attention preceded commercial phenomenon by several years. For while the most successful Western MMOs up until 2004 counted subscribers by the hundreds of thousands; World of Warcraft was released that year and gained a million subscribers in its first few months, and in subsequent years grew to a global nation nine million strong. Successful against all previous expectations, WoW (as gamers affectionately acronymed it) near monopolized the fantasy MMO genre, with competitors struggling to hold even a sliver of that audience or ceding the field altogether. To grow that large meant the game had leapt demographic hurdles and cultural barriers, escaping its hard-core gamer niche to become a true mainstream phenomenon, not just a game; in view of how it was grossing about $75 million a month, it was almost a new industry in itself. Internet guru Joi Ito went even farther than that and described Warcraft as a model for *all* work done online by companies, by government agencies, and by any geographically far-flung organization. To prove his point, he'd log into WoW and demonstrate the multilayered complexity of running a high-stakes raid in a dangerous dungeon, a task that often required a hundred-plus players on several continents acting in tight coordination, overseen by a leader whose management interface looked less like a wizard's lab than a mission control command tower. Now investors and corporations otherwise uninterested in the game industry began to take notice. If it could be so successful in this form, how much larger could a world grow if it offered a place that would welcome everyone, including those not especially interested in being elves or gnomes?

It's in this period of heightened awareness that Second Life emerges. Seen from the vantage of thirty years—all the worlds made before its arrival, all the imagination and utopian rhetoric devoted to the concept, and all the tens of millions of people around the globe who embraced the medium—its appearance might seem inevitable. *Of course* someone would attempt to build a self-contained world and an international community and a platform that has become, in the twenty-first century's first decade, the best candidate to be a key feature in the Net's next generation.

But as it happens, making the metaverse wasn't exactly the goal of Second Life's creators, at least in the beginning. It emerged through accident and afterthought, and numerous decisions of blind faith and intellectual daring, many of which went disastrously wrong and most of which still seems, even in retrospect, like desperate improvisation. And as a wise woman once observed, Second Life is what happens when you're making other plans.

Chapter 1

Touching Knowledge

From Virtual Reality to Real Company

If Second Life becomes an integral part of the Internet's next evolutionary stage, it's still quite possible that few will remember Linden Lab, the company that nurtured it in the early years. (Ask people who came of age in the twenty-first century if they remember Netscape, creator of the first commercial Web browser; expect blank stares.)

Building the metaverse wasn't even the company's main goal when it began operations in 1999, in a warehouse on Linden Street, a narrow alley in San Francisco's Hayes Valley. Like many parts of the city during the Internet's first boom times, the street teetered between gentrification and drug-addled squalor. On one end of Linden were upscale restaurants serving the arrogant young mandarins of dot-com excess; on the other was an unattended parking lot with a clientele who often slept in their cars. Linden Lab's immediate neighbors were wholly appropriate for the world that would eventually emerge from their servers: a dubiously grungy auto body garage and a fetish boutique.

Into this unlikeliest of spaces came Philip Rosedale, clutching the keys to his shabby new office. He'd just left his position as chief technology officer of Real Networks—then the Net's audio streaming software of choice—and plowed a million dollars of his own money to build . . . well, at the start, that part wasn't exactly clear.

Born in 1968, Philip Rosedale is tall and lanky, with a triathlete's build and the cheeky, boyish good looks usually associated with Hollywood teen idols. (To rib him on that front, some of his waggish employees once cut out a photo of Rosedale from a magazine profile, glued it into a collage of teeny-bopper stars from the eighties, then tacked the mess to the bulletin board at the company's front entrance. For months afterward, visitors to Linden Lab would get their first glimpse of the CEO as a disembodied head floating amid a montage of Mark Hamill, Michael J. Fox, and Emilio Estevez.) Rosedale has light-colored eyes, and during his rhetorical crescendos (which are frequent), they go wide with a kind of wonder that gives anything he's saying an aura of the inevitable or the evangelical, or both. He is prone to flights of gratuitous cosmology, though it's clear he sees these as directly related to the day-to-day of running his company. Then again, it sometimes seems like conversational judo to dodge oncoming practical questions by flipping them into the stratosphere. (A Second Life subscriber once asked him where Linden Lab was going as a corporation, and Rosedale answered by first talking about the birth and expansion of the entire universe.) Whether it's everyday chat or a bout of ontology, however, Rosedale's honorific of choice is generally "dude."

He spent his earliest years in Maryland, the oldest son of a U.S. Navy carrier pilot who later retired to become an architect and an

English major who left her teaching position to raise Philip and his three siblings.

"For a little while, because there was no good public school," Rosedale recalls, "I went to a born-again Baptist school, no kidding, in trailers, in single-wides, in Hollywood, Maryland. And it was so interesting because they just . . . preached fire and brimstone, and it was crazy, and it scared the crap out of me."

For a time, it turned him into a pint-sized proselytizer. "So I would go around and ask people, 'Have you been born again?' So I think that actually helped me critically examine the world around me in a really profound way . . . I [later] realized, this is driven by people, this is not driven by some fundamental truth . . . But it left me with a kind of appreciation of deep thoughts and meaningful things. I just think I kind of had to take that and make my own some sense of it at some point."

Traditional religion discarded, something still kept him yearning to visualize the absolute.

"I can remember standing in the backyard near the woodpile," Rosedale recalls. "Looking into the woods, I can remember thinking, 'Why am I here, and how am I different from everybody else? What am I here to do? What is my purpose here?' But I don't think I thought it in a real religious sense . . . I always had this strong [sense of], 'I want to change the world somehow.'" Thinking back on it now, Rosedale wonders if this was the ultimate origin of Second Life, when he began feeling about for a goal that would match that insight.

His experiences with computing would turn that sense of wonder in a practical direction. As an early teen, he read about a single-cell simulation conceived by theoretician Stephen Wolfram, intended to demonstrate how complexity could emerge from nature if a cell reproduced through very simple rules. Rosedale got Wolfram's simulation working to his satisfaction in 1982 on an

Apple computer owned by his aunt and uncle in Santa Barbara. Starting with a single pixel, the Wolfram program quickly transformed the monitor into a starburst of activity.

"You can see the pattern evolving," Rosedale recounts, "so when you get something growing, it's like a little Christmas tree going down the screen. So I looked at that, and I [thought], 'Oh my god, you can simulate . . . anything.'" That intuition was enforced a couple of years later, when he and a friend tinkered with a Windows program that displayed Mandelbrot sets, mathematical constructs that seem, at a distance, to be a single crystal form but as you keep magnifying, reveal layers of thriving intricacy. Once again, he saw the richness and variety of life, simulated through an elegant flourish of code.

Unlike most computer programmers, whose creativity is entirely consumed by the digital, Rosedale maintained a loop into the real world; he had a yen to tinker and reshape it. As a kid he wanted his bedroom door to slide up and down, like in *Star Trek*, so he got out some tools and made it so. Which is why his parents came home one day to discover that he'd not only taken his door off its hinges but had gone up into the attic, cut a deep groove through the ceiling, and attached it to a pulley system, instead.

And though it seems inevitable that Philip Rosedale would, through his interests and aptitudes, originate Second Life, it was his college girlfriend Yvette who first brought *Snowcrash* and its notion of a 3-D Internet called the Metaverse to his attention. She bought the novel for his birthday in 1992, but as he tells it, what Yvette really did was link Stephenson's book to a half-formed vision Rosedale already had, even before being aware of it:

"I remember the idea of this sort of digital genesis . . . floating in the darkness like an avatar, and you had like a tool belt, and the tool belt allowed you to make things . . . shapes, and surfaces and stuff . . . and they'd show up near you and you'd stretch them and shape them and everything." These changes would happen dynamically, he decided, and from the start, he saw what would become Second Life, for it was implicitly a shared space—other people would be avatars like you, and they would see what you were doing and have the ability to modify or contribute to your work.

He would think about this vision often, while he programmed; his dream interface would be the human body. "How can I do this, how can I be in the machine?" he'd ask himself while he coded. "Not to be in the machine and play Doom, but be in the machine and build things." The hyperviolent first-person shooter is often (incorrectly) credited with being the first fully 3-D game, but the title actually belongs to Ultima Underworld (1992), a cerebral dungeon exploration adventure created a year before Doom by a Cambridge studio bristling with mad-scientist graduates from nearby MIT. In Underworld, you were placed in a vast cavern; you could look up and down, swim in streams, and fly. There were rudimentary lighting effects that furthered the illusion of distance and mystery, and the sense of being inside a living world. Rosedale estimates that he played Ultima Underworld for a hundred hours—another affirmation of the ideas he was already germinating.

After moving to San Francisco when Yvette, now his wife, took a job there, Philip's Internet tinkering led him and a college friend to create FreeVue, a compression software company that enabled computers to stream video on the slow dial-up connections of the time. It interested RealNetworks enough to make a purchase offer, which led to a phone call from a Real board member named Mitch Kapor. Founder of the Lotus Development Corporation and creator of the company's 1–2–3 business software, Kapor is often cited right after Steve Jobs and Bill Gates on the roster of those who led the personal computer revolution.

But as Kapor remembers their first conversation, Rosedale didn't even know who he was.

"Which," as he wryly puts it now, "was a little surprising."

Acquaintances made, RealNetworks CEO Rob Glaser bought himself the FreeVue software—and a new chief technology officer. Rosedale moved up to Seattle to work for the company through the mid-nineties and toward the millennium. But he always considered it a means to the end of building the visualized world he'd been picturing in his head for so many years. (After catching the first *Matrix* film with some RealNetworks colleagues, Rosedale left the theater glum, announcing to them, "But that's what *I* was gonna make!") As he remembers it, he was just waiting for broadband and 3-D graphic technology to catch up to his vision.

"We all imagined the Internet to be social and 3-D," Rosedale argues now; "it's just that the technology didn't allow it. We all fantasized about the information superhighway; we imagined ourselves driving down it in three dimensions—with other people next to us." It's just that the Internet back then wasn't fast enough to complete this transformation in a way that was technically feasible or collectively accessible. (Then again, the entire history of the computer reflects this desire to give binary data a metaphorical physical substance. Take computing's icon-driven interfaces, which depict programs and files as pictograms of office supplies and other real tools, or in a "desktop" operating system, or in "pages" and "sites" of the Web. Digital information makes sense to most of us only when it has a real-world analogue.)

After Rosedale left Real in 1999, Kapor briefly brought him on as an "entrepreneur-in-residence" with the venture firm Accel Partners, yet another company where Kapor was a board member. With Kapor's support, Rosedale pitched variations of his ideas there, but he couldn't get funding. This would become a recurring pattern in future years, with Rosedale describing the concept that would eventually be Second Life to investors and getting hard stares in reply.

Looking back on it now, Kapor holds no grudges. "Virtual reality was already an over-hyped area; there had been a number of unsuccessful efforts at it." At the same time, "multiplayer online games, which was the only other analogue, had also been unsuccessful for a lot of people . . . [investors] didn't see what it could become and the only thing that it looked like were other things that had failed and it felt very risky."

This left Kapor free to personally invest in Rosedale, joined in this by Jed Smith from Catamount, another venture firm. Together they planned a "long runway" of development, designed to keep the company operating over an extended stretch on a limited budget.

"We should be prepared for several years before anything happened in terms of revenue, much less profitability and in terms of recognition by the outside world," Kapor remembers thinking. "Sometimes companies starve for lack of money, but sometimes they choke to death from too much."

Toward early 2001, Linden Lab officially incorporated. In the warehouse, Rosedale and his tiny staff sat in a small circle and started a conversation that's usually asked a lot earlier than two years into a company's life: What, exactly, were they in business for?

They had a few options from which to choose. While running early trials of what would eventually become Second Life, they were also toying with "the Rig," a virtual reality/touch-activated hardware prototype, with the vague idea that the two technologies could somehow interact. For starters, as first Linden employee Andrew Meadows remembers it, the CEO suggested that Linden Lab could get into the fast-food business: "'We now have a company, what are we gonna make? We could outfit [the warehouse] to make a restaurant; we can sell hamburgers.'" Meadows thinks Rosedale wanted to challenge his employees to put aside everything they had been working on up until then so they could improvise a totally new direction.

The hamburger stand, however, was quickly tabled. The tiny Linden team also decided (albeit reluctantly, for some) to abandon the Rig so they could concentrate on this world they were making—even though it was, at that point, just an untrammeled ocean that moved between two servers. (In the beginning, all was without form and void.)

San Francisco during the dot-com boom was a place where capitalistic excess and idealism overlapped and merged and from up close, seemed indistinguishable. Which is probably why Rosedale attributes the last facet of inspiration for what became Second Life to what he saw in the middle of a Nevada wasteland. In 1999, he and Yvette went, along with thousands of hipsters from around the Bay Area and the world, on the annual pilgrimage to the heart of the Black Rock Desert—Burning Man, a freeform, quasi-gnostic art experience and improvisational community that reaches its apex over the Labor Day weekend, then disappears just as quickly until the next year.

Out there on a playa that was nothing but sand, wind, and the unforgiving sun, a community suddenly appeared, where high-tech millionaires mingled with impoverished bohemians and everyone in between. To Philip, it was markedly better than the society he'd left behind. At Burning Man, real-world commerce and brands are looked down upon, with all economic transactions conducted through barter. (Rosedale remembers a Burning Man massage parlor, where you got a back rub, but only after you yourself had given one.) They attended a rave with a live DJ, held in a thin Airstream trailer, with Burners crowded knee to knee in the narrow space, undulating from a seated position; they watched daredevils on a flying trapeze, cutting long shadows across the Black Rock expanse; they saw

towers and spires and onion-shaped domes that evoked architecture from across the planet. Walking through the desert,
they found themselves at the entrance of a hookah lounge made
of hundreds of Persian carpets.

"So you'd lay on the pillows," Rosedale recounts, eyes twinkling at the memory, "and you'd feel like an exotic Asian king,
and you're looking out on the parched [desert]; the line of sun
starts at the edge of the rugs, and you see that hot desert, and you
imagine you're Kublai Khan on a bender." It was illusion made
concrete, and it led to an insight.

"They were just structures of the mind," Rosedale recalls,
thinking about Burning Man. "It reinforced that idea that what
we believe in or what we make of things is all that is real. It was
unreal because everything was clearly made of found materials
and was transitory. But it was real, because when you were there,
it was real to you."

And in that perceptual shift, something shifted in him, too. "I
was just blown away by the fact that I was willing to talk to anyone. That it had this mystical quality that demolished the barriers
between people. And I thought about it . . . 'What magical quality
makes that happen?'" Though it wouldn't exactly fit in a business
plan, it was an intuition he'd pursue in building Second Life into
a full-fledged online world.

And to do that, he began assembling a staff ideally suited to
that task. Among the first hires were a sex educator, a rock star, a
medical doctor, a late-night talk show producer, and, of course, a
weapons expert trained to work on a nuclear submarine.

Chapter 2

Imagining the Net in 3-D

Shunting the Datastream into Rivers and Sky

Had you come across Second Life in 2005 or later, you might have assumed it was conceived from the start to leverage the latest in Net business trends. Described by Linden Lab as "a 3-D online world created and owned by its users," the wording evokes both the concept of user-created content so in vogue during the Web 2.0 era of the Internet industry and the enormous popularity of online games like Vivendi's World of Warcraft. With even more succinct shorthand, you might even cite the Metaverse of *Snowcrash*. (As you might have spied, even reading this far, Stephenson's world already has a synonymous relationship to Second Life.)

Second Life was originally developed, however, with none of these things exactly in mind.

Second Life the beginning, Second Life was a chaotic and unformed place, and like an ecosystem just taking shape on an early planet, it evolved more or less organically, in a haphazard way the original creators did not at all conceive. They were like the "clockmaker" God imagined by Enlightenment philosophers, albeit one whose fumbling hands often spewed springs and gears everywhere, and with the added qualification that their creation, so to speak, showed them the way.

"In the very beginning, he wanted to make an interesting organic space," Andrew Meadows remembers, describing Rosedale's earliest ideas for the world they intended to build. "So some of the inspiration wasn't so much the Metaverse as described by Stephenson [in *Snowcrash*]." At the time, Rosedale was more inspired by computer-generated imagery he saw at a 3-D graphics expo, which depicted lush, natural settings with so much realism, the pixels seemed vividly alive. To Rosedale, the next step was taking those settings from static images to a moving simulation. "It was now possible," as Meadows puts it, "to model a natural world that had bugs and flowers and trees that grew."

Rosedale saw this as an Eden that he and Linden Lab would shape, and only then allow users to interact in. "[Y]ou would wander around in it as an avatar," Rosedale recalls imagining, "and you'd come across animals—maybe they'd try to eat you or something—that no one had ever seen."

Cory Ondrejka, who would go on to become Linden's chief technology officer, had not even read *Snow Crash* when he joined the company after a typically circuitous route. A decade earlier, he was serving onboard the *USS Lafayette*, a nuclear submarine, during his stint as a student at Annapolis Naval Academy. Dark-haired, with chiseled, Slavic features that vaguely recall Sal Mineo, Ondrejka has a military officer's gravelly, sardonic wit, leavened by a geekish delight in pranks and systems gone awry. (In-world, his Second Life avatar of choice is the Flying Spaghetti Monster, which he created as a tribute to the popular Net satire of "intelligent design," so Ondrejka is apt to roam the world he helped build as a mass of airborne noodles.)

Working shifts of eighteen hours under the Atlantic at the close of the Cold War, Ondrejka trained to operate the *Lafayette*'s reactor core, and he credits that education to an ability to act decisively and to "[m]ake good estimates of what you don't know. Because in the military, one thing they try to beat out of you is guessing . . . if you guess, people die." After mustering out, he wound up at a division of Lockheed Martin in New Hampshire, working on still-classified systems in electronic warfare that remain in active use in Iraq and Afghanistan. But a high school friend was developing video games in California and remembered the amateur computer games Ondrejka made back then; he coaxed Ondrejka out to the West Coast to help program a motorcycle racing title and, later, Armageddon, a cult arcade spinoff of the Magic: The Gathering card games. Somewhere in there, another developer friend told Ondrejka about the strange San Francisco job interview from which he'd just returned.

"I met these guys," he told Cory, still dazed. "Either they're gonna take over the world or they're crazy. Go up and do an interview and find out whether they're crazy or not." After a bit of wheedling, Ondrejka set up an appointment with Linden Lab.

One six-hour interview later, he called his wife, Jennifer, and told her they had to relocate to the Bay Area. Ondrejka joined the company in November 2000, motivated by a desire to work with Rosedale, more than anything else.

"We were going to build this living, breathing world," as he remembers it, "very much not the Metaverse." He personally saw it as a platform to reinvigorate game development, wracked as it was by costs that were starting to approach movie budgets and the exhausting cycle of new consoles for which the games were being designed.

And so, from an original demo of a world that was just an expanse of ocean, Rosedale and his team began to create a fuller reality, with gravity and terrain and the beginnings of flora and fauna. Taking advantage of his education as an atmospheric physicist (Rosedale was a fellow student at the University of California San Diego), Andrew Meadows did a fluid simulation of the air.

In their first conversation after Linden Lab officially became a company, Rosedale and its sparse crew discussed what the world was for and why people would pay to be in it. Meadows imagined users lying on the virtual grass, looking up at the stars. It would be an accurate astronomical simulation, so they would be able to zoom their display upward, into the explosion of constellations, and see whole distinct galaxies. Ondrekja talked about robot wars, where users would create and program battle 'bots to bash each other, sending rivets and sprockets flying across the landscape. Continuing the video game theme, Meadows suggested a touch-sensitive treadmill system in an arcade so players could control a giant, rampaging monster; other players would log in from home, get in biplanes and tanks, and launch army-versus-Godzilla attacks.

All worthwhile ideas, perhaps. And had they pursued any of them, they would have wound up making a technology with little relation to what we now know as Second Life. In all their grand plans, no matter how disparate and half-formed, was a confidence borne from the Internet boom still rattling outside. "Everyone had this feeling that we're going to change the world," Meadows remembers, "even though we were a little tiny startup in a converted warehouse." And while that prediction might eventually pan out, several cycles of failure awaited them first.

What they initially built seems almost a mash-up of all the ideas that arose during that conversation. They called it Linden World, and it resembled the Book of Genesis turned into an action movie. It wasn't exactly the verdant, untrammeled paradise that Rosedale wanted, but a post-apocalyptic place strewn with

half-formed cities and bridges—which really only existed to be
blown up by the guns and grenades with which Ondrejka and
his team had given their robot avatars. (To terraform the land,
you'd toss your grenades at the appropriate place and carve up
the ground from the blast.) There was a modest ecosystem, but
even that had a certain toothy appeal: Snakelike creatures called
Ators roamed the surface, trying to eat geometrically shaped birds
(which, in turn, ate rocks), and if an Ator caught enough birds,
he'd give birth to more Ators.

Along with being armed, avatars in Linden World were able to
fly on their own power, just as they later would in Second Life.
Apart from the occasional superhero-themed game, this was a rare
ability to give an MMO user. In later years, many Residents would
describe the liberating, dreamlike sensation of being able to defy
gravity in Second Life, to skim the surface of the earth, or to
climb high, unfettered, into the stratosphere. None of this, as it
turns out, was part of the original intent.

"We didn't want to do the animations for climbing," explains
Meadows. "It was all [about] cutting corners, getting things up fast."

Linden World was different from other MMOs in another key
respect. As an alumnus of RealNetworks, Rosedale was an expert
of streaming, the just-in-time delivery of content through steady
bursts of data over the Internet—not a single download, in other
words, but a continuous flow of data. Rosedale's streamed world
did not require installing a library of sound and graphic files on
users' hard drives beforehand; instead, almost all the objects in
SL are streamed from their servers to each Resident's computer,
and displayed only as they are seen. When you arrive in a Second
Life forest, for example, only the trees directly in front of you are

fully visible, while those behind and to your sides remain a gray-
ish blur until you turn to look directly at them. (Rosedale's technology is a literal application of Berkley's famed "If a tree falls in
the forest and no one's around to see it . . ." paradox.)

As a practical matter, streaming meant Linden Lab could create
a program that required little memory to install—about 25 mega-
bytes, roughly the size of a Web browser. (For this reason, too, the
Lindens colloquially refer to their software as a "viewer," since it
was basically a 3-D browser.)

From the very beginning, Rosedale and his team architected
their world to be a single contiguous reality, shared by all its
users. This is another crucial distinction, because while they
boast a large total subscriber base, players of MMOs like World
of Warcraft do not actually share the same world. Instead, their
subscribers play on several thousand separate *copies* of the world,
segregated by individual servers, which are generally inhabited
by only a few thousand players each. (And for bandwidth con-
siderations, this segregation is usually geographic, with European
players relegated to EU-based servers, Asians to Asia-based servers, and so on.) This kind of online world is known in the game
industry as sharded.

By contrast and by design, the Lindens' world was a single network of servers, where each server represented a sixteen-acre
cube of "reality," with all servers geographically linked together
so avatars could seamlessly move from one region to another.
When the population grew, Rosedale's plan went, so would the
world, with new servers added on a regular basis to make room
for new immigrants.

At the beginning, the Linden team would control the servers,
but, Andrew Meadow recalls, "Even back then we had the idea
of having a very distributed world so people could run their own
servers." In that future, they imagined a continent or hemisphere

that the company controlled but was linked to third-party servers, islands and alternate empires of reality that their subscribers
could visit.

Linden's streaming architecture made another feature possible: dynamic, collaborative creation. This was a realization of
Rosedale's vision of an avatar in the darkness with a tool belt.
Onscreen, it's portrayed as a kind of magic: Your avatar stretches
out a hand, rays of light trail out of your fingertips, and a wooden
sphere, cube, or other basic building block (called a "prim," for
"primitive") emerges from the world with a rumble. You can then
stretch or reshape the prim, giving it different surface textures
(metal, stone, and so on) so it seems to change substance. You can
even enable its "physics"—a reasonable proximity of Newtonian
mechanics—and make it subject to gravity and inertia. Create
another prim, merge it into the first, and a complex object begins
to take shape. Meet a friend in-world, bestow building permissions to her, and now she can add to it, too.

But the ability to create wasn't originally the central focus
of Linden World; the developers were more interested in creating a game out of their destructive avatars and rock-eating
birds. That changed at an early Linden Lab board meeting with
Mitch Kapor and other investors. At that point, Kapor was
really investing in Rosedale the man, in hopes that something
marketable would emerge from what was still just so much
warehouse noodling.

As Rosedale and Cory Ondrejka spoke to their financial back-
ers, a projector displayed a live video feed of Linden World on the
wall. Other Linden staffers were in-world, running a demonstration that the investors could watch. A few of them were using
the building tools the staff used to create content. And as the
demonstration went on, the investors' eyes drifted away from the
meeting and toward the screen.

On it, one Linden staffer was building a giant, evil snowman, while another was busy creating a mass of little snowmen, gathered around their titan Frosty to worship him.

This, everyone realized, was what made their online world unique, not an artificial ecosystem or grenade-strewn destruction. In no other place was it possible to build and see the results instantaneously; to share the act of creation with others; to riff off their work, and make it larger than its individual components; to collectively create. *That* was the uniqueness that they had stumbled upon, without quite planning it; that was the key feature that would distinguish Second Life from everything else on the market.

This presentation has become a milestone in SL mythology, recounted time and again by those who were there. For this was the moment of Second Life's true birth. And only after it did Ondrejka begin to see a connection to what they were making and Stephenson's Metaverse.

"People are going to build human artifacts," he realized. "And if you're going to have human artifacts, you're going to need to have people . . . which means avatars." (And *human* avatars, not what they had then: bulky, flying robots called "Primitars.")

The natural world they had been making up until then fell into the background. The birds and snakes and Ators fell away, too, replaced by a conception of a world for people, created by people. (To this day, the company-made trees and foliage of Second Life remain lifeless, little more than static imagery.)

So in a very true sense, Second Life as we know it didn't exist until its original creators had explored it long enough to realize what its purpose was. As paradoxical as that may seem, the original world remained a shapeless void and thought experiment until the Linden staffers had played in it long enough to discern what it *wanted* to be.

This realization brought Rosedale back to his time in the Nevada desert and the thoughts about what made his experience there so essential and transformative: "The other thing about Burning Man, obviously, was that it was this huge playspace for making things. It's just this wonderland of creative projection. . . ." And now they had something like a virtual Burning Man, captured in the technology they had initially intended as a combat game or simulated environment. Now they had another model to draw from—albeit one more generally associated with naked people caked in sand.

Through this realization, Linden World also began to resemble something like a commercial product. "It shared similar characteristics with SimCity that I felt had made SimCity so successful," Robin Harper remembers thinking. As an advertising executive with Maxis, the game studio of revered designer Will Wright, Harper had helped launch numerous spinoffs of Maxis's enormously popular build-your-own-world Sim games. Now considering a similar role with Linden Lab, she discerned similar potential—"The ability to set your own goals, the creativity, the pride of building and ownership that came with being able to make something out of ownership." Harper went on to become the first female executive in a company then (and still) dominated by young men, a kind of hip aunt indulgently sitting amid a sea of programmer and developer dudes, scarcely flinching while they whooped at each other during impromptu multiplayer matches of Battlefield 2 over the local network or launched unprovoked desk-to-desk firefights with Nerf dart assault rifles.

Linden World was opened to a trickle of Beta users in March 2002; the first to register chose the dubious name "Steller Sunshine" for her avatar. As the Linden staff exited the warehouse office for the night, they left Steller alone to wander the world, which was still a scarcely developed countryside with a small, modern town the team had built as a content creation demo.

The next day, they got a chance to see what their first citizen had made.

"We came to work," Harper remembers, "and there on the top of a hill, she had built a cabin with smoke coming out of the chimney, and next to it, a beanstalk that grew right up into the clouds."

Somehow, overnight, Steller had created not just a thatched-roof home, but a narrative, and a game. The object, she announced in a sign she'd left at the beanstalk's base, was to get to the top— not by flying, but by hopping from leaf to leaf. At the top, Steller had created a Cloud 9, her miniature version of heaven for those with the patience and ability to make it there.

It was the first instance of user-created content in their system, and to Harper, it laid the theme of everything that would come after. "I think it set the tone of the way Second Life is now," as she puts it, "with the expected juxtapositioned with the unexpected."

This is what I mean by "Bebop Reality," riffing off the framework and rules of the existing world to create a new harmony of the strange and fantastic. The beanstalk exists to this day, an ancient artifact that has survived dozens of iterations (though it's much more difficult to find now, amid the skyscrapers and Egyptian pyramids and spaceports that have since sprouted up around it).

As it turns out, it was inevitable that someone like Steller would be there, too. A mother of four small children, the Southern Californian was already a veteran of other online worlds. "My quest really was to try *any*," as she puts it now, "especially if they had any mean of customizing your environment." A Web designer with 3-D graphic skills, she was looking for a creative outlet in between parenting. "I was zooming in and out of the Internet and 3-D worlds back then," she says, "really literally looking for the 'right place' before I found SL." In this, Steller was not unlike the majority of Second Life's early pioneers, a technically savvy creative class (often underemployed), searching for a place where they could share their inventiveness with others.

The next challenge was to make Linden World a commercially viable product, and much of that task went to Hunter Walk, a business developer who'd just left Mattel, and prior to that had been a production coordinator with the Conan O'Brien show. Walk became one of the few early staffers to leave Linden Lab of his own volition—to take a prominent position with Google. (Also among the early Linden staff: Aaron "Phoenix" Brashears, a burly programmer with a walrus mustache and a penchant for leather, who in his off hours worked the phone bank for the San Francisco Sex Educator Hotline; Ryan Downe, an elaborately tattooed musician with an acclaimed run as a pop star on Elton John's record label; and James Cook, a wry, button-down programmer with a medical degree, who often practiced medicine at a clinic over the weekend.)

The management was pretty sure they didn't want to launch as Linden World, and Walk's goal was to find a better name that also distinguished itself from the competition.

"A lot of the game worlds were verbs which described what you'd be doing," he recalls. "You know . . . ever-questing! Or place names—Ultima, but online!" Linden was working with a branding agency to create the world's eye-in-hand logo, but remained stymied on what to call the place. Ever the Californian fabulist, Rosedale wanted a name that suggested a mystical dreamworld— Sensarra, for example.

Walk balked. "Using the world was already so unapproachable and was gonna be for so long, why put up another barrier, a strange name that people didn't understand? And secondarily, because of everyone bringing their different idea to it, I wanted the name to be a vessel that people could fill themselves, that would be evocative of the *promise* of the world, and then put that responsibility upon the user to fill the promise. So I didn't want to describe what they would find when they got there. I wanted to describe what it could be to them."

After brainstorming on a fitness center treadmill, he had it, or something close enough.

"I came back the next day with 'Life Two,' thinking about the Milton Bradley game Game of Life," he says. "That evolved into Second Life." And that provoked immediate resistance from other staffers: "That's really easy for people to say, 'Ha ha, you need a second life because you don't have a first life,'" Walk recalls them arguing. (So far this prediction, it should be said, has proved utterly on target.)

Still, Walk held his ground. "I said, 'You know what, let's take those slings and arrows. It's such a strong notion, it's such an idea, *everybody* wants a second life.'" He pointed to the growing ubiquity of alternate identities and little personalized icons, in e-mail and instant messaging software, on pseudonymously authored blogs, seemingly everywhere on the Net. "You see more and more people with avatars and screen names," he told them. "I think if we hit our stride we can sell this. It won't be geeky. It'll be 'Of course, why *wouldn't* you want one?' Because it doesn't have to be better or worse, it doesn't mean your first one is lame or great, it just means it's different, and you can be somebody different, and do something different." (At the same time, the name also had enough metaphysical connotations to satisfy Rosedale.)

It also offered a second chance at virtual community—an ideal promulgated by tech visionary Howard Rheingold in the early nineties, but one that had waned in the crush of the Net's first commercial boom. Rheingold was brought in as an early consultant to Linden Lab and perceived its potential to build on themes he'd first identified.

As I later learned, Rheingold's insights indirectly led to *my* joining Linden Lab as a contractor for a time. "I think it may have been when Robin first visited me to demonstrate SL," he says. Rheingold mused that they should hire a chronicler as the world began, saying that "it seemed to me to be a great opportunity to document the social life of a community from the very first."

At the time, I was a regular freelancer for Salon.com, the San Francisco–based online magazine, and just beginning to cover user-created content, which was slowly reshaping the game industry. It had long been standard practice for game developers to give out the editing tools to their games so players could create their own custom-made additions to them. Fans could swap the add-ons and extra missions they'd made with each other, and doing this extended the titles' shelf life. This activity grew into a tight-knit community of fans, many of them talented enough to remake some games into a version that was even more popular than the professional one. From this creative ferment came Counter-Strike, a terrorists-versus-commandos action title that used a modified version of the popular Half-Life game from Vivendi. Counter-Strike, by contrast, was largely created by a college kid in his parents' basement. Despite or perhaps because of this, it was the most popular online multiplayer game for a nearly a decade.

"Modding" (as this activity was called) democratized the game industry, and that was exciting; still more exciting to me was how modding changed the dynamic between consumer and producer. In fact, it more than changed it; it potentially extinguished the distinction. Second Life seemed to me like the ultimate modder's playground, a world that was defined to be self-editable. So during my own first demo, when Robin Harper offered me the chance to report on what Second Life's users were creating, I gladly accepted.

I reported for work in April of 2003 with a double-click, and the sight of a green progress bar crawling across the screen as the Second Life world appeared on my monitor for the first time.

By then, there were some thousand Beta users, and despite such low numbers, it was a chaos of creation. It was ugly and random; even in its earliest days, it was fully suffering the tragedy of the commons.

It was also, in fitful starts, beautiful and extraordinary. It was impossible to define with traditional terms because identity and reality itself were fluid and random and changing at a whim, based on what the individual or the group decided at any given moment.

A typical example: Shortly after I joined as journalist, I was standing by a river when a UFO descended and hovered above me. The freakishly thin alien pilot yanked me off the ground with a blue tractor beam. More from obligation than anything else, his midget copilot threatened me with a giant anal probe, then escorted me to the holding pen, which I wound up sharing with a hippy in a tie-dyed T-shirt and a talking monkey in a *Star Wars* uniform. Engines humming, we skimmed through the atmosphere at high speed, after which the pilot handed us parachutes and the UFO simply winked out of existence, and so we went falling from thousands of feet up until our parachutes deployed and we plummeted into the ocean. Once there, the alien pilot returned to human form, created several display panels, and began showing us photos of the person behind the avatar, while we stood around at the bottom of the sea. Anxious for more action, the monkey donned Army fatigues and took an M-60 machine out of his inventory. Happy to oblige, the pilot pulled a World War II fighter plane out of his own inventory. And so we clambered onboard the P-40, took off from the ocean's floor, and went flying over a war zone; the monkey now perched on the wing screamed "DIEEEE!" while he strafed a well-armed babe in a bikini below.

As a first-hand experience, it felt like sharing a lucid dream with hundreds of people bouncing 3-D riffs off each other, a sporadic cascade of imagery taken from pop culture, history, and art, some stuff that you recognized and a lot more that seemed incomplete or evolving—themes you could pick up and embellish with your own creative power. This was Bebop Reality, instant improv in an infinite multi-partner jam session you could join at any time.

The question then, of course, was whether there were enough people out there who would pay to be part of it.

Chapter 3

The Engines of Creation

The Alchemy of User-Created Content

Today, the main entrance into Second Life is a lush courtyard with a fountain, and more often than not, the first view new Residents behold when they enter the world is the skyline of a futuristic city, looming just at the horizon.

Called Nexus Prime, it's among SL's oldest collaborative projects, and for that very reason, it has been an ever-changing metropolis. In the earliest months, it was a gleaming city of soaring, neon-trimmed spires; soon enough, however, it started to corrode from below, becoming a dark and decrepit red-light district hugging the ground, crusted with the docks and seedy bars of a dystopian future. That gave way after the builders made the earth swallow it up so Nexus could be reborn as a city built right into a wasteland network of craters and ravines. Shortly after that, the entire city was set up high on a giant metal plate, held aloft over the canyon by steel stilts the size of skyscrapers. Then it was retrofitted into an arcology, a sprawling, self-contained artificial habitat tethered to a mammoth space station high overhead. Then it became a *failed* arcology, testament to human folly and hubris. Still further metropolitan makeovers followed.

It's this constant flux that makes Nexus Prime so essential to understanding Second Life and its infinite narrative of creation and destruction. Casual visitors are prone to stumble past Nexus as they teleport to the world's shops and nightclubs; real-world marketers recently apprised of SL's potential advertising opportunities usually ignore Nexus altogether, eager as they are to make their way to the latest corporate-funded island. And while these are also critical aspects of the Second Life experience, Nexus Prime is a vivid glimpse into the world's soul, revealing how it came to be and what is required to keep it thriving. It's also a microcosm of Second Life's emergence as a user-created content platform, and consequently a microcosm for what has come to be known as Web 2.0.

Understand the disparate coalition of people who built this city and what they needed to make it grow, and you understand the social alchemy that makes any great Internet community flourish. Appropriately enough, it was made by people from a vast range of real-life backgrounds, among them a female pornographer, a physics student, a military police officer, a gas station attendant, and a young woman squatting in an abandoned apartment building occupied by drug addicts.

Nexus Prime was conceived during Second Life's Beta period, in early 2003, shortly after Linden Lab added a "Group" function to the software. Similar to a guild or clan in a traditional MMO, the Group feature made it possible for Residents to affiliate around a common interest and communicate with each other on a collective Instant Message channel. Among the first groups was Tyrell, a nod to the mysterious corporate manufacturer of "replicant" androids in the movie *Blade Runner*. So Second Life's first prominent group was attempting to give substance to alternate worlds that up until then had only been imagined in books and movies.

"I think most of us were sci-fi fans, [and] we saw what looked like the beginning of the metaverse," remembers Spider Mandala, now one of Tyrell's informal leaders. They thought of themselves as pioneers, and in Second Life's pre-commercial era of dodgy graphics and a minuscule user base, they perceived the glimmerings of the place described in *Snowcrash* ten years earlier. "We were taming the wild, wild Web," as Mandala puts it. "So I think a lot of the early founders and early Residents had that mentality . . . we were the eternal Beta testers tilling the virtual land for future Residents to come in."

Their offline reality, however, was quite different from the vision they had for themselves. At the time, Mandala was managing a gas station in the Midwest and floundering in college. Tyrell's leader (appointed after a coin toss) was a bald giant named BuhBuhCuh Fairchild, in real life a student who signed up for SL's Beta program after realizing he was about to fail a class in quantum mechanics (even though it was his last requirement for graduating college with a double major in art and physics). "At which point," Fairchild remembers, "I was unemployed, applying for jobs at fast-food places, and not getting them because I was overqualified . . . basically maxing out my credit, doing some temp work. Starving, not able to afford my apartment." The perfect person, in other words, to lead the pioneering effort.

The same might be said of the avatar known as Bel Muse, in real life a woman in Southern California who was making a good living in the genre that helped transform the Web—online pornography. "I'm really a marketer," she tells me now, "so I worked with free sites that showed a little flash to entice the surfer to one of my sponsors . . ." Muse worked from home, and because she'd been immersed in Internet porn for the last few years, she saw Second Life as a fun respite. (For a time, she brought her work with her, in the form of The Pleasure Cove, perhaps Second Life's first sex resort.) She was also a gamer and enjoyed playing Electronic Arts' Sims Online, but was struck by the cultural shift offered to her in this new world.

"The Sims Online was so restrictive," Muse remembers. "It treated us like slightly retarded lab rats . . . and SL treated every Resident like they were an artist." Linden Lab had just announced a contest offering free acreage to groups who could create and sustain a themed area, and Muse convinced the Tyrellians to apply. This gave them a large plot of land to build on.

Tyrell broke ground on a sim they dubbed Gibson, in honor of cyberpunk author William Gibson. In the eighties, Gibson had reimagined science fiction as a gritty, urban experience, where technology and the mean city worked together in new and often disturbing ways.

Around that time, the Tyrellians asked Catherine Omega to join them in building Nexus Prime. Omega's avatar, a punky brunette in a form-fitting body suit with a utility belt, evoked a streetwise heroine from Gibson's novels—and by sheer coincidence, so did her real life. Because shortly after joining the Second Life Beta program, Omega found herself without a permanent address in real life. "I was only out on the streets for a couple weeks," she told me casually when I first met her in-world, in 2003. "But it was a while before I had a real place."

In the interim, she did find shelter of a kind: a condemned apartment building in the worst part of Vancouver. "Not a crack den," she allows. "It was sadder than that. People go out, buy crack, smoke it by themselves." She squatted in a flat above a shuttered store, without running water or readily available electric current. Despite all that, she still managed to hack back into the world of Second Life.

"I had my laptop with me," Omega remembers, "and I was using it as a router." She used a soup can to catch a wireless Internet signal from nearby office buildings. "Boosting electricity was easy enough because I have my multimeter and I know enough to not touch live wires." She scrounged through the hollowed-out building she was living in until she could find a live wire to tap as her power source. Since her laptop was being repurposed to receive the wireless signal, she now had to acquire a computer to actually run Second Life. "It turns out that a computer capable of running Second Life is difficult to come by when you're homeless," she observes wryly. "It took me . . . like a week." She found a partially damaged one in a dumpster behind a computer store, replaced the fan, and got it working again. All this activity affirmed her skills as a hacker—while distracting her from the desperate place in which she'd found herself.

Among all the Tyrellians I've talked to, none remembers exactly how Nexus Prime took shape, and all of them are generally hazy about who worked on what aspect of it.

"The city was built so that everything was modifiable by anyone else building," Spider Mandala recalls. "So we'd build one thing only to discover that the next day it had moved ten meters over, or shrunk in size, or someone else had moved an interior into it. The process was very organic, crystalline. The concept being cities do not grow according to some rigid structure and order. They're almost alive. We wanted to try to do the same." As a construction process, it was what Tyrellian and architecture student Nada Epoch would describe as "a 3-D wiki," similar to a group-editable Web site like Wikipedia, with all its strengths (self-correction, dynamism) and weaknesses (inconsistency, confusion).

And so Nexus Prime started rising up from the ground, with airborne Tyrellians skimming and zipping over their towers, their domed buildings, their complex network of tunnels beneath the surface, and their cantilevered walkways crisscrossing between them, so high they cut through the clouds. Since they agreed that building rights would apply equally to everyone in the group, any Tyrellian could alter any other Tyrellian's work. They would work together on separate parts of the city in small groups, or sometimes alone, until their individual pieces met; at that point, they'd improvise ways to mesh the parts together. The creation was a jam session in three dimensions, jazz riffs conducted with steel girders, planes of pavements, and sheets of glass—all made possible by the fluid nature of Second Life's Bebop Reality.

In Nexus Prime, those who were most inspired and driven would have the most impact on the whole. "[I]t evolves from who has time to work on it," as Buhbuhcuh Fairchild describes it. "So the more time you give it, the more it becomes your own."

While their work may seem inconsequential fun, their free-form collaboration actually resembles the activity that makes the Internet itself possible. Consider the informal open-source community of programmers who constantly improve the operating systems that power most of the Net's servers, not usually for any monetary reward but for the fun and personal satisfaction of improving the whole with elegant valuable bloc of code they can call their own.

That said, it is difficult to describe the mercurial nature of collaborative projects in Second Life, for they involve a group of individuals working together on an installation that exists only as a digital image streamed across the Internet. Oftentimes, collaborators do not even know each other's real names, nor any personal details beyond the objects and scripts produced by their avatars. Still, the best of them manage to work. I've watched astounding projects emerge from nothing—cityscapes and winter castles, surreal sculptures out in the empty desert—created over the course of weeks or months with a professionalism that would rival the output of seasoned graphic artists.

Most of these projects, however, fall short—after all, any volunteer can abandon the team by just powering off his computer, without suffering any blow to his real-life reputation—except for creating a social bond between avatars. And almost invariably at the heart of the collaborative process is a strong avatar with wit and galvanizing energy, keeping up the team's cohesion and morale. Often (almost always, it seems) that central figure is a woman, a Bel Muse surrounded by young men eager to impress with their creativity.

This is not to say that task is an easy one. "It was difficult balancing so many strong personalities," she tells me, unburdening herself now in a torrent of words across my screen. "Responding to drama, trying to find compromises when no one wanted to compromise, having to deal with the result of the compromises wherein everyone was unhappy and feeling cheated . . . at one point I was just logging in to be available for people to bitch at."

In the end, as she puts it, "There was to my point of view no real distinction between feelings, ego, and prims. If they involved people's work, they involved them personally." For many of the creators, it was their first chance to give their unique talents a wider audience; for many more, it was a creative escape from a real life that was unimaginably hard, or stifling. So it's not hard to understand how protective they could be. Or for that matter, how aggravating.

Despite all this, Bel Muse's bond to the group and the project kept her in Nexus Prime. And as her friends in Tyrell got to know her better, they learned that despite her California blonde girl avatar, she is African-American in real life.

"The thing is," she told me once, "if people ask me straight out, I always tell the truth. But most people never ask." Most of her compatriots absorbed the information without shock, though she suspects it heightened their awareness. "[W]hen my friends do know . . . they become a little more sensitive, aware that I might view some things differently." Leading a large group as an avatar was the first time she didn't have to preempt the prejudices an educated black woman is usually accustomed to encountering.

In the real world, as Muse puts it, "I have to prove myself. I have to make a good impression right away—I have to come off nice and articulate, right away. In Second Life, I didn't have to. Because for once, I can pass. I can't pass in real life."

So the city kept growing and changing, taking on new textures and shapes, and in the process, it took on a narrative of its own. In its first era, it resembled a prototypical city of the future; in its second, it took on the more corroded, polluted aspects of cyberpunk; in its third and fourth eras, it became a city seemingly struggling to survive some recent ecological apocalypse. This didn't stem from an explicit story they'd written, but it was more than enough to evoke one. And without Tyrell Corporation ever planning it, other groups of Second Life Residents began role-playing within the city, acting as if they were part of a future the Tyrellians had created on the fly. They began creating detailed story lines and characters about Nexus Prime, a kind of cyberpunk improv theater that wove the architecture into the plot.

This is emergence within emergence. SL is open-ended enough that whole communities and creative projects will, unplanned, come together, then inspire entirely new groups to branch off from their activity. This is the alchemy of Second Life as an Impression Society: One positive contribution leads to another; one form of quality content (urban architecture) attracts another, entirely different variety of quality content (dynamic role-play), to build on it.

As Spider Mandala puts it, "People get interested in something so they get involved, they promote and propel the thing forward and forge a community around it."

Though Linden Lab had originally donated the land, Tyrell eventually had to cover the land's usage fees; a couple of members now pay for it through anonymous donations. And as Tyrell's members became more successful and moved on to separate projects, Nexus Prime became a memorial to what they had built together, a prototype of collaborative creation at its earliest and purest.

By mid-2006 or so, the city's evolution had slowed to a crawl. Most of the Tyrell group were now too overwhelmed with professional Second Life contracts to keep Nexus growing. At one point, nearly a third of the Tyrell Corporation had been hired away by Linden Lab as developers and community managers. And as real-world businesses began entering Second Life (something we'll look at down the way), they went searching for seasoned content creators to make their own headquarters. Often, that meant hiring someone from Tyrell.

"Most of Tyrell is involved in professional development in some way," Spider Mandala notes, and he includes himself: The former gas station attendant became a full-time developer with The Electric Sheep Company, one of the first metaverse marketers, creating virtual-world locations for clients like NBC, Reuters, and Nissan. In this way, Spider and his peers were following in a tradition established by the developers of what he calls "the flat Web." In the early to mid-nineties, the Web was the province of geeky artists and hard-core techies, but the Net's first economic boom transformed these early adopters into successful Web developers with Fortune 500 companies on their client roster. Such was the case with Tyrell, only now in 3-D. And the Tyrell Corporation, a fictional company taken from *Blade Runner*, has become a real brand in Second Life. (In a way, it's the Parc Xerox of SL, the noncommercial arm of a for-profit company, with few products to their name but a deeply respected reputation.)

"I had ideals that we were going to forge the free idealistic Utopia," muses Mandala, thinking back to the days when Nexus Prime was a labor of love instead of the massive portfolio sample it has inadvertently become. "But . . . money makes things happen; it's in some ways an undesirable reality, but the benefit it has had to SL is immeasurable."

As for Catherine Omega, government assistance helped get her out of the condemned apartment, but it was her renown at programming in Second Life that brought her an income in subsequent years. Through 2004 and 2005, she made a decent living from her in-world contract work, hired by Residents eager to put the legendary avatar on their payroll. Toward the end of 2006, Omega became the full-time Second Life coordinator for a Vancouver Web developer, a high school dropout now working with a staff largely comprised of Ivy League alumni. Her business card lists both her real name, Catherine Winters, and the avatar name by which far more people know her. She lives in a better place, in an apartment far from the addict-infested drug haven where she first began her own second life.

"It's in a good part of town, with fun shopping nearby, and

I know my neighbors. It's pretty tiny," Omega allows, "but it's clean and all mine."

This is what I mean by Mirrored Flourishing, where an avatar's valuable contributions in-world lead directly to the betterment of his or her real life, as well. A gas station attendant is now a well-paid software developer; a talented black woman is able to exercise her leadership abilities without having to scale the unnecessary hurdle of prejudicial assumption; a bright young hacker who began in a place without running water but an abundance of drug-addled neighbors is now sought after by businesses who otherwise would not even consider her as an employment prospect.

As I'll come to later, real-world corporate sites in Second Life are mostly empty, and except for a jolt of visitors during special events, lie dormant. Time and again, it is instead the new Nexus Primes that attract the populace—cities with names like Midian, Kowloon, and Lost Angels. Were you to look for activity on most given nights, you'd rarely find it in places sponsored by real-world companies (many of them built, ironically enough, by Tyrell members). Instead, after the free money sites and nightclubs, the places that teem with constant activity are the sandboxes (where anyone can build without having to own land) and imaginary cities of the future and the past, usually built—like Nexus Prime—with love or little immediate concern for monetary reward by informal teams of creators as equally diverse as Tyrell. It may be culturally impossible for corporations to imbue that same kind of devotion in their own Second Life sites, but without at least trying to evoke it, their efforts are mostly destined to be sterile and unrewarding.

In its most recent incarnation, a visitor will find a Nexus Prime that seems like a summation of all that it has been up until now.

There are still the clean streets and gleaming spires of the future, but that's only on the surface. Slip through the cracks of the sterile walkways and you'll fall hundreds of feet to discover that this utopia has been built literally atop the ruins of an abandoned city of discarded cranes and warehouses. This is the locus for Residents who now make the city their virtual home, self-designated citizens in an unfolding cyberpunk story they created for themselves on top of what Tyrell Corporation had improvised. So even after most of Tyrell's members have gone on to make Second Life their career, these subterranean denizens keep the city thriving, and vital.

"Nexus Prime has been there from the beginning," says Tyrell officer Spider Mandala, "and I deeply suspect it will be there until the very end."

Chapter 4

The Unwisdom of Crowds

Object Lessons in Online-World Social Engineering

As Second Life crept toward its commercial release, Philip Rosedale, Cory Ondrejka, and Hunter Walk met constantly to design
its social systems. Attracted by Mitch Kapor's reputation, high-
tech luminaries stopped by to check on their progress. "I think
sometimes they just wanted to see if we could pull it off," Walk
muses, "whether we were crazy or not."

"People were so skeptical," Kapor recalls now. "Outside the
team, nobody thought this was going to work." He'd sit with
Philip at venture capitalist pitches and endure the salvos that
would get thrown back at them: "'It's [just] a game, the graphics
aren't good, users won't create content, the technology isn't going
to work, Philip can't run a company.'"

Still, he insists, "You got immune to it after awhile. We took
delight in overcoming these successive waves of skepticism on a
larger and larger scale." Kapor says his prior experience helping
launch the home computer revolution inured him. "I just find this

endlessly amusing," he says, "because this is about the fourth or fifth time I've seen this movie. People said the same thing about the personal computer back in 1978. If you updated people's hair-dos, you could shoot the same script."

Still, it's easy to understand the skepticism. The Linden team had tied their business model to user-generated content and, Walk remembers, potential investors were fixated on the idea that "[c]reativity was supposed to be a dark art that only Spielberg and Lucas could do."

Walk tried to tackle that skepticism by Socratic analogy: If you bought a Monet and your child gave you a finger painting, which one would you show off in your house? You'd display both, clearly; it's just that you would frame the Monet in the living room, where guests could enjoy it, and you'd put the finger paint-ing on the refrigerator, where the family could see it.

"They matter because of what they represent," Walk would argue, because of "the memories they provoke, who created them. And I felt like SL was going to be like that, a lot of mixture of Monets and kids' finger paintings."

This also happens to be the conceptual shift required to under-stand Web 2.0: For traditional passive media like film and televi-sion to work, the majority of content must appeal to a majority of the customers. But for a user-created medium like Second Life to work (or for that matter, social networks or video sharing sites), it's perfectly feasible that a majority of the particular content appeal to just a minority of the customers. What mattered was that you had a large bloc of creators making content for an even larger audience of consumers, many of whom were content cre-ators themselves.

"But," Walk notes, "it's hard to raise ten million dollars on that."

If this book were a traditional high-tech success story, this negative assessment would inevitably lead to the triumphal moment where the market refutes the skeptics and validates the creators as visionaries who saw farther, and were right all along.

But that's the long view, not yet decided. What's striking, when one goes back and looks at all the social engineering they tried in order to nurture creativity, is how utterly disastrous or wrong-headed most of them were. And no matter how utopian or idealistic the intents, these designs led to unforeseen negative consequences. At every turn, the company ran up against the dogged insistence of the Residents to make their own sense of the world, no matter how its actual owners coaxed and cajoled them.

But here is the paradox: It's difficult to see how Second Life could have succeeded to the extent it has without this litany of failures happening first.

The Prisoner's Dragon

While the world would be a place equally suited for finger paintings and Monets, the Linden staff believed its sustainability depended on users who created truly engaging content, experiences and events to which large audiences would regularly return. They wanted to build internal reward systems that would foster this level of excellence, but had little direct precedent from which to draw. Until then, most online worlds were fantasy-based and pre-made by the company's designers. (The ascendance of Facebook, YouTube, and other successful user-created networks were still half a decade away.) This meant Linden Lab had to start by sketching out a totally new social ecosystem that would make its vision thrive.

Second Life's civilization began, in other words, on whiteboards.

Ondrejka and many of his programmers came from the game industry, and they brought their experience with them. (MMOs and other online games had been building game-play that encouraged social interaction and other positive user behavior for years.) They also looked to the reputation systems of Web sites like eBay, where trustworthy buyers and sellers are literally rewarded with gold stars. But then, these were at best imperfect inspirations. In the end, a lot of their systems depended on intuitions applied to a medium that had never before quite existed in the form they imagined.

As Walk puts it, "[W]e just tried to do what felt right."

Although they had few precedents to aid their understanding of what worked, they did have a couple of examples of what didn't. A Silicon Valley startup called Makena Technologies had recently developed There, a sunny, cartoonlike non-genre virtual world. It came with limited building tools, but Makena required users to submit their designs for advance approval. Electronic Arts' widely anticipated Sims Online promised tools for user-created content—in an interview, auteur game designer Will Wright promised those to me personally—but when it finally reached the shelves, its user creation features had mysteriously been drastically scaled back.

None of this went unnoticed at Linden Lab. These companies were imposing artificial filters on their subscribers' abilities, which slowed or halted any kind of evolutionary cycle in content quality. Despite Wright's stellar reputation (and a cover story in *Newsweek*), Sims Online never quite reached 100,000 subscribers before waning. Their active user numbers remain unpublished at press time, but it's fair to say they haven't achieved anything like Second Life's active user base.

In any case, Rosedale and his team had an approach that went far beyond the precedents of game design. They characterized the challenge in Darwinian terms.

"We figured if this was going to be like the world, we needed to speed up the evolutionary cycle," says Walk. And somehow, they had to compress two million years of human evolution into about five.

"[I]f you have a genetic mutation that is better suited to the environment," Walk explains, "it'll replicate really quickly." That which didn't, simply disappeared. This was the mindset that shaped the systems they designed—not just tools for user-created content, but tools for other users to punish and reward that content.

When we think of social engineering in the real-world sense, we imagine government regulations or other explicit codes that prohibit or encourage behavior. But those deal in the realm of the possible. Linden Lab's challenge was to begin this social architecture from the very beginning, almost at an ontological level, with every early decision fraught with consequences.

Take avatars, the alter egos Residents choose to represent them. In classic fantasy MMOs, avatar choices are generally constrained to a narrow, Tolkienesque spectrum of elves, Halflings, and so on. But what if you were starting with the premise of an open-ended existence?

"Second Life is supposed to be about limitless opportunity," Walk remembers them thinking, "but you can't be a 10,000-foot dragon. We stood back and we said, 'Wow, this is Prisoner's Dilemma.' Like the first time somebody wants to be a 150-foot giant, then *everybody*'s going to want to be a 150-foot giant, so all of a sudden you're in this out-of-whack world."

After some deliberation, they confined avatar choices to humanoid and gendered, with size limits within a realistic scale. Instead of giving users an automatic, pre-made option to go beyond those confines, they created "attachment points" on every conceivable joint of the avatar body. If Residents wanted to be taller than the eight-foot maximum height, they'd have to create leg-shaped stilts and attach them to the bottom of their feet; if they yearned to be a multi-limbed alien, they'd need to create and attach those additional arms themselves.

In this way, limitations inspired creativity from the very starting point, in the choice of what a Resident would be. But if it was an inspirational restriction, it also enforced a common identity.

"I always liked the idea that if you saw somebody," as Walk puts it, "and they were an eight-foot Gundam robot, you knew that was a costume, and inside there was someone who looked just like you." Indeed, players in traditional MMOs often experience a kind of role-playing racism. (People who choose to play Orcs often refuse to socialize with Elves, for example.) By contrast, the Linden team coded everyone who joined Second Life with the same DNA, so to speak (no matter how strange and diverse each of them eventually became).

"You need limits to push against," went their reasoning, as Walk remembers it. "We wanted to figure out, 'What are the systems of scarcity that would help direct people's activity?'"

This is the paradox underlying the world's premise: If the Residents and their creativity were to flourish in what was explicitly designated as an open-ended universe, the company actually had to impose limits and restrictions on them from the beginning.

The Freedom of Self-Limitation

At the same time, many restrictions were self-imposed by the Residents themselves. As mentioned before, the ability of avatars to fly in Second Life actually began as a quick work-around, so the developers wouldn't have to devote time and resources to creating climbing animations. When it came to transitioning from Linden World to Second Life, the team opted to discard the jetpack propulsion but retain flying. For Rosedale, Walk recalls, the power to transcend gravity was "innately, strongly interesting to people," especially when it did not come from an external mechanical function but was a graceful, effortless ability that came from within.

But if flying is a universal dream, few Residents have embraced it in full. Where one might expect airborne societies of people frolicking in the clouds, the overwhelming majority of Residents insist on remaining earthbound for most of their time. When SL launched, Walk watched, perplexed, as the early users steadfastly kept themselves on the ground.

"They immediately started building—homes!" And not even fantastic, otherworldly homes, but realistic houses for the most part, fully appointed McMansions with utilities of no conceivable necessity. ("Why would you build *bathrooms and dining rooms?*") But that kind of artificial realism was the preference of the majority (and still is).

Given the chance to fly, Residents instead built homes that assumed gravity; many went even beyond that to defy *anti*-gravity. Steller Sunshine's giant beanstalk, the very first piece of user-created content, was designed to be a game where you chose *not* to fly, reaching the top of the stalk by leaping from leaf to leaf. An aerospace industry quickly emerged from dedicated users who'd learned to create, script, and ultimately sell all manner of flying machines, jet packs and fighter planes, rockets and flying saucers.

Why the fear of flying? Many have speculated that the sensation of self-propelled flying is too jarring for extended periods, and that people's visceral empathy with their avatars means they need to maintain a visual reference of themselves on the ground in order to feel comfortable. Whatever the case, flying remains a largely temporary behavior, sparingly used to quickly get around barriers. (Which was, when you think about it, the function's original purpose.)

Log Rollers and Rate Whores

If Residents rejected some of the supernatural powers given to them, they were also apt to abuse the power they had over others. Early on, Rosedale and his team implemented a ratings system for content creation. Originally, when a user was given a plot of land, he'd also get a hydrant-sized voting box. If passersby liked whatever the landowner was building, they could click the vote button.

Rosedale, says Walk, "loved the idea that you could rate somebody's build while they were offline . . . What a little shot of adrenaline and confidence." It was a personal reward that went to a larger good. Because if you aggregated these votes, the thinking went, you'd have a handy database of worthwhile content, as chosen by the people. Then Residents could use this to search for quality creations, as filtered by popular vote.

It's fair to say the voting boxes began to be abused almost the very moment they were introduced. Builders would simply ask their friends to grace their voting box in return for the same consideration; it was content-creation logrolling.

Mechanisms to reward socialization led to an even stranger emergence. "Because we wanted to create interaction," Walk explains, "we wanted to figure out other ways you'd benefit from meeting people." They introduced calling cards, which Residents could exchange with each other when they met. They added a Ratings metric to every user's publicly viewable profile, categorized by Behavior, Building ability, and Appearance. Every Resident could give a plus or minus to every other Resident in any or all of those categories. And so, the theory went, you'd know at a quick profile glance how popular, talented, or attractive a user was, as decided by democratic selection. The Linden team even created Leader Boards on their official Web site, so the top ten Residents in those categories and others would be known to all. In this way, democracy would reward talent and charm.

Ratings were enthusiastically manipulated from the start. Now Residents weren't working to be the most friendly or talented as an end itself, but just to have the official status on the boards. What's worse, those who did make the boards didn't always want the recognition because it just meant that new Residents would harass them for handouts of Linden dollars, SL's virtual currency.

Walk still believes that the ability to negatively rate other Residents was a wise implementation. To bestow a rating, Linden Lab designed it so that the Resident had to be in-world and within physical proximity of the person he or she wanted to rate. In that way, a negative rating would be personal, and a touch awkward for both the rated and the rating. This would convey the seriousness of the disapproval—and, it was hoped, inspire the negatively rated to reform themselves.

At least the first part of that theory succeeded, all too well. "Neg rates" became Second Life's equivalent of psychological muggings. Sometimes they reflected one person's genuine disapproval of another; but just as often, they came in collective waves. Cliques would gang up on a perceived miscreant, neg rating him or her en masse, all at once. On the user profile, these minus ratings were depicted on a small panel, but they might as well have glowed in the dark. Residents branded with the dread scarlet letter of a neg rate would often append footnotes to their profiles, to explain (or at least excuse) its existence. Even a few months into Second Life's Beta period, with a community comprised of only a few thousand, I began to receive reports of "lynch mobs," riding the world armed with collective opprobrium.

But it wasn't just negative ratings that were causing widespread social fallout—even *positive* ratings fell under a pall of distrust. Those with high positive ratings would get wracked by accusations of being "rate whores," trading favors for their high numbers.

Sitting to Succeed

As the Linden team's efforts to engineer personal behavior failed, most of their attempts to create community misfired, too. Much as city councils build public parks in underdeveloped neighborhoods in a bid to revive them, the company tried to create civic spaces.

Instead, many Residents went off to create neighborhoods of their own, such as Elven villages or cyberpunk cities (as we saw with Nexus Prime), elaborately planned and organized. Some even came with elaborate charter agreements, like the rules laid down by real-world homeowner associations.

And as these subcommunities and commercial locations began to thrive, Linden tried to reward landowners who were already interested in running social gatherings and special events. And, as always (or nearly so), the outcome to that was totally counter to what they planned.

"Improvise, Adapt, Oversit"—Spring 2006

Sometime in recent months, the world was taken over by zombies. They now comprise much of the population. You'll visit a crowded club with music blaring, but instead of a dancing throng, you'll find a dozen Residents in the hunched-over, "puppet without a master" pantomime that indicates someone is away from his keyboard.

The theory behind Traffic Incentives, a monthly kickback of Linden Dollars to landowners who brought visitors to their property, was pretty simple. Without imposing any expectations on how they attracted foot traffic, Incentives rewarded property holders for getting them there. In practice, of course, this meant the big Traffic Incentive winners were usually nightclubs, casinos, or free sex parlors—or even more often, clubs with a dance floor, casino games nearby, and a secluded basement or maybe a cloud-shrouded skybox to which you could teleport for sex with willing partners (or the kind who were willing with enough money up front). And if that seemed like a crude result to some, who was Linden to judge what people wanted in their world? They were coming into SL to enjoy content, and it was up to them to decide what sort of content they were looking to enjoy. As long as the traffic kept rolling, Linden kept paying. It was an elegant bit of social engineering that unleashed Resident creativity with little oversight by the company.

The thing was, sometime around last fall, people started coming into Second Life to sit. Just sit.

The camping chairs, as they were called, offered a unique value proposition for the cash-poor Resident: sit down on one, and the landowner paid Linden Dollars in proportion to the amount of time your rear end stayed seated in her chair. Payouts were low— L$2 per five minutes, or about 10 cents an hour on the open market. But then, you were just sitting. Someone speculated how at that rate, you were probably paying more for your electric bill to even be in Second Life than you made from the camping chair. Factoring in the broadband subscription fee with the utility bill, it wasn't an implausible claim. But hey, free money!

Somehow (and I have noticed this time and again), more than enough Residents are more than willing to devote themselves to virtual work that pay them pennies by the hour. Through the transformative magic of being in this alternate world where the currency went that much farther (if you didn't mind the sports car or the evening gown you were buying not actually existing, that is), the activity didn't seem like work. Some land barons cleverly merged camping chairs with animations of menial labor, so when a Resident sat on one, it looked not as if he or she was sitting, but instead, scrubbing the mall floor or cleaning the windows of a nightclub. Now Residents were role-playing as unskilled laborers, and many jumped at the opportunity to do even that. (It made a certain existential sense: Spend a couple of hours mopping the casino entrance, then take the few dollars you earned, blow it on the slot machines inside, and go back for another cleaning shift.)

And every month, the lure of free money was enough to connect thousands of Resident asses to hundreds of chairs. They were housewives who sat in-world while they did house chores, or office drones who let their avatars sit in Second Life while they did slightly more meaningful work on another program on their computer. They were also (in several cases I know) high-powered executives trying SL to see what the fuss was about, or popular personalities from a well-known punk-flavored erotic Web site. With a single button's click, they all could have bought thousands of Linden Dollars for a few real dollars. But again, it was free money.

In some of the most popular places, Second Life started seeming like a Potemkin village, a virtual world where participation was also virtual. Not to say the world as a whole had been zombified, for all the same crazy freeform creativity and deep social connecting was going on everywhere. But when it came to the spots that were supposed to be the most popular, the camping chairs gave a uniquely metaphysical meaning to Yogi Berra's immortal observation, "No one goes there anymore; it's too crowded."

"Well, I see it as this," one casino owner reasoned to me. "People want money, and they will do anything to get it. So they come and sit, and maybe play some. People who sit in the chairs aren't the type that will build Second Life. The people who really make SL what it is won't be found in a chair because they are building and creating."

Condemned by Dots

After Traffic incentives were ended, however, the camping chairs remained; landowners still found value in paying Residents a stipend, for they could still exploit another feature of Second Life that wasn't even intended as a social mechanism. Viewable with one click, SL's Map button displays a dynamic overhead view of the entire grid. In it, every Resident in-world is represented by a green dot, like ants slowly moving through a maze of content. This became a visual shortcut to see where other Residents were in the world and what they were doing. In various locales the green dots would congregate in large numbers, and the immediate inference was obvious: If people were going to these places, something interesting must be going on. And so any noticeable clump of green dots would attract more, and as those grew, more would follow—a feedback loop that came to be called "the green dot effect."

Pay Residents to occupy space—and only occupy space—and a business owner could use them to bait more Residents. And since many of the campers spent their slight earnings on the establishment they were already in, it became a cycle of dormancy and spending.

Residents, in other words, were now leveraging the system to socially engineer each other.

For a time, Linden Lab would feature twenty sites of high-quality content every week—beautiful gardens, soaring castles, rip-roaring theme parks, and more. But staffers grew weary of exploring the world to refresh those choices, and weary of community accusations that they were engaging in favoritism. So the Favorites panel was removed from the SL viewer.

And so the green dot phenomenon continued to thrive; alone and unguided, users would careen around the map and wind up following the jade trail into the most active places. Almost invariably, the most popular would be nightclubs, sex havens, or free money campsites. And while other, smaller-scale activities abounded elsewhere, it was easy to assume sex, clubbing, and camping were the world's defining themes.

This somewhat mistaken impression was solidified even further by Popular Places, which listed the twenty sites with the highest foot traffic. In terms of unique users, this chart captured the daily activity of roughly 10 percent of all visiting Residents, and as the population grew, an even smaller percentage. But what were the other several hundred thousand people who were also in-world at the same time doing? (High-quality content areas, in terms of artistic beauty and ambitious design, usually achieve a medium level of popularity, depending on word-of-mouth and a long tail of attention.)

When a media backlash against Second Life reached crescendo levels in late 2006 through 2007, one of the chief complaints centered on the questionable quality of the experience. Put plainly, critics claimed that SL was a cesspool of sex, gambling, and other vaguely questionable or illicit activities. And so a popularity listing that had been gamed by social engineering was also defining (incorrectly) what the world was to outside observers.

Democracy and the Impression Society

The ready suggestion here is to put systems like these up for a worldwide vote. But while Residents as a whole love their freedom, they have never shown any collective love for democracy's more strenuous duties. In 2004, Linden Lab asked Residents if they were interested in self-governance but garnered a tepid response; in 2005, the company introduced a voting mechanism whereby the community could nominate new features for the Lindens to work on—which attracted, at most, a mere 478 voters. A Resident-led petition in 2006 against a widely reviled property-rights abuser tallied fewer than one hundred signatures. Another petition, in mid-2007, was directed at Linden Lab itself, demanding the company fix a number of system-debilitating bugs. It gathered a mere 4,540 signatures—less than 2 percent of the total active user base at the time. Responding to the petition in a Second Life–based Town Hall meeting, Cory Ondrejka begged Residents to register their complaints on the company's bug-tracking database so they could go after the bugs with the most votes. A few weeks later, the highest-ranked bug had all of 147 votes.

None of this is to say Residents are socially apathetic; rather, their collective sense of Second Life is reminiscent of Americans' relationship with their country: deeply patriotic to its ideals on an emotional level, eager to rally in its defense when threatened by external forces—but come most election days, still not likely to show up at the polls.

But this also placed the company in a prisoner's dilemma with its paying customers. Any effort to discern the majority's wishes was ignored, while any attempt to implement a system was gamed by an active minority.

There's a broader reason why most of these systems failed, and it involves SL's status as an Impression Society, where any cultural, economic, or social contribution is valued in direct proportion to its organic creative flair and sustained effect. Lindens Labs' social mechanisms imposed artificial metrics on what had become, even in the earliest months, the social coin of the realm. Quite literally installing voting machines on creativity, personal behavior, and in-world activity cheapened genuine expressions of admiration and appreciation. And when these mechanisms began getting abused, it was a direct affront to the Impression Society.

Over time, most of these systems were grandfathered out. For Ondrejka, the important thing was not whether their social engineering systems ultimately failed, but, he tells me, "which of them are failures—and which of them served a purpose when they went in." Whatever their tendency for self-implosion, he believes they did their part to get the economy and the culture flowing to a point where they were no longer needed.

If one is inclined to squint, of course, it's easy to discern real-world analogies to all this. Any top-down distribution of rewards that depends on the honest participation of all is doomed to fail. Let even two people within the group collude to exploit it, through rate whoring and camping chairs—or for that matter, trading food coupons and work assignments—and others will decry the behavior as cheating (and then use it as justification to do so themselves). Had something like Second Life somehow existed a year before Lenin was stowed on a sealed train to Petrograd, seven decades of global tumult might have been avoided. Still, as Ondrejka's words suggest, it's too simple to invoke the failures of collectivism. All along, the company's plan was to gently nudge Residents from social welfare onto a path of libertarian capitalism (a course with its own perils, to be sure, but more on those later).

What the Linden creators learned is even easier to apply to other Web 2.0 sites that leverage what has often been called (but rarely is, in James Surowiecki's sense), the wisdom of crowds. Fans of video-sharing sites like YouTube know that ratings rarely reflect a video's actual quality; news-aggregating communities like Digg are regularly wracked by coordinated takedowns of stories that small groups of users deem undesirable. To keep the social mechanisms useful requires a never-ending arms race of reforms and tweaks against a constant siege of exploit-seekers. In the end, Linden simply withdrew from that conflict altogether. It's one thing to create a system of democratic evaluation; it's another to keep it truly acting like a democracy. Then again, that lesson hasn't been fully absorbed anywhere, two thousand years after Athens.

It's a final irony that a social mechanism that *did* work is one that utterly failed at first. In the very early stages of development, Hunter Walk designed a First Life panel for users' in-world profiles so people could add details about their real lives for others to see. With these, Walk says, "I wanted people to say, 'This is the other side of me.'" But for the longest time, most First Life profiles remained blank. With the world so new, few were inclined to project their actual identity into it.

But in the years since then, the First Life profile has become indispensable, widely employed by active users; it's become a quick way of determining who are genuinely committed to being part of Second Life. (It became even more crucial when real-world businesses and organizations came in and wanted a way to start validating true identity.)

Which speaks to Walk's last point: Social engineering *does* work, if and when a group of individuals decide on their own that they're truly ready for it. And sometimes, the only thing for the engineers to do is stand back and give them time to embrace the constraints.

Chapter 5

Self-Made Mankind

Identity and Role-Playing in the Digital Generation

At the start, Stella Costello was beautiful by most standards of either the real or virtual world, with a slender waist and a neck framed by perfect crests of blonde hair. But something seemed off, for the woman who owned Stella would look at her on the computer screen and feel no relation to the avatar she was controlling with her keyboard. It had to do, she realized, with the avatar settings for Stella's size, making her svelte and petite—which Stella's owner was, admittedly, not. Her solution was to adjust her avatar's girth and weight with the system's internal appearance settings.

"[I]t was a gradual shift," Stella's owner recalls. "I'd look at her and feel distant. Then I'd slide the slider up and feel more honest with myself and more connected to her." Gradually, Stella became full-figured—making her unlike nearly every other female avatar in Second Life, who are almost invariably slim. She doesn't denigrate that choice in others. But her own avatar, she decided, would defy those beauty expectations, and the honesty of her size became a tiny victory for her.

"In a cheesy, cheesy way," as she puts it, "Stella taught me to love myself more, so I let her be me."

In its early years, the very first choice confronting a new SL user was how he or she wanted to appear to others. After installing and running the program, Linden Lab dropped the initiate onto a small tropical island, built with a winding walkway studded with numerous information stations, each a short instructional on movement, chatting, and more. But many would-be Residents found themselves meandering at the first station, which showed them how to customize their avatars. This was achieved by using numerous adjustment panels and a slider interface that let them instantly go, for example, from being four to eight feet tall. Seemingly every aspect of a humanoid person was changeable—not only gender, size, and hair color, but features far more granular, like thickness of nose bridge and length of ears.

The combinations were nearly infinite. And often for that very reason it was here that many users quit in frustration, overwhelmed not only by the variety of possibilities but also the challenge to create the ideal alter ego they had in their heads. (I have seen many users remain at this part of the Prelude tutorial for hours, by turns fascinated and aggravated by the options afforded them.)

In Second Life's first few months, by Hunter Walk's estimation, perhaps half the avatars were fantastic and strange, and would enter the community freakishly tall, say, or with spiky multicolored hair and other flourishes of gratuitous silliness. This rapidly changed, for the first cottage industry to emerge from within the community was customized avatar enhancements. (Nearly all of them made the choices for the female avatar more beautiful and fashionable. Linden Lab's avatar customization interface was created by male programmers who were, for all their copious coding talent, not exactly on the cutting edge of glamour.) And while the default options for a woman's avatar were vast, nearly all the choices somehow managed to be remarkably unflattering.

With a few notable exceptions, the early Residents who took matters into their own hands were women. Washu Zebrastripe, Resident name of a girl from the Midwest, invented wigs that were actually attachable prims sculpted to look like hair, and they quickly supplanted Linden's own hair interface. Nephilaine Protagonist, a young mother from the South, became so renowned for her elegant, Goth-inflected clothing that she launched Pixel Dolls, among the first virtual fashion lines. They were part of a quiet uprising, as the talented women of Second Life reclaimed a sense of beauty the system had denied them. One upshot was a panoply of choices that never quite existed for average avatars in this world, or any that had come before. The other was a chance to imagine oneself into another form, and maybe become the better for having done so.

Once inside an online world, Sherry Turkle argued in *Life on the Screen* (1995), her influential book on computer-mediated interaction, computer users would find themselves "swept up by experiences that enable them to . . . challenge their ideas about a unitary self." She was describing how all varieties of online role-playing—either in the virtual-world sense or in an anonymous chat room or message board—would give us new ways to play with different aspects of our identity. Freed from the accidents of birth that define who we are, to ourselves and the people around us, the anonymity of Internet-based communication would give us new ways of playing with the things that seemed most fundamental to us and finding out just how essential they really are. Class, race, even sexual orientation would be fluid.

Looking back at the statement now, it still seems far too optimistic: In contemporary, fantasy-based MMOs, players' choices are usually limited to the expectations of the universe they're joining, which usually means selecting a template derived from *The Lord of the Rings*. If you're a heroic, fireball-casting wizard, does that really challenge your ideas about a unitary self? Are you really going to learn anything about who you are (except, perhaps, that you like fantasy games)?

But as it turned out, Turkle's observation was simply ahead of its time. Creating a constantly revolving theater of role-play first required a system expansive enough to make every attribute fluid, and believably so. It also required an economy and a culture vibrant enough to make those shifts in identify meaningful—and, at times, painful.

"The Skin You're In"—Spring 2006

Normally, Erika Thereian's avatar is blond and California tan, nothing less than the archetypal white girl of the world's dreams. Recently her friend Chip Midnight asked her to model his latest "skin"—not an unusual request, since Midnight is a long-established master of customized avatar skins that Residents make, buy, and wear when they're going for a look that Linden Lab's own interface can't achieve. She'd wear Midnight's latest skin around Second Life to build up word-of-mouth and generate sales.

"I often throw her my new stuff to take for a spin," Midnight explains to me. "She's very social, so she's a good way to get feedback." (Viral marketing, in other words, at its most immersive.)

But when she wore one of Midnight's recent skins, it also became, as Erika tells me, "almost a *Black Like Me* thing." (She's referring to the landmark sixties book in which a white man attempts, through painstaking but not very convincing makeup, to experience life as an African-American.) This is because Midnight's latest product happened to be the skin of a staggeringly photo-realistic, attractive young African-American woman—someone akin to tennis star Serena Williams, say, set to avatar form. Many gasped in admiration when Thereian appeared in public in her Midnight skin. Some, however, did not. She found that out after she randomly teleported into a location where a couple of avatars were standing around.

One man took a look at her and announced, "Look at the nigger bitch."

Another said, "Great, they are gonna invade SL now."

She spent three months in the skin of a black woman. Some of her friends shied away, she believes. Then there were, she adds, the "guys that thought I was an easy lay, for lack of a better term." She was astounded at the reaction, especially when an avatar's racial appearance is changeable with a single mouse click. Other reactions were more muted: A couple of close friends in Second Life simply stopped talking to her, and when they randomly ran into each other, greeted her with a polite chill. ("You know how you interact and something changes and no one tells you?") Another friend framed their problem with her in a uniquely para-doxical query: "[L]ike, when are you going back to being you?"

Thereian told some of her black friends about her experience in Midnight's skin. "And they were not surprised at how I was treated, at all," she says. As it happened, some of them are also Residents of Second Life and play as *white* avatars. "Some [of them] because there were no good black skins available," she explains. "Others because they felt more accepted that way."

And though she didn't alert the Linden creators to the racist speech directed at her, she had street justice schemes of her own cooked up. She waited for the right moment to spring it on one of the men who'd aimed the hated racial epithet at her.

"Listen," she tells me, laughing. "I waited 'til he was with a group of his buds. I went in and thanked him for the wonderful sex, and left."

"Thanked him as a black lady, you mean?"

"You betcha," she says, chuckling. "They were congratulating him. 'Til he denied it most vehemently." Which only got them asking why. "Showed him for the bigot he was."

Which was really the larger lesson she learned in her three months within Midnight's skin.

"Showed me who were good people and who were fakers. That is a good thing to know."

"Being black as the litmus test for the virtuous?" I suggest.

"Yes," Thereian tells me.

By anecdotal estimate, some 70 to 80 percent of the Resident population stay within the human register. A selective list of those outside that spectrum would include robots of all sizes, shapes, and functionality; angels; vampires; elves; *anime* characters; walking sunshine and storm clouds; six-foot phalluses; famous sculptures and paintings (including Van Gogh's self-portrait and Duchamp's *Nude Descending a Staircase*); aliens; political caricatures; penguins and ponies; and a pile of talking feces. For most of them, the embodiment is a surface novelty, but for others, it's a deeper transformation. I once interviewed a female art student whose human avatar, Kazuhiro Aridian, was fused into a robot exoskeleton of terrible beauty, all rusty gears, inverted metallic limbs, and spiky claws. She described the process of becoming Kazuhiro as "sensual," an erotic becoming. "Pain is the strongest physical feeling," she told me, "and it's an attractive expression, visually."

Several of the most prominent avatar types represent Internet subcultures that have existed long before Second Life. Among the most identifiable racial minorities, so to speak, are the furries, Residents who role-play as anthropomorphic cartoon animals. By one estimate in mid-2007 (derived by the number of avatar costumes sold at retail), furries comprised some 6 percent of SL's active community but include some of the most recognized and talented content creators. In a sense, they are the Amish of Second Life, a relatively insular subculture that many find strange, but whose skills as nurturers of the world are respected.

They also represent a summit of the avatar experience: a striving for transcendence into an alter ego that's so idealized, it's no longer even human.

"Furry Like Me"—Spring 2005

"I made it for you," Relee Baysklef tells me, giggling. "I know you're interested in us furries, and I thought you might like to look the part when you report on us."

The veteran squirrel has invited me into her lab (the palmlocks on her sliding doors are paw-shaped) and given me a mysterious envelope to drag over my avatar.

And when I do, my human head goes bulbous, my body goes round, and my torso shrivels.

"Ahh, there you go," Baysklef says, watching with approval. "Shrink shrink shrink. Since your name is Hamlet, I thought you might like being a hamster."

In seconds the transformation is complete. As is my discomfort. And then I notice the hirsute nub growing out of my backside.

"What's this thing sticking out my back? Looks like an extra vertebra!"

"That's your tail! Hamsters have really little tails." She takes a photograph of me in full fur. "You look good with your suit on."

One morning, Hamlet Au woke from uneasy dreams to find himself changed into a giant hamster. I stood there for awhile, trying to find the words to describe the experience of looking at this new avatar of mine. I didn't feel like myself. Looking at my avatar provoked a sensation of awkward self-consciousness. I do feel like myself when I'm in my default Hamlet Au avatar, who mostly resembles me physically (as a glance at my author photo will attest). But this, well—this felt like something else entirely.

The reason most furry Residents make their own avatars, Baysklef goes on, is because there's "a spiritual connection to animals, or a specific animal . . . Some furries are more fluid, though, like Arito Cotton, who has been a dragon, a fox, and a bat." Cotton is among the pioneers of the furries, leading like-minded people from other online communities where the subculture thrived; he created the first furry avatar template, attachable items that transformed a human Resident into a walking cartoon, from fuzzy ears to hind paws.

In real life, Baysklef tells me, she's tall and overweight, and that is the source of her desire to change. "My real body feels awkward and strange compared to the body of my fantasy," she says. As with many furries, this sense of kinship with adorable mammals has existed since childhood. In her case, choosing the particular species took some time.

"It's been years now [as a squirrel]," Baysklef tells me, "but I've been a furry longer than that. It takes a lot of time to really find yourself." This search for a personal association with a cute animal (or a cartoon variation) extends beyond animals that exist, for the subculture of furries includes Otherkin, Residents who re-create themselves as fantastic animals, such as werewolves and dragons—and here again, the impetus is often inspired by the person's sense of his or her real self.

"While it's debatable," Baysklef tells me, "most of them do have mutations or chemical allergies that match the myths and legends of their mythical connections." So, for example, Otherkin who are dragons will often have scaly skin from eczema in real life.

This sense of avatar identification is so profound, it often transcends self-awareness—or skirts around it entirely. More often than not, one meets furries dressed in *Star Trek* uniforms, or swords and sorcery regalia, or powered battle armor (with a special chrome sheath to protect the tail). It is not enough, in other words, to role-play as a six-foot raccoon; even that has to be embellished with the fantastic.

In another interview, I put this point to Tasrill Sieyes, a Resident who had brilliantly fashioned his avatar into a walking incarnation of *Nude Descending a Staircase*. (The experience of being embodied as a twentieth-century masterpiece, Sieyes noted dryly, was "an interesting feeling. Kind of . . . freeing.") After awhile, I asked him to revert to the avatar in which he felt most himself—and without hesitation, he transformed himself into a robed purple fox with octopus tentacles protruding from his back.

"[S]ome people are so attached to their furry form," he explained, "that it is them in all ways. And adding their other likes to it is just natural to them, as a person adding [clothes and other attachments] to their human avatar."

With such an intensity of role-playing in such comical personae, it's not surprising that furries in Second Life are often the target of mockery, as they have been in other Net-based communities. In what can only be called geek bigotry, ironically the worst attacks come from gamers and other Netizens. In fact, shortly after becoming a recognizable minority in SL, members of a popular gamer Web site came streaming into the world en masse, declaring open season on Second Life's furries, ransacking their events with machine guns and ridicule. And if it's a little odd that some people go in-world so they can be anthromorphic creatures, it's even stranger when another group of people go in-world to make fun of them for doing so, since to do that, they also have to take on an alternate form themselves. Then again, this is just one more skirmish in the class war of geek cultures, Trekkers, *anime* aficionados, video gamers, and innumerable others, each struggling to depict themselves as slightly less socially inept than those they ridicule.

"What we do is pretty silly and different from the norm," the squirrel Relee Baysklef acknowledges. "Us furries tend to be strange or exceptional people." People looking for closeness. "Don't be too surprised if a lot of people start hugging you," she warns me. "A lot of furries love to hug!"

No doubt they do. (Indeed, the need for physical touch, protected by a shell that makes contact safer to give and receive, seems to be a core motive for the furry experience.) Still, I'll politely refrain from any furry-based embracing in the future.

If you want to know who you really are, try on a role that is decidedly not you. Relee Baysklef takes on the form of a squirrel and feels a connection to a form she's always wanted to be. Hamlet Au takes on the form of a hamster, by contrast, and feels as if he's walking around in public wearing a scuba-diving suit made out of lime-green sandpaper. And while there's nothing exactly wrong with publicly wearing a lime-green sandpaper scuba suit, I still wouldn't quite feel like myself inside it. I'd also worry that people would form their impression of me just from the scuba suit, and not see who I really am.

These are valuable things to learn, if you can stand to have the nub of a tail sticking out your backside for a time.

A man I know joined Second Life, and when it came time to create an avatar, he chose an alter ego that was also male. But something about his personality and language made the people he met and befriend in-world think of him as *motherly*. Not for his sexual orientation (he was heterosexual in real life); it had something to do with the endearments he used and the way he nurtured the people he cared about. They even began suspecting he was a woman in real life, who was only pretending to be male. Eventually he relented and flipped his avatar's gender switch. He took to wearing exotic female clothing—a sex change by popular demand.

When the deepest identity change is possible with a single mouse click, the opportunities to gender play—and the motivations for doing so—are endless. They are not always sexual, except in a roundabout way. (Some men just enjoy creating and fully controlling their ideal woman.)

Club hostess Eboni Khan once explained to me another reason men gender-bend their avatars, something that seemed so implausible I'd not have considered it otherwise: as a way to seduce women.

"Sensitive and tender?" Khan asked rhetorically. "Pretend to be a girl, and seduce the girl of your dreams. Then tell her you are a man, and hope for the best." (Unsurprisingly, one of the most common ethical dilemmas in Second Life is whether a gender cross-dresser should feel obligated to reveal his or her real-life sex to a virtual world romantic partner—and if so, when.)

Whatever the motivations, creating an identity of the opposite sex is a substantial part of the culture: In mid-2007, Global Market Insite conducted an extensive survey of Residents; 23 percent said they played a different gender. (For that matter, 22 percent said their avatar had a different skin color than theirs in real life, and mysteriously, 11 percent reported having an avatar with a different *political* orientation.)

And if the motivations for gender play are numerous, so are the opportunities for learning more about who you are when you become the opposite of what you were born to be.

"Man and Man on Woman on Woman"
—January 2005

So there's this man who's male in real life but a woman in Second Life (even though in real life he's into women), and then there's this other man who's also heterosexual in real life whose avatar in Second Life was male for awhile, but then he decided to be a woman instead, and then, guess what: These two straight guys met in Second Life and fell in love, and so now they're married there.

So, you know, just another avatar-based romance.

"We haven't really been too sexual," Jade Lily clarifies for me. She's a petite brunette with a button nose. "We're like two people who are becoming very close. It's like I have no concept of gender in Second Life . . . so the only way I can think to qualify my heterosexuality is my attraction to a female figure."

I stopped awhile to chat with Jade Lily and Torley Torgeson, the female figure in Jade's life. As it happens, I knew Torley when his avatar was a slim Asian guy in flowing neon clothes. But in deference to his wishes—and what else *can* you defer to, where identity is so malleable?—I'm going to abandon the male pronoun when I mention Torley from now on, too.

As it happens, the shift is easy enough. With some judicious tweaking, Torley now resembles the sister of his earlier self: a leggy Asian woman with stiletto heels and a rose between her teeth.

"Jade's the type of person who I felt I 'knew' early on," she tells me, "even if I didn't talk that much to her to begin with. It's kinda like . . . you have your Pokémon cards or pieces of the puzzle and whatever, and you suspect someone else has a bunch of the missing pieces. Well, as time went on, I found this to be true."

We're sitting in the courtyard of Jade's library in-world. To make things more complex, we're joined at the table by someone who has a real-life history with Jade: Sage Maracas, a muscular man wearing dark sunglasses—who's controlled, in this case, by a woman.

"I thought it would be interesting to have a relationship with a guy in Second Life who was actually a girl in real life," Jade continues, nodding at Sage, "and we thought we wanted a relationship at the time."

"You mean in real life?" I ask.

"Something like that," Maracas grunts.

"[A]nd I think we wanted to salvage that [relationship]," Jade continues. "It didn't really work out for either of us, I suppose."

Which brings us back to the relationship that *does* seem to be working out, at least for the moment, involving the two brunettes, who stand up and lock into a warm embrace.

"Mmm," murmurs Torley as her hands grip Jade's waist, "it's hard to let go."

I ask them what it feels like, when they see their avatars hug each other.

"It feels like I'm hugging a girl when I hug Torley," says Jade.

"Same," says Torley.

But since Jade told me earlier that sex isn't the emphasis for the relationship, what about it, exactly, is "romantic"?

"If I imagine him as a female," Jade answers, "which isn't difficult to do with his new female avatar, I'd say he's an ideal partner for me, personality-wise. What makes it romantic, I think . . . are the long conversations that we have about who we are and where we fit in the world. How we think. We ask each other deeply personal questions. Trying to understand one another . . . I just treat him like a girl, and he treats me that way. And it's fun."

However, she adds, there are boundaries. "We've agreed that it can never leave Second Life. SL is the enchantment."

"Do you think you might be bisexual, in real life?"

"I'm not attracted to guys physically," Jade answers flatly. "But I think I could find a guy's personality attractive . . . I think a lot of people have homosexual tendencies. It doesn't necessarily mean they're gay in real life. In real life, I'm clearly attracted to women. In Second Life, it gets shady. I see my avatar, Jade, and I'm compelled to play a female role . . . because it's what she's supposed to do, I guess. I dunno. SL has either taught me a lot about myself or created more questions. Maybe both."

Jade and Torley did consider meeting each other in real life, but that never came to pass. And in later months, they grew apart.

"It gradually faded," Torley tells me. "And before the silence got uncomfortable, we talked about it and did the proverbial 'moving on' [conversation]."

Now Jade is dating a woman he met apart from Second Life.

"I have learned from Torley how important it is for me to have a partner who has a positive outlook on life," he tells me, "someone optimistic, passionate, and motivated." He says this aspect of Torley's personality will be the standard by which he'll select the woman he eventually marries.

As for Torley, she was randomly exploring SL's sandboxes one day when she came across a beautifully crafted, ornate table, and sent a message to the person who made it. "It took awhile, but we started talking about our views on the world," she says. And that's how she came to know Ravenelle Zugzwang, a woman in both worlds. Their relationship flowered into something deeper.

"I consider Ravenelle Zugzwang my wife," he adds. "We haven't met in person yet. I hope we will soon, though."

The Internet is being repopulated by alternate identities. Consider the Gartner Consultancy's projection of 80 percent active Net users in an online world (and by definition, with an avatar) by 2011; recall the eruption of social networks, teeming with users who idealize themselves as sexier and more successful than they really are, an avatarization of their real person; and remember the unimpeded growth of online worlds for children and teens, which boast tens of millions of avatars even now. See them converging at a single point, and see them then as something else. Avatars could very well be the e-mail address of the future Internet.

The most energetic Netizens will likely maintain several avatars in numerous worlds, some for business, with immediate links to their real-life person and their financial/government credentials. Other identities will be for recreation and experimentation, and most people will keep these separate from their offline physical self in order to explore other facets of self and desire.

Is this a good thing? To answer that question, we need to consider the principle of Mirrored Flourishing, the expectation that positive activity in the metaverse can and should lead to genuine value in the real world. In some cases, as with furries, the question will be contentious: Does role-playing a nonhumanoid creature with such an intensity always contribute to the healthy development of the person offline? But few will doubt the value in trying on the attributes of another race, to experience the world (albeit a virtual one) from their vantage point. As for exploring different varieties of sexuality, as with "Man and Man"—there again, opinions will probably diverge, depending on personal and moral convictions about sexuality. On one side are traditionalists who consider even fantasizing about illicit sex to be corruption; on the other are those who see value in it—even as a necessary kind of frolicking, to find out who you really are.

Somewhere between those poles, the majority will fashion a new kind of gender ethics that will define the future rules of interaction on the avatar-based Internet. And as avatars become as universal as e-mail, this will shape our understanding of identity—on the Internet and offline, too.

Chapter 6

Making Love

And the rib, which the Lord had taken from man, made he a woman, and brought her unto the man. And Adam said, This is now bone of my bones, and flesh of my flesh: she shall be called Woman, because she was taken out of Man.— Genesis 2, 21–23.

In Second Life's Beta period, avatar-based sex was so artificial and cumbersome that engaging in it at all was more of a technical challenge than an erotic experience. Avatars come into the world without genitals, like child's dolls; making these in SL was easy enough, a matter of rolling and molding wooden primitives into something fleshy and attachable. (So widespread are they now, some Linden Lab employees half-seriously suggested licensing King Missile's alt-rock cult classic "Detachable Penis" to use in Second Life commercials.)

But it's important to tell the story of virtual sex, beyond whatever momentary fantasy or genuine engagement those who participate in it gain from the activity. Most anyone online has engaged in some kind of Internet-based courtship, even if it was merely a flirtatious e-mail exchange. But the generation that came of age in the twenty-first century has inextricably merged its intercourse (in the word's two meanings) to the Internet, be it through come-ons conveyed in text messaging or the elaborate role-playing and webcam-fueled erotic presentation integral to social networks. From that perspective, Second Life's lovers are moving Net-based sexuality to its inevitable conclusion, when the larger part of our seductions will be depicted and experienced online.

After creating genitals, the next step was getting avatars to physically couple in a way that looked even remotely convincing. For this, Residents started tabula rasa because the company never got around to creating animations so that avatars could hug one another, let alone copulate. Virtual nature finds a way, however, and the initial hack involved taking nondefault default postures and gestures the company had made and repurposing them for the user's own erotic innovations. (So, for example, a gesture meant to describe an avatar crouched down riding a motorcycle was remade for obvious ends.)

At its most heated, this was a visual reference, and a disarmingly childlike one—GI Joe's steely thighs scissored together with bare-ass Barbie. Most often, any genuine erotic heat was passed along through private instant message. (In the early days, I vividly remember flying into a mountaintop tree house—only to find a petite redhead and a catwoman already there, standing inches from each other, silent, naked, and entirely still, as some gale wind of private erotic chat surely flew between their keyboards.)

Despite so much suppressed lust, the full sexual renaissance arose much later, in 2004, when Linden Lab introduced a means of creating customized avatar animations and binding them to your character, as a controllable series of moves you could initiate at will. Staffers had a running bet when the first sex animation would appear in-world; as I recall, it came the very day the technology sprung, so to speak, into existence.

By the time you read this, the mechanics of sex will almost certainly have been upgraded. (In June 2007, Linden Lab introduced location-based, real-life voice into the world, and an insider with the metaverse adult entertainment business told me it became a key selling feature even when still in testing. Linden Lab has also announced plans to integrate "puppeteer" technology that will enable Residents to animate their avatars in real time, and no doubt, erotic pioneers will be among the first to latch onto it.) But from 2004 to at least three years onward, the technical means of making love, generally speaking, has more or less gone like this:

A custom animation is embedded within a spherical object, colloquially known as a poseball. When an avatar sits on it, the designated pose or animation possesses him, as if in an erotic fugue, launching him into whatever stylized movement or pose is contained within it. Just as often as not, such poses are nonsexual: Popular uses include dancing, game-play animations, or "gesture overrides" to customize ways of standing or sitting that replace Linden Lab's default body language with more personality-rich poses.

Put several of these poseballs together, however, and through basic geometry, sexual congress is achieved. Place one avatar on a blue poseball, for instance, and it starts him into a wild, motion-captured loop of pelvic thrusting; position another avatar on a pink poseball just underneath him, and it will instantly cause her to perform the complementary motions. This is why sex beds in Second Life seem to be strewn with clusters of multicolored softballs, every set containing a new position. (Miss the timing, or hop on the wrong poseball, and the session becomes comic, with one lover pumping away at the empty air, while the other help- lessly bobs and squirms on the other side of the bed.)

This element of the silly keeps SL sexuality viable, remind- ing Residents of its artificiality while allowing them to maintain a level of ironic humor and playfulness about it. Rarely have people described their Second Life sex to me without mentioning this madcap quality. What they instead describe, even at their most sensual moments, seems less like a grimly serious, role-playing escapism than a lighthearted digital lark, generally done with a half-grin. The same might generally be said of Residents who act out the *consequence* of sex, too: Two years after all that animated humping began in earnest, "birth clinics" began opening up so couples could become proud parents, a process that usually began with a "nurse" showing the expectant mother how to make her avatar look pregnant and culminated (after a sped-up birth cycle) with her spread-eagled on a clinic bed, as an animated "baby" (a prim-based doll, really) was extruded beneath her.

For most residents, I think, only in sporadic moments does the sex act become fully and genuinely erotic. Lillie Yifu, avatar name of an MFA student who makes spending money as a willowy call girl (sometimes earning the Linden Dollar equivalent of about $40 an hour), once described such an instance with a client to me, when all the elements converged perfectly to evoke a similar mem- ory from her real sex life. That parallel made what was happening in SL, she told me, "[A] golden moment that rushed through my veins and explodes on the back of my eyes even now."

After what must be one of the strangest deliberations of journal- istic ethics ever, I decided to pass on trying virtual sex myself— even if that meant missing a first-hand sense of the experience and understanding what drove so many to risk real relationships with it and often create new romances from the provocative mingling of pixels. For me to do it in my official avatar would be too disrupting to my reporter's identity, and were I to try it out through a secondary anonymous "alt" character, that would have quandaries of its own.

As a compromise, I visited a sex club and asked two of the regulars to demonstrate.

After a long pause, a broad-shouldered man and his lingerie-clad blond friend assented—but only if they could change out of their usual avatars first.

"We're not really together," the woman told me cheerfully, "so we don't want you taking screen shots of us doing it and make our partners jealous."

That moral boundary set, they rummaged through their inventories for the ideal erotic models, then took on new shapes. These new avatars were totally unlike their default personae—in fact, were not human at all.

Which is why the first time I saw sex in Second Life, it was between two zebras with psychedelic stripes fornicating on a water bed. Thus established, they proceeded through a series of Kama Sutra positions that would likely be impossible for humans, let alone zebras.

But here is a rule that generally applies in Second Life: The degree of virtual sex is in inverse proportion to the true emotional depth of the participants. The more casual the acquaintance, the more sex; the deeper the relationship, the less avatar-driven coupling, if any. Often this is because romances appear where the Residents were not searching for it; I'd estimate that only 40 percent of the active members are social gamers who go in-world looking for such activity. At heart, Second Life is an Impression Society, and impression is the standard that usually defines attraction: The most alluring Resident is not the player with the sexiest avatar (for anyone can buy a dazzling persona off the rack), but the one with the wittiest or most empathic conversation, or the strongest commitment to the community, or—most valued—the greatest creativity in all its forms. The expectations of the Impression Society drive the most serious relationships, leading to long-term commitments that often escalate into the real world, even into marriage. (I personally know of several marriages that began in SL. In most, one partner had to leave his or her home country to take the relationship to the next level.) Those are also the relationships where the virtual version of sex seems superfluous, except perhaps as an occasional lark. For the most part, virtual sex remains a social icebreaker or light erotic role-playing, as a prelude to casual friendship or an end in itself.

But still underlying that fun are the tensions that come from any game of casual desire, where lust merges into affection or even love—and both sides of the couple quietly wonder who will be the first to flee, or to escalate.

Making Love —Summer 2005

Phil Murdock had a hankering for his neighbor Snow Hare; to launch a romance with her, he hit on the most logical solution available: He got on his motorcycle and rammed it through Ms. Hare's living room.

"Break the ice," Phil shrugs. "Nothing like a motorcycle crash and a 'sorry.'" A brawny, bare-chested guy with close-cropped hair (not unlike the photograph in his First Life profile), he keeps a nickel-plated .45 crammed in the front of his leather pants. "It's been love ever since."

Their first month together in-world was a whirlwind of clubbing, shopping sprees, and building. Soon after, they started creating custom sex moves to sell. Phil would design them offline with animation software, then upload these files and attach them to their avatars, so they could try them out.

By that time, however, they both knew their feelings for each other were real and deep, and not just confined to their avatars. The trouble was, in real life, they lived several states and seven hundred miles away from each other.

And so to move things along in that realm, they hit on the most logical solution available to them: They created a kiss. Not just a friendly embrace, either; by then, those already existed (first invented by Frances Chung, a petite Asian with pouty lips and a programming degree). What Phil and Snow had in mind was a kiss worthy of the name: full-bodied, open-mouthed, devouring.

"We stood toe to toe, and I wrapped the animation to our bodies," Phil recalls. He had to modify the animation to make all the body parts come together just right. He also worked on making it more passionate, with his fingers tracing up her back, their bodies pressing ever closer. And though this kiss really only involved a depiction of their two animated characters together onscreen, he says, "The first Second Life kiss was awesome and special. Just as special as the first in real life."

Other animations on the market were not as sensual. "We didn't like what was out there already," Snow Hare remembers. She's a delicate and lithe brunette with bright eyes (not unlike the photograph in her First Life profile, as it happens), in bare feet and jeans. They set out creating new animations, Phil using his configuration skills, Snow Hare acting as his model and his inspiration. (And later, she'd make the furniture they'd embed with their sex-infused poseballs.) They created these for their personal enjoyment, but there was also a market out there to serve.

Their enterprise is named PM Adult; an American flag and a giant red arrow point the way into an emporium of their animations, selling all manner of positions, in all levels of explicitness, for several kinds of erotic taste and orientation. One of their hottest sellers is a bookshelf that, at command, drops down to the floor, revealing a bed on the other side, thoughtfully arranged with several poseballs.

On a whim, I asked them to demonstrate it, and without a moment's pause, they hopped on the bed and proceeded to merrily screw in a fluid, perfectly choreographed series of positions that would make a porn star blanch with envy. (Many of their moves were actually motion captured from adult film clips.) And after an uncomfortable pause, I realized they were genuinely arousing, stylized enough to resemble an erotic cartoon yet detailed and evocative enough to remind you of the real thing. To my surprise, I realized how many people could make this into a weekly entertainment.

Since opening PM Adult, Phil Murdock and Snow Hare have sold tens of thousands of sex animations and furnishings like these, as well as items from their crystal display chest of dildos, vibrators, and other toys—virtual reproductions of artificial simulation devices, in other words. For awhile, they say, PM Adult was pulling down some L$2,000,000 per month.

The figure makes my head lurch. I actually have to calculate the conversion on pencil and paper, to make sure I'm reading it right. "That's like, uh, $8,000 a month!"

"Yeah, about that for a bit," Murdock allows. "When we first hit the scene, was making the ton. But like the Internet boom everybody got it and it's slowed—but it is still nice."

Nice also was a Labor Day weekend, when Snow Hare and Phil Murdock had their first real date in the world outside. To do that, they got in their cars and drove several hours each, meeting at a motel roughly halfway. I ask them whether they wondered what would happen if, after driving all that while, they only discovered they weren't as compatible in real life.

"Probably would have just gone our separate ways, I guess," Phil muses.

"We agreed that we'd still work together, though," Snow adds, "but deep down we knew we'd hit it off; it was pretty much a sure thing."

And so it was. It's not often that two people who've spent so much time creating sex simulations get a chance to finally engage in the thing itself. I ask Snow Hare about the impact of their avatar lovemaking on what eventually became a real relationship.

"It wasn't the only reason that we decided to move on to real life," she tells me. "As everybody knows, there's more to a relationship than sex. But I would say yes, it did have an impact, positive, in such a way that I knew what to expect . . . before real life, I knew what he liked and enjoyed, and vice versa. Since we were honest with each other and were very compatible, it was easy to know what to expect in real life."

"It was almost like meeting an old friend and a lot of the nervousness of a first date wasn't there," Phil tells me later. "This medium definitely lets two people share their feelings and desires for one another, and that is a powerful thing in itself."

So their avatars' love calisthenics really meant something after all. And not just as a catalyst for their offline romance—there was also that nest egg of Linden Dollars they now had. Phil converted enough of it into U.S. currency to buy them a truck and a washer/dryer. And then he converted even more, so he could help Snow move into a new house—this one only a couple of hours away from Phil, so they could meet and be with each other a lot more often, with a lot less travel time in between.

I wonder if Snow Hare ever fantasizes about the real-life version of their romance while in Second Life, or vice versa.

"Not in real life," she answers. "I don't fantasize about Second Life. And in SL, well, sure, I do fantasize about real life, 'cuz it's obviously better. Who doesn't want the real version?"

I should also note that nothing in this chapter should be read as suggesting that sex is the main content stream of Second Life—a notion that's managed to take root despite a dearth of evidence. (For awhile, the dubious claim that one-third of the content is sexual made the rounds, and it still occasionally springs up.) It's a meme that recalls the first brush of public awareness of the Internet, in the early 1990s, and with it, an unfounded hysteria that depicted the Net as largely an unbounded porn haven, which led to attempts to ghettoize it or, worse, burden it behind walls of government regulation and private filtering.

It is narrowly true that about one-quarter of the most popular sites in Second Life have sexual activity as a primary selling point. (This is an estimation based on a measure of raw foot traffic to these locales, but as mentioned before, the activity of tens of thousands of people in the very popular locales says little about what several hundred thousands of other residents are doing during the same day.) And unlike the real world, all content in the role-playing/game areas of Second Life are made for entertainment, not utility. So even the world at its most pornographic—picture the main bedroom of a virtual bordello—is still dominated by nonsexual content: the furniture, the fixtures, the facets that comprise the building, the avatar's clothing, jewelry, and hair—all of it not sexual in itself, and entirely transferable to non-erotic contexts. To express this as a rough ratio, every time two avatars engage in sex, untold dozens of content makers have spent untold hours creating aspects of the environment they're in that have little to do with their specific activity. (In terms of landmass, the company recently estimated that only 18 percent of the total world had been designated by Resident leaseholders as having mature content—only a subset of that amount being mature in the sexual sense.)

In that sense, then, Second Life pornography is at best a secondary market dependent on a much larger, multivaried economy. And as I'll discuss in later chapters, adult clubs are not exclusively sexual and are often more socially complex than the category suggests. (At one leading gentlemen's club, I once interviewed a top stripper who liked discussing Ray Kurzweil and transhumanism with her clientele while she disrobed.) Since animations are largely automated, adult nightclubs function on two levels, with avatars providing a visual complement to a social network that's largely created through instant messaging. To visit an adult club is to be inundated with light and streaming music and the voice of a live DJ as you watch nude performers in cages or writhing together in a steamy onstage shower, and at your periphery, perhaps a flurry of sex off in a corner divan or in the VIP room in a private skybox high above the club; and most of this goes on silently. The real drama is in the space where the seduction takes place, relationships (virtual or increasingly real) are formed, and the dramas that emerge largely go on quietly, in the private middle space of IMs.

While avatar sex is but one part of the world, it's also true that it's among the most powerful kinds of interactivity—at least for those who are willing to suspend belief long enough to feel its draw. At some point, all those who have felt something like attraction in-world reach a chasm where they have to consider the leap, as Snow and Phil did. Or, alternatively, withdraw, abandoning contact with a single click, or with self-imposed boundaries meant to protect themselves or the people who already love them. Or in the case of many, to have this decision forced on them.

Which would include, I should say here, me. Second Life was the first online world where I interacted with female avatars that seemed to cross the Uncanny Valley, the term robotics engineers and computer graphics animators use to describe a simulated human that looks real, but somehow, creepily off. Not so in this world: Here, the women were distinct from the generic female avatars of fantasy games; they seemed distinctive enough to have, for lack of a better word, soul. Avatars are coded by Linden Lab to make eye contact with each other, so that if you were in first-person mode, they seemed to be staring directly at you—a mesmerizing effect. And so I felt another phenomenon for the first time—the awestruck, stupefying giddiness a man usually feels when in close proximity to a beautiful woman. Though my physical contact extended no farther than a hug, I was surprised and a bit embarrassed to discover that even a friendly embrace was sometimes enough to shoot a tickle of electricity through my scalp. (To me, this remains the most visceral proof that avatars have finally vaulted across the Uncanny Valley.)

In fact, my girlfriend (now fiancée) clearly sensed this, too, expressing irritation every time she walked by the computer that I was "talking to some half-naked woman." With time, her annoyance largely faded as it became clear that I was ultimately, engaging in the most fundamental of journalistic practices: conversation.

In an online world like Second Life, the emotional intimacy is directly injected, mind to mind, enhanced by a visual representation that becomes your mental picture of the person somewhere out there on another computer. But the point, I think, is clear: The interaction is so realistic, so powerful, it can inspire the full gamut of human emotions, including desire, rage, and jealousy. Even from someone who just happens to glance at it as she passes.

"Watching the Detectives"—Spring 2005

Laura Skye had an inkling her lover was unfaithful and had gone back to tomcatting in the racier nightclubs, where the working-girl avatars come with loose clothing and even looser morals. So she hired herself a private investigator to do some snooping.

"I found out he went with an escort," she tells me, "and we had a big argument. But I didn't trust him." So she clicked on the "Find" button—Second Life's equivalent of the yellow pages—and typed "detective" in the search slot.

Which is how she wound up at the office and private cave hideout of Markie Macdonald, P.I.

"We set up a honey trap," Macdonald tells me there, picking up the story. "You know, nice female avatar . . . flirted quite a bit."

In a honey trap, a gorgeous woman or handsome man is hired to approach the target of an infidelity investigation, lay down some seductive patter, and see if the suspected philanderer takes the bait.

"We charged L$1,000 . . . it was a one-night job," says Macdonald. She's a slinky, voluptuous redhead in a form-fitting gown; were she in a Raymond Chandler novel, she'd be the ingénue who undulates into Marlowe's office pleading for help. Instead, she's the one who owns and runs an investigation firm, with several undercover agents in her employ. (When she's not overwhelmed by her real-life job as an IT manager for a multinational based in Scotland, that is.)

And as odd as it may seem, Markie Macdonald isn't the only private detective in Second Life.

"It appears as if infidelity is a big problem here," Bruno Buckenburger notes, chuckling. A friend once asked Buckenberger to investigate her cheating boyfriend, and this gave him the idea to hang out his own for-hire shingle. "Through word of mouth, we've gotten referrals. Again, women (mostly) want to check up on their men, and so they introduce the agent to the boyfriend, and the agent hits on the guy, and in all cases . . . the guy bites and winds up cheating." But Buckenburger is careful to make sure his employees don't run afoul of the law—i.e. Linden Lab's Terms of Service agreement—which punishes stalkers.

"We do review TOS with them and make sure they don't wind up stalking the guy just to get the job done," he says. "We make sure the client introduces the agent to the boyfriend so it doesn't wind up being stalking.

"So far," he adds, "the boyfriend always winds up hitting on the agent right after the introduction."

To prove their case, Bruno prefers that his agents take an incriminating screen shot with the target—or, just as good, have the agents teleport the client right to their location, so she can see with her own eyes her unfaithful partner in a compromising position.

Like Markie's, Bruno's roster of undercover sting agents is secret; and in his case, at least, they're even secret to themselves.

"The interview is where people get tense," Markie Macdonald tells me. After an interview in her public office, she takes clients to a private cave surrounded by a security barrier so they can tell her their story in total privacy. Many clients treat this as a lark, until the reality hits: They're about to pay someone to find out how serious their virtual relationship is, by spying on their lover. Some walk out at that point. Macdonald presses them on this, to make sure it's what they really want. Because as she's learned, many of her clients have a Second Life partner who also happens to be their real-life lover.

Which was the case with her client Laura Skye. Dave Barmy wasn't just her partner in Second Life; in the material world, they also share a home together. They don't log in-world at the same time, however, since they have two computers but only one working monitor.

"We take it in two-hour shifts," Laura explains. So only Dave was in-world when she passed by their monitor, looked over his shoulder—and found his naked avatar in a tangle of limbs with a voluptuous avatar prostitute.

She was not happy about that, not at all.

"Why, exactly?" I ask her, when I meet with her at my office on Shipley cliffs. "It's just in a computer, right? He's not really cheating."

"He says the same thing," Laura says, "but I don't agree. I feel it's cheating with me. Because it's something I don't agree with . . . he knew it, and it hurt my feelings."

In Second Life, it's possible to designate another Resident as your Partner and have him or her listed on your in-world profile as such (a way of giving virtual weddings substance beyond a public marriage ceremony, though those, too, are an important part of the social fabric). Laura Skye and Dave Barmy had designated themselves as Partners, until she walked in on him and his paid companion.

"Then I divorced him in-world," she says, then throws her head back, laughing. "He got an e-mail saying I'd left him."

She made him promise that he'd never seek the company of another in-world woman again. And he did make that vow, but she still had her doubts.

I ask her how it would change their real-life relationship if she caught him cheating on her again in Second Life.

"It would be the end of the relationship."

"You would break up with him in real life?"

"Oh yes."

At the time, Dave Barmy was engaged to Laura Skye in real life. But the episode with the avatar whore put a kibosh on that.

Instead, Laura set the agents of Markie Macdonald on Dave and waited to hear what happened. The investigators began compiling a detailed roster of his comings and goings through Second Life.

"Markie reported back to me every day, with timings," she says, "where he was, and at what time . . . Like he went shopping, went to a few nightclubs, stayed at his house."

Then he met Macdonald's honey trap, a gorgeous and apparently willing woman. And they set to talking.

"And guess what," Markie Macdonald tells me later. "He talked about his partner all night! Who says men are all bad!"

Given the opportunity to cheat, Dave Barmy had just talked about Laura. And Macdonald reported this back to her client.

"I was very relieved," Laura tells me.

But I'm a bit curious about how Dave felt. "Was he angry with you?"

"A little, but I had every reason to do so . . . I don't want to seem like I'm a control freak or anything like that, 'cause I'm not. I've just been hurt a lot in the past . . . I'm a very emotional person, and I do allow my feelings to come in here."

For his part, Dave Barmy described himself as "shocked" when his real-life partner told him about the in-world test he'd just passed, albeit with flying colors.

"I had nothing to hide, so I didn't really mind—if she wants to waste her money on a private dick, that's her problem."

The test of faith seemed to improve their real-world romance, Laura tells me. "Still a few little arguments, but every couple has 'em . . . there isn't so much tension as there was before."

But that's just in their day-to-day world offline. They still haven't become a couple again in Second Life.

"Maybe one day when I feel ready," says Laura Skye, "then I might take him back in-world."

Meanwhile, business is good for Markie Macdonald, and the other detectives in the same line of work. So the undercover agents keep roaming the world, unknown to anyone but the investigators who employ them, seeking out their targets in secluded places, looking for some crucial breach of trust or some momentary loss of faith. Or on better days, an opportunity to digitally validate the realness of love.

Chapter 7

Building Walls, Defending Territory

Border Disputes and Culture Clashing in War's Shadow

They left their world to escape the war, but in the end, it followed them there.

For the first decade of its popular use, the Internet has been a marvelous way of bringing people from around the world together online—mostly so they can learn just how much they can't stand each other. For every instance of individuals and communities coming together online in a positive way, there are surely thousands more where the interaction is fraught and divisive. The most popular political blogs and Web sites are not those searching for common ground along the ideological spectrum, but those where opponents are villainized in scathing rhetoric, roiling a readership that has echo-chambered itself away from external dissent. In the end, for most people, others exist on the Net only as words on the screen. But what happens when those words take on substance and refuse to budge from the place you call home?

Second Life was born in a time of war, so it's not surprising that armed conflict would be part of its early days. But to fully understand the battles that are fought, and what causes them, it helps to understand the concept of the magic circle, an expression attributed to Dutch culture theorist Johan Huizinga. It is the self-contained world that people step into when they play games, taking on roles (such as king, warrior, or thief) and engaging in behavior (tyranny, murder, adultery) that would be antisocial or impossible or both, outside its boundaries.

Ultimately, this is the territory being defended down the way—not physical space, but the perimeters of the playful imagination. And as virtual worlds grow into a primary channel of Net-based interaction, it's inevitable that these circles will determine the shape of future conflicts. Sometimes they will remain strictly fantastic; at other times, as they did at the Jessie Wall, they will mix the wonderful with the painfully real.

"The War of the Jessie Wall"—Summer 2003

I asked the red man with the devil horns to tell me what happened at the Jessie Wall, but he just shot me dead.

Getting gunned down is actually the kind of response you should expect in the Jessie region, once known as the Outlands, where wanton violence is expected, even encouraged.

Nowadays, it has almost crumbled away into obscurity. But in its prime, it resembled a cross between the Cold War's Berlin Wall and a giant dam, built to hold back the kind of trouble you come into Jessie to seek.

The Lindens created the Outlands to be the place where Residents could let their id rage, and on that standard, they succeeded. Because in April and May of 2003—right after full combat operations began in Iraq—the Outlands became a free-speech fire zone, where political debate raged in three dimensions, accompanied by property destruction, failed peace treaties, and robot turrets.

After the authorities stepped in, the final parting shot was several rows of giant cubes floating above the Wall, left there by an angry Resident. On some was the flag of Communist China—inset with Second Life's official, distinctly New Age-y eye-in-hand logo.

On other cubes was a message in a similar vein, but slightly less subtle:

> *"For all you Liberal Pinkos out there in Second Life,*
> *this is an official FUCK YOU!*
> *. . . Enjoy living in the USSSL (United Soviet*
> *States of Second Life)!"*

After the first Gulf War, French theorist Jean Baudrillard argued that it had effectively never happened, since it had been reduced to computer game graphics at Pentagon briefings and video footage taken from missile-mounted cameras. And now in the summer of 2003, I found myself literally in a computer game, often while watching the latest firefight coverage from the Sunni triangle on the television at my periphery. It seemed sordid, even disrespectful, to characterize what I was witnessing in Jessie as a war.

I finally opted otherwise because what happened at the Jessie Wall—including everything leading up to it, and everything after—still strikes me as a microcosm for many things. It's about what happens when cultures clash and territories are disputed; when people misinterpret rules or misapply them. It's about political debate and what we believe to be political at all, depending on where we're from, and what assumptions we take with us when we come here. And because you often learn the most about yourself when you come into conflict with others, it's also about the Second Life community's first challenge to define itself.

But first, maybe it's important to describe what it's like to die.

Because the thing is, death isn't so terrible a fate in Second Life. When it happens, you just get transported back to the last "home" point you set. (This is in contrast to most traditional games online, which oblige you to lose some of your avatar's inventory or wander the world as a disembodied spirit until you can find your corpse.) That said, death in SL can still be irksome because it means you have to spend time traveling back to whatever you were doing before you got killed.

It's even more obnoxious if you're not the kind of person who is in the world to shoot or get shot at it. And at the time, most Residents in SL were decidedly not in that category, for more often they were artistically inclined Web developers and graphic artists, most of whom were not "gamers" and were unaccustomed to shoot-'em-up fun—and perhaps just as often, simply not comfortable with weapons in general.

World War II Comes to the World

In the first weeks of April 2003, a group of World War II Online players trickled into Second Life, attracted by the free-fire anarchy promised by the Outlands and the ability to make their own WWII–era weapons and buildings. The game is a complex, massively multiplayer simulation, and so the people who play it tend to be older history; many are veterans, active-duty military, or Army brats. These first settlers used Second Life as a kind of online central command, from where they could plan combat strategies for their main game.

This group represented the "First Wave" of World War II Online fans, and for the most part, the WWIIOLers, as they named themselves, were welcomed by the Residents, providing as they did a fresh new element to the world, which was still sparse in combat at the time.

Meanwhile, in the world outside, the coalition invasion of Iraq was reaching its apex. A day after a game site published a story about World War II Online fans in Second Life, U.S. tanks rumbled into Firdous Square in Baghdad. The statue of Saddam was ripped from its pedestal and hundreds of Iraqis poured in, with shoes to pound the toppled sculpture and kisses to welcome the American troops. But the debate surrounding the war did not end; among its most dedicated antagonists and proponents, it actually grew even more bitter.

Ironically, according to Eukeyant Skidoo, his WWIIOLers originally hoped Second Life would offer a respite from the politically heated Iraq-related talk that had scorched their game's off-topic discussion boards, in the run-up to invasion. They learned about Second Life just as their own forum boards were lighting up with extremist anti-war posts. SL would be just the place, many of them decided, to take a breather from all that.

But inside this world, verbal debates can take on solid form. And as the mechanized war came to a close, a conflict very much related to the larger one in Iraq raged to the surface in Second Life.

Meanwhile, the gamer article was drawing a second flood of World War II Online émigrés. By all accounts, this wave was far more aggressive, and much less inclined to assimilate into the community as a whole.

Some longtime Residents watched all this transpire, bemused.

Other Residents turned the internal building tools against these occupiers—even against the many WWIIOLers who were interested in peacefully contributing to the larger community. This was the case with Davada Gallant, who began building a bunker/weapons shop/WWII memorabilia gallery. Outside the war zone, Catherine Omega's mansion was located just over the ridge from

Davada's bunker, and displeased, she told Gallant (as he recalls it) that she'd "show me 'the true meaning of shock and awe.' This struck me as rather corny, so I told her to bring it on."

Omega denies ever saying that—in fact, as a Canadian anti-war activist in her real life, she says it's unlikely. Both sides, however, agree on what happened next. Even though Gallant had never shot at her, Omega began erecting a fifty-meter-high wall around his bunker, to isolate it from the rest of the neighborhood.

"I went to the Welcome Area one day," Resident James Miller recounts, "and there were forty WWIIOLers fresh from [the newcomer orientation area] shouting 'WHICH WAY TO BUNKER?' The WWIIOLers had sent their *own* liaisons to pick up their people and transport them to the Outlands to help fight off the original Residents living there."

By then, many Residents had started homesteading in the war zone, but not to fight—it was simply free Arcadian land by the sea, ideal for creating a new life. It was a thriving suburbia by the time the WWIIOLers appeared on the coastline, fully prepared to carry out the pillaging and combat the Outlands promised them. It was their playground, the invaders decided, and the game they were there to play was full scale, no-quarter carnage. A woman who ran a nearby weapons store was soon doing record business.

Some Residents welcomed the anarchy, but it didn't sit well with many others—particularly those already settled in the Outlands, who would rather just be left in peace.

Nothing doing: WWIIOLers swooped down and used the Outlands' homeowners for live target practice. And because most Residents set their reincarnation point to their home property, those who lived there found themselves stuck in an infinite cycle of violence. They'd get shot on their land, die, get resurrected, and get shot again; this would go on until they logged off entirely, or their antagonist moved on.

All of which was perfectly permissible by Linden Lab—since, after all, this was precisely what the Outlands were designed for.

Some natives fought back. A musician named Malaer Sunchaser gathered a sizable group of armed Outlanders and confronted the WWIIOLers in the adjoining Hawthorne region, where the newcomers were building a giant fortress next to an art gallery. His entreaty quickly backfired.

"[W]e told them to suck it up, or thereabouts," remembers Skidoo, who was in the bunker when Sunchaser's coalition arrived, "and they didn't like that either."

The ensuing firefight lasted the entire evening.

Making the Jessie Mandate

As the bloodshed continued, the complaints mounted, and Linden Lab stepped in, attempting to act as a kind of United Nations to impose peace between the aggrieved factions. Three WWIIOLers were suspended multiple times and finally left altogether. The Lindens also brokered a new land partition to accommodate the warlike settlers. Their solution, implemented in late April 2003, was to designate three of the four Outlands sims as no-kill areas—and from that point on, deadly war games were restricted to the Jessie region.

Meanwhile, inside Jessie, the WWIIOLers got the war they wanted. Through the rest of April, while the news networks featured coalition troops engaging violent insurgents and looters in Iraq, Jessie became a savage battleground between the WWIIOLers and a cyberpunk-themed group, the Noise Tanks. Their ongoing battle became an escalating arms race, powered by ever more powerful weapons technology. One Noise Tank created a bulletproof sphere and floated inside it high over Jessie, sniping WWIIOLers at will. To counter that, the opposition spent a week inventing a voice-activated turret that could fire shield-penetrating seeker bullets. It was the world's first widespread Bebop Reality war, bizarre new weapons clashing together like dueling soloists.

Watching from the sidelines was a Linden contractor with a unique portfolio: Randy Farmer, co-creator of Habitat, the first commercial virtual world. In between projects, he'd taken a short stint with the company to test the scripting and land ownership system for exploits. ("Better now than with paying customers later," he recalls the reasoning.) He'd already warned Linden Lab that their creation tools would lead to system-debilitating grief-ing and suspected the Jessie battle would inevitably reach that culmination, too: "I'd built and run too many worlds and seen this kind of thing end badly so many times that I just stayed out of it."

Until inspiration hit, and he decided to create the world's first WMD.

Using his skills with the Linden script language, Farmer built (he remembers now with evident relish) "a tiny invisible floating grenade that would explode as invisible tiny fragments in a sphere, flying outward at maximum velocity . . . then, to avoid detection, immediately teleport to another location in the simulator."

It was undetectable, unstoppable, and absolutely lethal. And so the developer who initiated one of the first conversations on the ethics of virtual killing lobbed several of these supernatural gre-nades at Jessie's combatants, slaughtering them all. (Having made his point, Farmer somewhat sheepishly disabled the grenades after a Linden staffer inquired after his smart bomb.)

As the conflict roared on, real-world politics had yet to enter it. Into mid-March, the only political statement near the Jessie Wall was a rather noncontroversial one—in the United States, at least—in support of Bush and the American troops still in Iraq. All the chaos on the other side of reality was still contained by the

Wall, but that was quickly about to change; the Wall itself would soon become a part of an even greater turmoil.

The Battle Over the Wall

In Jessie's heyday, when it suddenly became the only simulator for combat games, the sixteen-acre territory bristled with gun turrets, tanks, and cannons. Someone imported audio clips from *Full Metal Jacket*, so R. Lee Ermey's deranged, hyper-obscene drill sergeant rants echoed through the place, giving it that extra tinge of madness. Jessie was home to most of the WWIIOLers in Second Life, but at the same time, many of them felt boxed in from all sides by hostile communities. Outsiders made frequent guerrilla raids on Jessie, targeting group members at random—but when the WWIIOLers got their guns and went after them, the invaders would flee into an adjoining simulator, where violence was now forbidden. Attacking them there meant risking the wrath of the international authority—i.e. Linden Lab. (Many did anyway and were duly punished with suspensions.) To be sure, their previous, unchecked mayhem had provoked much of this, but they were still isolated in a single geographic area where they could be easily targeted and antagonized.

And that's about when the Jessie Wall itself became the stage for a giant political war.

On the wall where the message of support for President Bush and the troops hung, someone added a message of his own. It also featured Bush—but on this poster, Bush's image had been set alongside one of Osama bin Laden and the words "Fear creates patriots."

Rage ensued. The WWIIOLers covered up the Bin Laden poster with American flags and other images. By now, other SL residents had joined this odd battle of ideological iconography. And they went at it with gusto: putting up posters, for example, depicting a turtle helplessly flailing on top of a wooden post—only with

President Bush's head poking out from the shell. The other side covered those up with the image of a crying baby, with the title "The Official Seal of the United States Democratic Party"—but then that was covered over by rows of posters with a single word: "Leftist." So it continued back and forth, as if both sides were trying to defeat each other by sheer force imagery.

Then gunfire over the pictures broke out: A pack of WWIIOLers spotted a homesteader in the demilitarized zone near the Wall who had put up the Bush turtle poster. ("In the spirit of equal time," he insisted to me later.) Outraged, they spilled over the Linden security barrier and descended on his land, kicking and shooting him while denouncing him as a traitor.

This political to and fro was basically trumped when a WWIIOLer named Syank Nomad began adding a symbol that totally changed the debate: the Confederate flag (or to be more exact, the Confederate Naval Jack). That distinction didn't impress many Residents, who saw the flag as a symbol of racism and slavery. On Linden Lab's Web forum, an extended argument broke out, with several members arguing that Nomad had violated the company's Community Standards forbidding hate speech.

"At the time I posted the Confederate Naval Jack," Nomad told me later, "I honestly did not expect to stir up a heated political debate." To Southerners like him, he argued, it was a race-neutral expression of regional pride. "I am not a bigot or a racist," he added heatedly. "I am half Hispanic and part Native American."

Whatever role the Confederate flag had on their decision, Linden stepped in and ruled that from then on, no one but the company would be able to attach anything to the Wall. The surface was returned to its original state of blank, gray stone.

And just like that, the war was over.

The repercussions, however, would continue long after.

After the Wall

"A virtual world acts as a kind of fun-house mirror room when it comes to our offline culture," says Kathy Yamamoto, reflecting on the Jessie Wall incident. Claiming the Yippies of the sixties counterculture as her inspiration, Yamamoto was the one who had emblazoned the wall with her "Leftist" banner. "Distorted or otherwise, this world only reflects our offline world. I didn't expect to escape brutish behavior when I came here."

I wonder aloud if we'd see more conflicts of this kind, with Second Life about to open to the public.

"I plan on it," says Kathy.

"Hope, or plan?"

"Let me put it this way," she replies. "I believe cultural change is driven by conflict . . . I think conflicting ideals do the most to motivate change."

I ask her how Linden Lab should respond, and whether these kinds of thrashes cause people to quit in disgust, with Linden beginning to lose subscribers.

"I have a lot of faith in democracy," says Kathy. "If they are brave and ride it out, more will come in to replace any who leave because of the mess."

Other Residents weren't as sanguine about the idea of turning Second Life into an online experiment in democracy.

"If you feel strongly about guns, flags, freedom of speech, and many other issues," Mac Beach wrote on SL's discussion board, "then by all means write your Congress-person, march in a picket line, sign petitions. But please don't bring those things into Second Life because hashing those issues out in SL won't do a darned thing to solve those differences in the real world, and the process of all the endless debates will make our collective second lives miserable."

"If I wanted to invest the time," Catherine Omega tells me, "sure, I could go around telling everyone I met that I was queer, or a socialist, or [offer] my opinions on reproductive medicine, genetics research, religion, etcetera." She now regrets building a literal wall around the first WWIIOLer she met and wonders if such topics have a place here at all.

"The problem is that the vast, vast majority of people really do not care at *all*," she says, "or if they do, simply don't want to be bothered to argue the point . . . SL gives us all a freedom beyond nationality or birth, or conventional perceptions of resources or wealth.

"Real-world politics," Omega concludes, "simply don't matter there."

Perhaps so. Because many weeks after the war had ended, and the wall had grown half-eroded from misuse and neglect, the peace activist Kathy Yamamoto met the WWIIOLer leaders in a tower above Jessie, where the American flag and the pro-Bush message were still flying. It was striking to see them together, a young Japanese woman dressed like a Berkeley artist surrounded by armed and burly men in combat fatigues with Confederate Naval Jacks emblazoned on their motorcycle jackets. After agreeing the whole propaganda war had gotten out of hand, they made a truce to keep Jessie apolitical.

"Here's the deal," Kathy finally said. "You don't shoot me and—as I said before—I will not bother your stuff, shoot you, post posters, talk naughty, or look mean. That's the deal." And the treaty lasted for quite awhile.

Until, that is, the 2004 election.

In retrospect, there are two chief reasons why the Jessie war was so divisive, besides its parallel to the Iraq campaign. As an Impression Society, Second Life values creative contribution above all else. The war of the Jessie Wall, however, exposed a deep ambivalence about the coolness of virtual combat; many embraced it, while others evinced total cultural discomfort. At the same time, the principle of Mirrored Flourishing expects that Residents who do well in SL will somehow benefit from it in the material world, but it's supposed to reflect from Second Life *outward*. The war of the Jessie Wall reversed this, casting all the painful turmoil of the real world back into the metaverse. To this day, many Residents resent this intrusion into a place they see as a *respite* from all that.

In *Anarchy, State, and Utopia* (1974), influential Harvard philosopher Robert Nozick rejected every single vision of the ideal society that had been proposed by thinkers who'd come before him. True utopia, he argued, was not one unifying rule set, but a libertarian state sufficiently open to allow a variety of utopian visions—many of them inevitably conflicting. The pacifist arcadia of the early Second Life natives was interrupted by gun-toting frontiersmen, causing an epic clash over what kind of world SL was supposed to be.

In subsequent months, however, the WWIIOLers who remained were either grudgingly accepted or simply ignored. As their final peace treaty suggests, the mutual sense of avatars sharing a single place made it possible for diametrically opposed individuals to see each other as people, apart from political differences.

As designed, Linden kept adding new land in direct proportion to new Residents, and as the world developed into two continents, Jessie became a forgotten geographic pinprick of history. The war zone lost its physical centrality, and with it, its cultural significance. Private islands sprouted everywhere in the surrounding ocean, and this made the cultural landscape even more diffuse. Some isles are home to subcultures of strange sexuality or bizarre role-play, but Residents who might otherwise be offended are often oblivious that they're even there. By default, then, coexistence became the norm. (As it turns out, intractable views of the good virtual life need not conflict when there's enough elbow room.)

Combat continued, but with so few areas designated as combat-enabled, fighting became an opt-in experience among dedicated role-players. Numerous "mafia" families stage regular feuds, attacking rival gangs' nightclubs with shootouts and firebombs, but largely maintain a rigid code of *omerta*, declining to report such Community Standards–violating activity to Linden. Rival space navies with armadas of star cruisers and gunships battle in the skies above Second Life while far below, dance parties and shopping centers continue bustling, unaware of these galactic struggles.

But the arms race unleashed by the Jessie War has continued unabated and inevitably keeps spilling out of the combat zone.

"In the end," says Randy Farmer, "very little was done to mitigate the design of WMDs like mine, and I was told that to 'fix' the problem would put serious limits on the creativity of future users." In later years, Farmer's teleporting grenade would seem benign compared to what a burgeoning (and often illicit) arms industry would later concoct: nukes capable of blowing every Resident out of a region, or far more destructive still, gray goo bombs that release infinitely reproducing, self-replicating objects that overtax servers, causing whole areas to go offline. (To stop one particularly virulent gray goo attack, Linden Lab preemptively powered off a ring of servers around the metastacizing goo, creating a firebreak of nonexistence that prevented it from spreading any farther.)

After several of these incidents, Linden Lab began reporting the attackers to the FBI, on the rationale that disabling their virtual world was comparable to hacker sabotage on the general Internet. (The Feds duly scratched their heads, and as of this writing, no suspects have been arrested.)

As for Catherine Omega's belief that politics and other outside concerns were insignificant in the metaverse, that was true for a time. As is often the case, however, the real world's troubles found other ways to keep pouring in.

Chapter 8

Burning Down the House

Democracy as a Business Model

At first glance it may be hard to see how an eighteenth-century philosopher could have any relation to a twenty-first–century Internet startup, but somewhere between interviewing the cackling midget with the dancing rats and the Thomas Paine figure who resembled a giant cat, the name "John Locke" most assuredly popped into my head.

Second Life launched commercially in July 2003, and given its unique qualities, it received a disproportionate level of attention for a service that still had but a few thousand free Beta users. The Linden staff watched hopefully, expecting these free users to convert to paying subscribers.

The subscriber counter hardly flickered. "First day it was [only] like hundreds of people," Hunter Walk remembers. And many of those who did upgrade to subscription level were soon to be disgruntled.

At launch, Residents paid a monthly fee (much like traditional

MMOs) and were given a weekly stipend of Linden Dollars, an allotment of land, and a set number of objects they could create on their homestead. Create more prims than that reserve, and Linden automatically deducted a bloc of Linden Dollars from their account—in effect, a "tax" on excessive building. As with other social engineering mechanisms mentioned earlier, the tax system was conceived with the best intentions—penalizing too much building would curb server lag and place a Darwinian punishment on low-quality content.

Instead, it led to beautifully catastrophic results.

It was Locke who most clearly enunciated the concept of a social contract, the sometimes formal, sometimes tacit agreement governments make with the governed. In Locke's formulation, this contract mostly covered protection of person and property; in later interpretations, the contract became broader and included a mutual vision of the good society. In contemporary thought, John Rawls offers the most provocative version in *A Theory of Justice* (1971); in Rawls's take, the best way of thinking about a social contract that animates good governance is not literal, but hypothetical, as an agreement that rational parties would enter into if they had no prior knowledge of either their individual advantages and skills or their deficiencies and drawbacks. This was an agreement into which both the rich and poor, the talented and untalented would willingly enter if they didn't know what they were destined to be.

But we come into the material world with those attributes already thrust upon us. What Rawls described was a theoretical position, where we could hypothetically deliberate about the kind of society we wanted to live in before we lived there. But in a very literal sense, this is the position in which both the creators of and would-be subscribers to an online world find themselves. The customers have a range of worlds from which to choose, and are often already paying for membership in one or more; the developers need to attract an audience by offering a unique society they can enjoy.

For just about every prominent new world that goes online, thousands of people will leave their current virtual residence to visit and evaluate it. With every significant policy change or fee increase, thousands more will depart their usual world in search of a place that offers a better vision of the good society. If they like what they see in the no-risk trial and decide its stewards (i.e. management and customer support) run their state fairly, these visitors may eventually get dual citizenship—or make a permanent move to the new homestead, encouraging their friends from the old world to join them.

In that sense, the business of running a successful online world—or for that matter, any social network—demands a careful negotiation and ongoing conversation between the company and its clients to determine whether their two versions of the good world remain in sync. The trouble is, the company is often hard-pressed to determine when a policy decision will wreak havoc on that alignment, or even to get a fair read on what their customers will make of it, until they can see the negative consequences with their own eyes. Before then, most are notoriously uncommunicative or seemingly apathetic. Up until the very moment, that is, when they're inspired to lash out.

Thomas Jefferson had John Locke and social contracts in mind when writing the Declaration of Independence, and he added the clause "to secure these rights, Governments are instituted among Men, deriving their just powers from the consent of the governed . . . [and] whenever any Form of Government becomes destructive of these ends, it is the Right of the People to alter or to abolish it, and to institute new Government, laying its foundation on such principles . . . to effect their Safety and Happiness." And while the long-simmering American Revolution finally erupted over a relatively modest stamp tax, its metaverse counterpart was provoked by a more fundamental contradiction.

"Tax Revolt in Americana!"—Summer 2003

The first blow was leveled on Americana, a themed area and building project launched, implausibly enough, by a Resident named George Busch. By the time I arrived late one night, the Washington Monument had been buried by a stack of giant tea crates; in the center of Fenway Park, a pyramid of crates had been cluttered atop the pitcher's mound; the Route 66 gas station had been set ablaze by an insurrectionist midget in giant shoes, who stood there at two A.M., gleefully shooting off seditious fireworks, while several flag-waving rats he'd created danced at his feet.

It didn't begin like this. As originally conceived, Americana was among the first user-created public works projects of Second Life's commercial era. It was a vast theme park built like a microcosm of America, with many of the country's greatest icons represented in life-size proportions, including a Mississippi riverboat, an Independence Hall, and along the shoreline, a credible replica of the Statue of Liberty.

To create it, Busch gathered like-minded builders together to form the Americana group, through which they could pool their resources, their land allotments, and much of their Linden Dollar stipend, to cover the taxation costs. Over the months, Americana's skyline rose, built with love as a gift to the larger community.

But regardless of their civic-mindedness, the taxman came calling for them. It was an ambitious project that required thousands and thousands of prims to exist, and each member had to suffer the tax penalty. As their project grew, so did the tax cost, with no deductions allowed, leading to a weekly, mechanical deduction that hit them all. So even as their Empire State Building reached toward the sky, taxation made it impossible for the group to build any farther.

Across the world, signs and billboards took up their cause, bristling from homes and lawns and street corners: "Born Free—Taxed to Death!" Tea crates the size of small apartments floated in the rivers and were stacked up incongruously in the middle of shopping malls and dance floors. Muskets were fired, and more buildings were sent alight.

The revolt even had a moral voice, but fittingly for Second Life, the would-be Thomas Paine was a six foot, black-and-white–speckled cat named Fleabite Beach. I sent Fleabite a series of messages, asking to know about the rebellions, and got back a missive worthy of Thoreau. It was a broadside against Mad King Linden—not an avatar, Fleabite was quick to point out, but a symbol of Linden Lab policy gone amuck:

> WHAT IS YOUR GROUP CALLED, OF WHO IS IT COM-POSED, AND WHAT IS ITS PURPOSE?
>
> We are PATRIOTS to the man, woman and cat, as are all loyal subjects to the King who watch from afar as common sense and conscience are compromised, until liberty wells up in their hearts and they are forced to action. King Linden's laws have no power to make a man more just; and commonly, by means of their respect for it, even the well-intentioned are daily made the agents of injustice.

> WHAT ARE THE PARTICULAR CAUSES OF YOUR GRIEVANCES?
>
> The subjects of King George Linden serve the King, not as subjects and taxpayers and pay-to-players merely, but as machines, with their bodies. They are the Builders, the Scripters, the Texture Makers, the Event Coordinators,

the Tour Givers, the Mentors, the Resident Instructors, etc. In most cases they are treated akin to horses or dogs, expected to serve and to work, not by conscience, but by dint of a much heralded way and an unreasoned loyalty to a Mad King. A wise man will only be useful as a man and will not be submitted to the realm of beasts of burden.

WHAT DEMANDS DO YOU MAKE OF "Ma.d. KING LINDEN"?

The thoughtful consideration and realization of a means by which all Loyal Subjects can work toward the greater goods of community, god and country without the abdication of their moral relevance . . . Without true Representation there is nothing in SL but pixels that labor to arrange other pixels for the glory and prosperity of Kings.

WHAT ACTIONS DO YOU THREATEN, IF THE KING MEETS NOT YOUR DEMANDS?

Regarding future consideration by the Callous and Cavalier King George, we expect that our demands will fall on deaf or uncaring ear. Should this be the case, we shall make of ourselves soldiers of the heart, embracing Liberty and Justice for all; and rejecting law and dictate made in haste to the detriment of just and free-thinking men, women and cats everywhere. To the Mad, Mad King George we shall say, "You and your kind will rue the day. To you, sirs, Tea Crates in the Bay."

What ultimately drove Fleabite and his cadre was the belief that Linden Lab had failed to keep the vision it promised: With the tax system, it was not a place of freeform imagination, but a world where stringent limits were set on that creativity. Worse still, it

conflicted with the company's rhetoric of an improvisational, collaborative, community-minded world. (Then again, isn't that what
usually catalyzes social upheaval: an unresolvable clash between a
society's stated values and society as it actually is?)

So the protest roiled on; it even spurred a backlash of coun-
terrevolutionaries, or as they called themselves, Linden Loyalists
(the rebels simply called them "redcoats"). And the tax rebellion
struggled for continued relevance, as I discovered after barging
into a semi-covert meeting of the lead insurrectionists (the cat, the
midget, and a statuesque brunette who resembled a professional
wrestler) discussing revolution in the penthouse of an Americana
skyscraper. After threatening to kidnap me and hold me for ran-
som, their debate continued. In essence, the revolutionaries were
wondering if they were achieving the right balance between pro-
test-as-ironic-entertainment and protest-as-serious-statement.

In any case, the revolution frittered away, largely smothered in
the embrace of Linden Lab (the company made concerted efforts
to praise the dissent). In September 2003, it culminated in a series
of thematic events, from debates on taxation to musket building
to Burr-versus-Hamilton–style dueling. But the core systemic flaw
that provoked it remained: Ambitious creativity was still constrained by the State (i.e. Linden Lab).

And while the rebellion fell to inertia, Linden the company had
concerns of their own. Months after its commercial debut in summer 2003, subscriber numbers were still floundering. While it's
too simple to say one directly caused the other, the tax revolt was
the most visible representation of what was happening to the company as a business. My blog report on the tax revolt was widely
featured on the Internet, and this was the first time I realized how
many truly serious people were fascinated by online worlds: It
was originally picked up not by a gamer Web site but by the blog
of Yale Law School, in an analysis of the jurisprudential issues

inspired by players' rights. From there, it was mentioned on Slash-dot, the influential technologist blog, and traveled by chain reaction through the Net.

Seen one way, this was great viral publicity. Seen from another angle, it was now widely known that Linden Lab was selling subscriptions to a service with offerings that were so flawed, they were causing open revolt with muskets and arson. Perhaps for the first time, an Internet revenue model was quite literally provoking an armed uprising.

As a direct result, the company broke up into teams to figure out better ways to foster group-based projects. For Linden's main investor, Mitch Kapor, the revolt reflected a natural reaction to the company's value proposition.

"When you build a world in which the Residents feel and actually deserve a kind of psychic ownership to a degree," as Kapor puts it now, "you will get these extremes of people who take it literally and think they really own it." By contrast, he cautions, "We're interested in the aggregated wisdom of the group, not just the extreme . . . I had lunch at Henry's Hunan yesterday and had kung pao chicken, but I picked the peppers out and put them on the side; I don't bite down on them." He laughs. "You know they're there, they have an influence, but that doesn't mean you've got to eat them."

In any case, the company was feeling for a revenue scheme that would do away with taxes altogether.

"We started to reconsider the business model," Linden vice president Robin Harper recalls, "and walk away from the subscription model, which was informed by what we knew about gaming, and start thinking about it more as a world." That process was greatly informed by a consultation between three leading minds of Net culture and gaming: Lawrence Lessig, monumentally influential Stanford professor and founder of the Creative Commons movement; tech journalist Julian Dibbell; and economics professor Edward Castranova, who revolutionized the academic study of online worlds. It was a corporate advisory meeting; it was a congressional hearing on economic development; it was a counsel of elder gods lending assistance to a junior deity whose people were stubbornly refusing to embrace the gifts he was offering them.

As Harper remembers it, they began with a broader question, not just on the business success of other online worlds but on the wealth of nations: "What makes a country successful and helps a third-world developing country, for example, grow? It's the ability of the people who live there to build something. In order to do that, they have to have access to land because land serves as both a place to build and also as collateral."

In this, they were invoking the thought of Hernando De Soto, the Peruvian neoliberal economist whose book *The Mystery of Capital* and other works had garnered praise from both Bill Clinton and Ronald Reagan. De Soto argued that the informal economies of the poorest countries could be harnessed and transformed into long-lasting prosperity once the right structures were in place. So, too, perhaps, with this smallest of developing nations that existed only on Internet servers, and in the consensual reality, its users were willing to inhere in it.

"They have to be able to reap the benefits of their labor," as Harper puts it. "Which means that they have to have both ownership and financial reward."

From this discussion came a new revenue model, more radical than anything that ever had been attempted. Instead of monthly subscriptions, Linden Lab would sell virtual land and charge usage fees for its regular maintenance. They would also allow Linden Dollars to be bought and sold on the open market for real dollars (an activity nearly all other MMOs expressly prohibited, with their own virtual currency). Most unprecedented of all, they would allow Residents to retain the intellectual property of the designs and depictions of the 3-D objects and scripts they created in Second Life.

On this point, Lessig, who had once argued on liberalizing copyright before the Supreme Court, pressed Linden's executives most passionately.

"I asked the question about who got the rights," Lessig recalls. "My sense was that no one had really thought much about it, and so [people] were simply following the normal lawyer rule—take everything." This despite the company's own slogan, "Your world. Your imagination." Now Larry Lessig was suggesting that they live up to their own rhetoric. "When I suggested the opposite—give the creators the rights and encourage sharing of the rights—everyone was completely open to the idea." It was also a competitive move, something no other virtual world was offering. "Everyone understood [the change] as a way to differentiate Second Life and also encourage a wider range of creativity."

In this insight, Lessig effectively became SL's Thomas Jefferson. And though Linden's upper management was receptive to his vision, Linden's lawyers (as Lessig might have predicted) were not.

"That was a real battle with our lawyers," Linden CTO Cory Ondrejka remembers. "They didn't get why, they didn't get the sort of long-term implications of it."

No other corporate-owned MMO or online world had ever added such a clause to their Terms of Agreement, a document that traditionally expects subscribers to suspend all rights.

These changes would also mean, of course, ending the tax policy. And though no Linden Lab staffer has ever admitted that a tea crate uprising orchestrated by a humanoid cat and cheered on by an obstreperous dwarf and his pet rats had caused them to rework their business plan, the rebels were all too happy to claim the credit afterward.

In a larger sense, the revolutionaries *were* the galvanizing force behind the change. The subscriber-based model wasn't working, and the tax revolt was the clearest demonstration of that fact, mentioned by staffers time and again when they explained the policy revision. Without the rebellion, these course corrections might have come later. Without such a vivid reference, however, the need may have seemed less pressing; without the fundamental contradictions heightened to such surreal levels of wackiness, identifying the reasons for their lack of paying subscribers may have seemed less obvious.

As 2003 and the tax revolt reached an end, Linden management decided to take drastic survival measures to save their company.

"The runway . . . wasn't long enough for us to be confident that we wouldn't run out of money before we could raise more," Robin Harper remembers. "So we decided to scale back." And with that, two-thirds of a staff that had grown to thirty-one were cut down to just eleven, in a single depressing day. For the employees forced to leave, the revolt had come too late.

But most revolutions inspire their own contradictions, and Second Life's was no different. Almost three years to the day, another rebellion would tear at the world. As hoped, the new policy of intellectual property rights and virtual land and exchangeable currency inspired an economic boom and mounting interest by companies and entrepreneurs, both real and virtual. In particular, the clause acknowledging the intellectual rights of Resident creators unleashed an internal economy of virtual businesses in clothing design, engineering and architecture, entertainment, and beyond. It's a topic we'll explore further, but key to understanding the second uprising in 2006 is this: Many in the world considered it not just a policy, but a moral vow. It was another vision of the good society that the company could maintain to the strictest letter—but as many suddenly realized, not always in spirit.

"Copying a Controversy"—Fall 2006

If the earliest days of Second Life resemble the first century of American history, then the most recent years of the world seem to be replicating the last two decades of the Internet, albeit in minia-ture form. Throughout 2004, Second Life was an obscure medium for gamers, techies, and assorted early adopters—not unlike the Net's Usenet groups of the eighties and early nineties—and then sometime in mid-2005, it began attracting substantial interest from real-world businesses and the mainstream media. Which, much like Netscape's initial public offering in 1995, led to a mini dot-com boom, with massive brick-and-mortar corporations throwing money at the world with a kind of frantic urgency.

Right on schedule, the peer-to-peer open source movement that consumed the Internet of the late nineties arrived in Second Life toward the end of 2006. It began with the idealism of talented hackers creating cool applications but quickly careened into wide-spread protest, accusations of IP theft, and economic chaos.

Welcome to the Napster era of Second Life, where conflict between content creator and sharers come to a head. This time, the part of Napster's collegiate founder Shawn Fanning is played in part by a tiny pink cat, while everyone else in the world gets to be Metallica. But if I recall right, drummer Lars Ulrich never tried to crush Fanning with a giant boulder.

First came the hack. It began with libsecondlife, a group of Res-idents attempting (with Linden Lab's explicit blessing) to reverse engineer a modified version of the Second Life program. Their ultimate goal is to create limitless versions of the client, operating on thousands of independent servers, ensuring Second Life's spread through the entire Net. While the group has been operating for months, in late October 2006, they introduced an in-world demonstration of their client that very quickly became the buzz of the community. The libsecondlife team had figured out a way to log automated avatars into the world.

"From the server's point of view, it looks and acts exactly like a normal client logging in to the grid," Eddy Stryker explained with evident enthusiasm while he showed me the technology. (Fittingly, he resembled the shade-wearing Agent Smith from the *Matrix* films.) Perfected, Stryker went on, it would be a way of finally introducing artificial intelligences and nonplayer characters into the world, creating endless possibilities for game development, simulation, and more.

But that wasn't even the coolest part. Because not only had they figured out how to create artificial avatars, they'd also hacked up a way of cloning existing avatars, clothes included. Not just one or two clones, but *dozens*, dropping out of the sky all around me.

"[The program] logs into SL, reads the appearances of the closest avatar, and sets its appearance exactly like that person had theirs set," Stryker told me, as I stood amid an emerging forest of copies of myself: nearly fifty goateed men in white suits, clustering on Stryker's laboratory dock. This was the first public demonstration, but clones had already been released into the world, he added, "silently teleporting from sim to sim collecting data, or running tests on private islands."

"So the one bad thing I see with this is designers of clothes and stuff bitching," an exotic, vampiric brunette named Talila Liu observed after her run through the cloning process. Intellectual property theft, in other words, had an entry point into the virtual realm.

But while libsecondlife's cloning bot didn't save any information about the avatars it imitated, a similar application, CopyBot, did. Designed by libsecondlife to be an offline debugging tool, it existed in their site's publicly accessible directory. And someone took advantage of that to compile a version—and start selling it in-world. Then several more people got into the CopyBot sales business.

Within a few days, as Liu had predicted, CopyBot was savaging the community of Second Life content creators. But they did more than bitch about it. Couldn't CopyBot reproduce all their products free?

Many expressed their fears to Linden Lab. An announcement from Robin Harper on Linden's official company blog addressed their concerns, but did not generally resolve those worries. For it began by saying, "Copying does not always mean theft. There can be legitimate uses for copying, just as there are on the Web." Which was a totally valid observation to make, but it seemed to suggest Linden Lab was taking a neutral stance on CopyBot, telling content creators to take up their complaints with a lawsuit.

And so the initial concern became panic and anger. In protest, many landowners closed down their shops and nightclubs in protest. Within a day, over a hundred locations were shuttered, including some of the most popular sites in Second Life. It was quite possibly the largest and most substantial collective protest staged against a Linden Lab policy since the tax protest of 2003; and like that tea crate rebellion, it was an open display of no-confidence in the company's commitment to a core tenet of the society. The tax revolt was fueled by a policy that seemed to penalize excessive content creation; fairly or unfairly, the CopyBot boycott of 2006 was driven by fears that Linden Lab would not be an active defender of users' intellectual property rights.

But the protest didn't stop at the boycott, and the Residents who were selling the CopyBot program soon found themselves swarmed by Residents waving signs and shouting slogans.

One of them happened to be a tiny pink cat, selling CopyBot as a money-making opportunity, a way to grief worried Residents, or both. In an incoherent interview, the cat told me he'd sold over a hundred copies of CopyBot and that he was well in his rights to do so, since Linden Lab "said it was okay to use, as long as you weren't violating copyright." When I arrived to interview him, he was standing next to his vending machine, trying to keep it clear of obstructions. Not satisfied with mere sign-waving, protesters kept creating large wooden barriers that would block the cat's vendor—which, in turn, the cat kept deleting away.

He was a football-sized miscreant, and in the face of several dozen Residents swearing and chanting at him, he stood there silently, which seemed to enrage them even further. One Resident created a massive boulder next to the vendor, and as it grew one hundred meters in diameter, flung cat, protesters, and embedded reporter skyward in every direction.

Within hours of this, Linden Lab reasserted its authority, in tones both apologetic to the community at large and angry at the exploiters. Thenceforth, senior developer Cory Ondrejka announced, use of the CopyBot or similar technology would be considered a violation of the world's Terms of Service. Violators were now subject to permanent exile.

And with that, in the span of a few days, the CopyBot controversy—at least in terms of an active protest—was resolved.

The fallout, of course, continued. CopyBot showed that Second Life had finally reached a place on a par with the Net as it is now, where arguments over digital rights management and file trading still rage. On the larger Internet, those debates generally pit large corporations, movie studios, and record labels against their consumers—the Recording Industry Association of America and the Motion Picture Association of America versus, well, everyone else. But in a user-created virtual world, *everyone* can become a content-creating entrepreneur with a few clicks. So the debate became egalitarian, pitting creator against creator, each with his or her own personal view of what constituted theft and fair use and degree of faith in having a creator's IP rights kept sacrosanct in Second Life.

"I find it amusing but perhaps educational to see how freely people rip off MP3s or movies or applications or games without thinking twice that they are effectively violating other people's copyrights," leggy redhead metaverse visionary Gwyneth Llewelyn observed, "but in SL [these people] suddenly understand what 'content piracy' is all about!"

Attempting to soothe the outraged Residents, Linden Lab promised to implement fixes: Creative Commons licensing, creation date watermarks, and other tools that enabled Resident creators to make more plain what content they created and when, and what compensation they expected for its use. (At this writing, nearly a year later, none of these fixes have manifested.) Maybe features like these would be enough to restore the confidence of those who felt most threatened by CopyBot. Then again, as the world has kept robustly growing since then, perhaps they won't matter.

As for libsecondlife, a group widely admired for its hacking skills, they are now anathema to many who depend on the creation of SL fashion and other content for their livelihood.

"Some are just plain scared," LibSL member Baba Yamamoto tells me. "Some hate us . . . we've had people leave the group because of the reaction their friends had . . . we've been banned outright from what sounds like half of Second Life, if you believe the forums."

Despite such vehemence, actual damage from the CopyBot was ambiguous. I went in search of Residents who were directly harmed, but no one replied to my interview requests. A survey of Residents I conducted overwhelmingly faulted Linden Lab's handling of the CopyBot crisis, but the company reported that fewer than one hundred complaints had been filed. In retrospect, it's likely the Second Life community experienced an information cascade, a collapsing domino reaction based on incomplete knowledge and the behavior of influential individuals, leading to a rush of boycotts, protests, and shop closings. And, of course, giant boulders.

For several weeks after the CopyBot uprising, numerous clubs and store owners created and installed an automated anti-Copy-Bot defense, a program that spewed non-English text in chat; supposedly, this prevented CopyBot from stealing graphic textures, though precisely how was never quite made clear. So before the panic waned, visitors to these many places had to contend with a barrage of umlauts, tildes, and *accent de gues* fluttering across their screen.

The only obvious evidence of CopyBot's harm, in other words, was the defenses created against it.

But libsecondlife's Baba Yamamoto still sees a positive outcome in all this.

"I tried my best to explain what CopyBot is, and why it's inevitable," he says. The group regrets making the technology freely available, he insists, but does not regret "the exposure of the problem we face because of it. CopyBot does nothing that an open source client couldn't do. It deals with only what the clients are sent." In other words, while CopyBot may have been obliterated from the world, the fact still remains that computer graphics that are visible over the Internet are, by their very nature, copyable. Which means, on the surface at least, anything in Second Life.

"Until now people felt safe, sort of," says Yamamoto; "they figure the content is protected."

And while few are inclined to be thankful, CopyBot has liber-
ated them from that illusion.

In May of 2004, shortly after Linden Lab had instituted their new
land and IP rights policies, Philip Rosedale told technology reporter Daniel Terdiman an extraordinary thing: "I'm not building a game," he announced. "I'm building a new country." The
statement has dogged him since, for being either unsupportable
hyperbole or a goal that was genuine in some substantial way.
Or sometimes both. By giving their world's users a legally meaningful sense of ownership of what they create in Second Life,
Rosedale and his board had unleashed a ferocious level of content
creation and investment that would have been unthinkable otherwise. (Toward the end of 2006, the Linden team estimated that
the content already existing in-world would have required, had
it been done professionally, a 7,700-person development staff at
a burn rate of $800 million a year.) The policy also gave the prin-
ciple of Mirrored Flourishing a legally enforceable claim: Creating
quality content in Second Life not only led to fame and admiration in-world, but also in material reality, a copyright notice they
could hold in their hand. And in 2007 (fittingly enough, the week
before Independence Day), one renowned entrepreneur named
Stroker Serpentine exercised those rights, suing another avatar
for copyright infringements over his sex bed.

By contextualizing this policy as the progress of a nation, the
Lindens created a sense of patriotism and collective destiny that
would not otherwise exist. (I can't count the number of times
someone would pause in building an intricate sky tower or elabo-

rate strategy game or equally ambitious project and explain that
the motivation for so much labor wasn't money or even fame, but
"wanting to do something for SL.") I mentioned how Second Life's
community is an Impression Society, where the standard of cultural value is sustained creativity; Rosedale's rhetoric about a new
country gave this standard a national anthem.

This is worth highlighting, for Internet communities and social
networks are notoriously fickle, prone to dissolving without
warning, provoked by bad policy, poor service, or a Gladwellian
tipping point pushed by a number of variables. By contrast, any
incoming Resident who endured the initial new user experience
was more than likely to become a regular user. Looking over the
retention rates, Rosedale once remarked, "If they stay more than
four hours, they stay forever."

But this wasn't due to Rosedale's software, because in the first
few years, SL's user interface was notoriously user-unfriendly.
Most people abandoned the effort in frustration even before leaving Prelude, the small orientation island where all new avatars
began.

Instead, it was several thousand Resident volunteers who
devoted their own time and resources to helping out new users
themselves, often without Linden Lab's involvement, at Resi-
dent-owned locales like New Citizens Incorporated, founded by a
brashly glamorous black avatar named Brace Coral,where helpers
range in the hundreds. When Prelude failed to actually provide
orientation, these volunteers became the guides and translators
at an Ellis Island of their own design, familiarizing immigrants
with an interface that unintentionally became SL's naturalization
exam. Little of this would have happened for as long as it has were
it not for all this talk of a new nation, and enough practical policies that seemed to justify it.

At the same time, this also meant embracing the disruptions

that real countries face: The tax revolt and the anti-CopyBot uprising were provoked by a sense that the nation's core ideals had been betrayed. And this feeling of ownership has marked nearly every rupture since then. At its worst, an online community's anger doesn't seem like customer annoyance over a company's poor service, but vehemence for a nation's failed president.

But after all, a virtual world isn't a country—at least, not yet. Unlike in a real country, metaverse citizenship can be dissolved just by hitting the power switch. Real nations are largely about scarce resources (natural or economic) and rule sets to protect them. In SL, by contrast, the only physical scarcity is server capacity where the virtual land is hosted.

In a widely cited jeremiad against Second Life, NYU professor Clay Shirky argued that this disjunct between perception and reality undermined SL's promise at the root. "CopyBot was able to cause so much agida with so little effort," he declared, "[because] it was working with the actual, as opposed to metaphorical, substrate of Second Life." Destroy the illusion that all these vehicles and fashions and other items of virtual commerce were not truly tangible goods, but 3-D graphics easily copyable like any other digital imagery, and the economy implodes.

But this argument is wrong for many reasons, chief among them this shared sense of national identity. The strongest protections against IP violations in Second Life are not the Digital Millennium Copyright Act notices one Resident can file against another. (At this writing, the Stroker Serpentine suit remains the one in thousands that have proceeded to an actual lawsuit.) Far more stringent is the community of content creators who watch over each other and report on instances of theft or more vaguely defined "copying." This is especially true of the fashion and avatar enhancement business, perhaps the most powerful industry in Second Life. Woe betide the designer who is thought to be imitating or exploiting the work of a leading designer—the imitator is sure to be boycotted and ostracized by a coalition of fashionistas. If anything, this method of enforcement can be even more ruthless than the DMCA, for sometimes these accusations are actually motivated by personal feud and overreaction.

But the ferocity of the CopyBot backlash revealed something hopeful, in the conflict between media corporations and their customers. As Gwyneth Llewelyn suggested, a hack like CopyBot suddenly thrusts amateur content creators into the same position as a Sony, or a Vivendi, or for that matter, Newscorp/HarperCollins, publishers of this book. As will be seen in later chapters, while Linden's IP rights policy encouraged a dot-com boom of real-world company sites in Second Life, most of them managed to attract but few visitors. By and large the community preferred "native" sites and organically created virtual items. And while there are, of course, Resident-made knockoffs of real-world brands, these remain a small market, with customers preferring those created by established Residents.

And in the end, this is the state of affairs the tax revolt caused: a nation of IP equality.

Chapter 9

Avatar as Entrepreneur

In the fall of 2003, Philip Rosedale gathered his employees together in the foyer of Linden Lab's new office on Second Street, in San Francisco's South of Market district. Since the mid-nineties, innumerable Internet and multimedia businesses had been launched in that quasi-industrial neighborhood, fueled in large part by the cyber-utopianism of *Wired* magazine, a block away on Third Street. Almost all of these companies had been undone by lack of funds or the indifference of the market, and at the moment, Linden was plummeting toward a similar end.

After painful calculation, Rosedale and his management team had just taken the drastic move of laying off two-thirds of the staff. So there was more than enough room for all the survivors to sit on the sunlit rug and hear Rosedale describe the board's new business plan.

They were now tying their fate, he explained, not to monthly subscriptions, or any other proven revenue model. Instead, their aim was nothing less than creating a vibrant, robust economic system based on the production of goods and services that did not, in the strictest sense, exist. And instead of subscriptions, they would charge customers to live on property that also did not, in the strictest sense, exist.

Though the notion of paying for virtual land seems strange at first glance, it really put Second Life more in line with an Internet hosting service than a game. When you sign up for a blog, or an e-mail account, after all, you're really just paying a company to maintain and organize the data for it on their servers. With Linden Lab's model, the same scheme would roughly apply to Second Life. It was just that the data their users paid to store was represented in three dimensions.

"[I]t made more sense to focus the growth of Second Life on creating a powerful economy," says Robin Harper, recalling the shift. "And for that to be successful, there needed to be a basis for it in land. And people needed to be able to retain the rights over the things they created." This assumed that content creators would embrace their world not just as a gift economy of freeform creativity, but as a platform for commerce, too.

Many Internet companies attempt to reach profitability through dubious or financially untested strategies, but what Linden Lab was planning involved a whole other magnitude of risk: In effect, they were gambling the company's fortune on the most fundamental principles that inform the wealth of nations (at least in theory).

It's difficult not to see a parallel to the early years of the United States and its first century encapsulated in the space of a year. In Second Life's first few months, the world was an unsettled country inhabited by nomadic, close-knit communities. When discovered by the public, the natives clashed with subsequent waves of frontiersmen, many of them aggressive and territorial, and in that struggle, communal utopia gave way to a property-centric, libertarian society. As that society took shape, disenchantment with taxation in particular and a lack of ownership in general led to open revolt. This, in turn, pushed the company to redesign the social contract with a kind of Declaration of (intellectual property) Independence and coin an official currency that had a universal market value within its borders and outside its territory. They then established the virtual-world equivalent of a Homesteading Act, in which citizens were offered a chance to explore the continent and claim a portion of it as their own—leading to a new Manifest Destiny, an explosion of commerce, and the rise of a merchant class.

To extend the analogy further, many of Second Life's most successful early entrepreneurs were immigrants fleeing other failed economies, virtual and real. Had it been launched at the height of a real-world economic boom, it's hard to believe as many technically skilled people would have invested so much time and effort creating content in it. The 3-D builders and artists who became SL's fashion designers and architects would have found ready job offers in high tech; out-of-work programmers who became proficient LSL scripters, even more opportunities.

But in a time of recession—and not insignificantly, in an era of war—there were more than enough takers willing to build this virtual version of the American dream.

"Post-war Reconstruction"—Spring 2004

A year before joining the metaverse, Jason Foo found himself face to face with a *fedayeen*. The man's AK-47 had jammed, but setbacks like that are inconsequential to Uday Hussein's elite cadre of suicidal commandos. And so the *fedayeen* pointed the business end of his bayonet at Foo and came charging.

When I first met Foo in Second Life, however, the setting was a bit less dangerous. It's late February 2004, and he's standing in an open-air disco with flashing lights and pounding techno, the nightclub he's built with his rapidly accumulating earnings.

"I kinda turned into a realtor in here," he tells me proudly. "Made L$7,000 today, just selling land. I realized two days ago that the gray areas on the map are unclaimed land. I buy it up, and sell 512 [square meter] plots for L$1,800." His enthusiasm pours across the chat screen; judging by his avatar birth date, he's been a resident for less than three weeks.

"I got my first plot in Stinson on a land rush," Foo explains, "248 square meters. Sold it that night for L$1,000 . . . Then I noticed five plots in Green went public. I bought them for L$1 per square meter, chopped them into 512-square-meter plots, and sold each one for L$1,800." In a very short time, he'd become a mini-tycoon in the newly burgeoning enterprise of virtual land speculation.

While we talk, I notice that Foo has a picture of himself in full dress uniform in his Resident profile. I ask him if he's serving in the Marines.

"I just got out last week," he says. "Trying to find a job [now]. I have massive amounts of computer experience, and no computer jobs [in my area]. I also work with UNIX, and networking, and all sorts of stuff."

"Were you in Iraq?"

"Yep," he says. "And Afghanistan. And the Philippines. Last year."

"And saw three conflicts?"

"Yeah, in one year . . . all within eight months, actually. Modern warfare, man."

His stint ended in Afghanistan. "Unfortunately I lost a quarter of my kneecap, and my leg is permanently damaged. Land mine. I got lucky. My best friend stepped on the mine. Killed him. Injured me."

I tell him I'm sorry to hear that, but Foo seems unruffled.

"It's war," he says. "People die. We know that. At least we know we die with a purpose. Trust me, this is nothing compared to other wars. We lost more people in one day in Vietnam than we have since this war started. We are lucky."

In any case, that period of his life is over now. "Well," he says, "I served my time and my country. Now I serve the Second Life community. There are a lot of interesting people here, a lot of talent." Because for Foo, the massing of so much land and money isn't an end in itself.

"It's all about the community," he tells me. "I have always been one for helping people. I know how hard it was for me to first get land here in SL. I want to alleviate that problem, and also give alternate options to owning land. We are going to build condos and apartments. And I want to be the largest realty company in Second Life. I want to be the one everyone comes to for help and land and rentals. A place where people can share creativity and sell ideas."

I have to leave Second Life, so I promise to pick up this conservation when I can get back in-world, and he readily agrees.

"I'm collecting unemployment," says Foo, "so I'm here a lot."

When we meet again, Foo takes me through the headquarters of Realm Development. It's still under construction, but it already boasts a disco in the basement of a multilevel glass-and-steel building, standing by the sea. I ask him how his mine-ravaged knee is doing.

"Still feels like someone is stabbing me with a knife when I walk up the stairs," he says. "I'll live, though. No big deal. I just need to get a cane." I ask him for how long, and he laughs. "The rest of my life."

"Will your Veterans Administration benefits be enough to cover you?"

"Nope. 'Cause technically, I can still work."

"So they only give you partial benefits?"

"Yep. Doesn't matter," he says, unfazed, "I'm starting a business. A fitness center, I am starting with my mom."

That's in the world outside. Meanwhile, I'm here to see how his Second Life businesses are going.

"This is our new club," Foo tells me, taking me out on the open-air deck, "I sell property so fast that I can't buy it fast enough. We average about L$10,000 a day." (This is roughly $40, by contemporary exchange rates.) "We want to make sure every noob can get a cheap plot of land," Foo adds.

Foo's acquisitions were part of a larger trend, for only months into Linden's experiment in land sales, Residents like him were already grabbing up large swaths of real estate far beyond what they would personally use. In successive years, these estates would become large islands, these islands whole continents, owned by groups and individuals, gated communities or mini-countries attended to by large staffs of Residents they employed.

In between telling me about his plans as an avatar-based entrepreneur, he tells me about his experiences overseas.

In the Marines, Foo was a communications specialist, which is the Corps' taciturn way of describing forward reconnaissance well ahead of the front lines. "I wanted to test my skills to the max," he tells me, explaining why he volunteered. "It was the biggest honor. Together with our [individual] specialties, we could smash a computer to pieces and put it back together with bubblegum, wire, and sticks, and make it work . . . [like] using a tree to communicate with a satellite, by rigging up a satcom system to the tree and connecting an amplifier."

When enemy troops don't interrupt them, that is: "My unit got attacked at least once in each place we went."

"From how far a distance?"

"I have an Iraqi bayonet," Foo says, by way of explanation.

Which brings us back to the *fedayeen* commando who wanted to kill Jason Foo, another world away from this deck above the digital ocean. The man had an assault rifle with a bayonet, and he was charging down on Foo.

"His gun jammed, and he went to run me through," he says, casually. "I grabbed the gun, detached the bayonet, and cut his throat."

I didn't speak with Jason Foo for most of March and much of April 2004. Events in Iraq began careening to the edge of chaos, while construction of Foo's real-estate headquarters was completed, with a casino on the main floor and an art gallery on the balcony. He gave me a tour of the place, while patrons hovered over the crap tables and the slot machines and music from a live DJ thrummed through the hall.

"I already have about fifteen employees," Foo tells me, "and job positions are pretty full." Some of the employees sell real estate; others play hostess in the casino. He was looking to hire more for future projects he's planned.

But for all his success in Second Life, Foo's computer skills still hadn't translated into a real-world job in the place where he lives offline, even after many months of being back home from the front.

"The lack of high-technology businesses here is keeping me from getting a job," he says. "I play Second Life on a daily basis, now that I am still unemployed."

And with this unemployment, his original ambitions to become a kind of benevolent tycoon, giving away land at bargain rates to beginners, have changed somewhat. The economic recovery in the world outside had still not reached his hometown, and his veterans' benefit checks were not sustaining him.

"I really don't want to use the game to make money," he says, "but I really have no choice anymore. I need money to survive."

So now he was selling some of his Linden Dollar earnings to other Residents for real cash, to cover some of his necessities in the real world.

"Coming back to civilian life after going to war, and not being able to find a job, is very frustrating," Foo wrote to me later in a long message. "I have many times thought about going back into the service . . . it would be easier. But my thoughts are shattered when I come to the realization that I cannot go back in because of my injuries . . . I am doomed to live the rest of my life in the civilian world, and leave everything I was behind me. Talking with my buddies who are still in the Marines makes me a little sad and depressed. I want to be there, I want to fight . . . I will not ever believe that my closest friends who fought next to me in combat died for nothing," he finished heatedly.

I walk with Foo as he greets his customers, waving at them, announcing upcoming prize giveaways and the like. I follow him to the top deck, where we can keep talking in relative seclusion.

"I just wanted to have fun and help people," Foo says, "[but] I need to consistently make L$100,000 a week at my casino to transfer into U.S. $450 real-life money. The market is constantly changing, so I don't know if I will get enough real-life cash for my sales of game money the next week."

Despite this, he insists, "I will not let this keep me from providing a great environment for people to hang out and meet people, and I will not ever push people to spend money. I am not greedy, and never will be. I just need to do what I can to pay my bills, and stay alive."

But even that might not be enough, which is something he dreads. "I may have to leave my hometown here in the backwoods [in] a place that doesn't even show up on the map, to go find a state where I can find a job. I would also have to leave behind the rest of my family here again, as I did when I went to war. I left once; I don't want to leave again."

So for now, he stays where he is, expanding his in-world empire from the computer in his one-bedroom apartment, taking from it what he needs. "It keeps me off my feet," Foo says to me, "which is good for me to heal, and it keeps me from going insane . . . It keeps my programming skills honed, and my creative talent on queue." This was Mirrored Flourishing at its most grim, activity in Second Life bettering his real-life options—but given his position, and the national policies that seemed to leave him behind, only barely, and so unfairly.

Before he finishes the interview, Foo tells me about a donation box he's built in his casino and plans to erect in sites all over Second Life, on behalf of the Disabled Veterans and POW Fund. "Every L\$5,000 collected gets transferred into U.S. \$20 for donation to the charity," he says. He has even created an alternate avatar, a grizzled man with gray hair but an upright gait.

"Just wanted to make him look like an old veteran," he explains. And so with this, his enterprise expands to support not just one wounded veteran, but all the thousands returning home. Broken but yet unbowed, still soldiering on any way they can.

By 2005 and into 2006, the population of Second Life had grown large enough that you could identify numerous discrete subcommunities, as broadly defined by their predominant in-world activity. By my anecdotal estimate, some 40 percent of the active users would qualify as Social Gamers, residents who frequent nightclubs, parties, casual gaming locales, and other regions where social intercourse or casual gaming is central. About 20 percent are best termed Fashionistas, for early on, avatar appearance as an end in itself developed into such a pervasive culture as to become its own social circle, not only of designers and consumers, but of an avatar-based modeling industry and a runway-show fashion circuit. Another 20 percent or so would fit the rubric of Role Players, residents who are denizens of fantastic user-created RPGs played within SL, or in highly defined subcultures like the Furries or Goreans. At about 10 percent, Innovators are the world's builders and scripters, and code hackers; far larger during Second Life's Beta period, they've since become the hermit shaman class, individualistic and standoffish, for the most part, but with skills that are highly treasured.

The final 10 percent in this eyeball survey, of course, are the Capitalists, whose dominant SL activity is running a business; by August 2007, they comprised well over 42,000 residents with a positive cash flow, earning more Linden Dollars from their enterprises than they were paying Linden Lab for virtual land and other services.

And as frontier settlers became landed gentry, a Gilded Age power elite among the entrepreneurs quickly emerged. The most successful plutocrats are those skilled at satisfying the most basic desires of Second Life Residents, which fall into two broad categories: personalized avatar identity and instant gratification.

The first refers not just to fashion, but to all the personal accessories that distinguish an individual, from hair to jewelry to customized skins, even weapons and other genre signifiers. The second is more complex, but essentially means easily accessible enjoyment that Linden Lab refused to offer new users, most of whom show up in the official welcome area utterly bewildered. Many or most expect a traditional role-playing game with specific goals to accomplish and prizes to win and instead learn that they are more or less alone to fend for themselves. In concrete terms, this means casual gaming centers, nightclubs, and varieties of adult entertainment—easily understood, enjoyable activities for new users that are reassuring in their familiarity. (I often refer to these as "the Donald Trump or Donna Karan business archetypes.")

This also meant providing immediate access to virtual land. In the first few years, Linden's system of selling and distributing land was confusing, and often unfeasible. (Buying land initially required a credit card, which Europeans rarely use, for instance.) And even beyond that hurdle, the sign-up process required multiple steps, from finding available land in-world to upgrading the user account on the Web site, and more. (While still a contractor with the company, I vividly remember noticing a whiteboard in the Linden office. On it, a staffer had created a multi-part flowchart for buying land, a process that required about twelve steps. "I cannot *believe*," someone nearby groaned, "that *this* is our revenue model.")

In that sense, it was the company itself that provoked the rise of so-called land barons, who very carefully and judiciously bought up vast swaths of land, then charged a rental fee to other Residents to live and play on that acreage. Again, they were providing instant gratification for a desired end: Instead of enduring the tortuous official process, thousands of Residents opted to pay a fellow user directly to handle it. The most successful began buying private islands from Linden Lab, using them to create "themed sims" made to resemble a Japanese landscape, say, or a futuristic city. On the main continents, the explosion of small landowners had resulted in a chaotic jumble of disparate styles and urban blight, a sex club situated next to a church near a rocket launch pad and a garden of hallucinogenic mushrooms. And everywhere one looked were billboards, rotating signs, and advertisements for

SL products, evidence that the internal economy was working all too well. As an alternative, the land barons offered their themed sims as tightly regulated, gated communities.

The most successful of these in the early years was a cheongsam-wearing avatar known as Anshe Chung. In real life a Chinese-German woman working with her husband, Chung took baronage to even greater heights. She didn't just provide numerous themed areas, but basically became Linden Lab's unofficial outreach director in Europe, providing alternate payment plans for EU Residents and multilingual staff workers available at EU hours, when Linden's California staff was fast asleep. By late 2006, she owned more than $1 million in virtual land. Her islands expanded into a continent and required so much upkeep and development that she eventually returned to her home country of China to set up a virtual world facility. The metaverse, in other words, has been outsourced.

Shortly after their IP rights policy was announced, Linden staffers speculated excitedly over the new businesses and projects that would soon emerge. Residents would create Second Life machinima, animated movies created through video capture taken from the SL viewer, and these would become pilots for cable TV shows, movies, and more. Resident fashionistas would create avatar-based styles that became so popular, they'd license their designs to real-world fashion companies.

But as with many other decisions, the company's intents have not been fully borne out by their community. For the first few years, there was only one unambiguous example of a "home-grown" concept making the leap from Second Life and flourishing outside its borders.

"The Tragics of Tringo"—Spring 2004

In the nineties, a Canadian kid working out of his parents' base-ment used the level-editing tools of the popular first-person computer game Half-Life to create a mini-game he dubbed Coun-ter-Strike. It got so popular, people began buying the original Half-Life just because you needed to install it to play the kid's game. It became so popular, in fact, that it had a broad impact on multiplayer gaming and did much to change the game industry's attitude toward user-created content.

In a similar way, I once predicted, a Resident would one day create a game that was so addictive and popular, people would end up logging into Second Life just to play it. That would be the tipping point for the Second Life community and the way it was perceived by people outside it. But as it turned out, the Counter-Strike of Second Life was really a simple, innocuous-looking, casual game that involved nothing more spectacular than a bunch of people sitting around poking at two-dimen-sional boards.

I'd noticed Tringo's arrival when it first went on sale, but by the time I recognized its significance, it had already pushed past that tipping point, both in the online and in the outside world.

So it was awhile before I met its creator, Kermitt Quirk, a non-descript gentleman except for his greenish hair (though his avatar often resembles a humanoid lizard). Quirk is based in Australia (he's originally from New Zealand), but despite our distance, the quality of our connection is just fine. As it happens, he'd just bought a premium graphics card.

"I just got a new graphics card yesterday," he tells me. "Second Life runs smooth as silk now."

"Bought it with your Tringo earnings?" I ask the lizard.

"Pretty much, yeah," he replies. "Not actually from Second

Life money cashed in, though. I haven't done that yet. I'm gonna just keep it in there as a nest egg, I think."

Disarmingly simple, Tringo consists of a display board to track scores and pieces in play, and game cards for the individual players. After they place their bets in a winner-take-all pot, they compete with each other to fit their pieces together onto their cards. In effect, it was like slow-motion Tetris on a 2-D playing field.

A business programmer in real life, Quirk and another Resident developed an algorithm that would calculate the placement of the pieces without overtaxing the servers, which is why Tringo is so fast even in a crowded region of Second Life.

The game was easy to learn and had a gambling aspect that heightened the excitement and the competitiveness; but even then, it might have remained a modest success. Kermitt Quirk had more in mind, however, for in Tringo he had created a franchise operation. He sold it to landowners, and if they ran Tringo matches on their property, they could retain a cut of the profits from the gambling pool. That gave them an easy-to-sustain revenue stream, while ensuring the spread of Quirk's game across the grid. At L$15,000 (about $60 each, in contemporary market rates), he had sold hundreds of franchises by the middle of 2006.

"I ran it as a Beta for a few days," he says. "And even then the word seemed to spread really quick. After I released it for sale, it just went nuts, with people buying it over the first couple of weeks . . . I broke the $L1 million profit mark just a couple of days ago."

An indication of its success is not just found in the number of Tringo-related events in SL (which on some days make up more than 25 percent of the total event listings), but in the veritable subculture of Tringo groups Residents have started up. There are over two dozen, with names like Tringo Busters, Tringo Sluts, and Tringo Zombies.

In a testament to its influence, Jinny Fonzarelli, a British philos-

ophy/theology student and Resident who runs Thinkers, a group
devoted to discussing political and metaphysical topics, launched
a debate on "The Tringoization of Society." "Between Tringo and
pointless contests," Fonzarelli told me, "I know many people feel
their Second Life has been immensely devalued." So a cultural
debate was held within a game about the mini-game that's beginning to impact the community of the larger game.

But Quirk's franchise operation was just the start. In later
months, an offline company called Donnerwood Media would
buy the non–Second Life rights to Tringo and develop a version
for the Web, and then a version for Nintendo's Gameboy Advance
system. There was even talk of a British *television game show* created around Tringo.

You can pretty much find a match of Tringo in Second Life at
any hour. At three A.M., I found one going strong at Ice Dragon
Resorts, often the world's most popular sites. On what used to be
a hill of driven snow now stood a raucous mini-mall of stores,
floating billboard cubes, a ceaselessly blaring stream of pop
music—and at the center of it all, the Tringo game room, done up
in chrome and flashing colored lights.

When I arrive, a leggy brunette supermodel, a humanoid dragon,
and a punk rock demon are playing a round hosted by Dragon
employee Ezri Martin. It's largely an international crowd of players, with a few in Australia and at least one in France. And it
occurred to me that Quirk's Tringo had transformed more than
SL, for here was a chattily competitive get-together, not unlike a
neighborhood poker night or a night of pub trivia contests, a communal third space made international and more than a bit surreal.

"Late-night international tragics!" Magenta Eldritch adds from
the bleachers.

"Great headline for you there, Hamlet," yells Martin. "In Australia," she continues, "when someone is addicted to a sport or

pastime, they are referred to as a 'tragic.' E.g., a cricket tragic, a football tragic.

"And now—a Tringo tragic!"

If allowing subscribers to retain their IP rights did not unleash an immediate explosion of SL-to-RL economic activity, it did energize internal commerce and innovation. As of this writing, few creators have realized the Second Life dream as Quirk had through Tringo, creating a virtual prototype of content, then making it so popular that the outside economy clamored for it. Still, they could at least build their business and brand in relative confidence that Linden Lab would not suddenly co-opt it.

(I should qualify that statement, since it quickly became evident to content creators that they might end up competing against the company itself. So much so, the community coined a verb for it: GOMed, named after Gaming Open Market, a Resident-run Web site that was once the leading Linden Dollar currency exchange outlet—until 2005, that is, when Linden Lab introduced the LindeX currency trading service on the company's own site, effectively rendering GOM obsolete. While their rights remain secure, innovators still run the risk that their business may be depend on a feature or even a system flaw that will be added or corrected in a future update.)

So in SL's first few years of existence, the ironic beneficiaries of Linden's liberal IP policy were the large real-world corporations and organizations that needed no such protection for their SL-based content. What it did was protect the sanctity of their real-world IP rights, since with the policy in place, they didn't need to get a licensing agreement from Linden Lab to launch their marketing efforts. No matter how genuine the rhetoric, the vision of Residents free to prototype their virtual world creativity to an eager external market did not come to pass (at least in the early years). Instead, the prime beneficiaries flowed in the other direction: MTV, American Apparel, Warner Brothers, and other stalking horses of real-world commerce. Not avatars, then, but corporations—that other nonexistent entity that nevertheless enjoys many of the same rights as a person.

But as is often the case, this was a Linden policy that succeeded in ways that weren't quite planned: It created an entirely new kind of entrepreneur.

"Chasing Aimee"—Fall 2006

I first met the avatar known as Aimee Weber in 2004 at a virtual bar modeled on a real-world Manhattan dive. Aimee was (as she is now) a lithe brunette with librarian-sexy eyeglasses, a fashion sense that trended toward punk rock ballerina (a tutu worn with combat boots, ripped and torn stockings with a tiara, that sort of thing), and butterfly wings sprouting from her back—violet-blue, idly flicking open and shut, as she interacts with the world. The ubiquitous wings were the gift of a random stranger who gave them to her very shortly after her "birth" in Second Life.

In its earthly incarnation, the Bellevue Bar was a semi-notorious joint in Hell's Kitchen known, as *New York* magazine notes, for its "sordid vibe, with beat-up couches and aging local barflies propped up against the bar." Aimee had built the in-world tribute because she was a regular at the real place. She designed it to be as skanky as its real-life counterpart, right down to the graffiti in the imitation toilet. Back then when the world was still relatively Arcadian and fantasy-themed, it seemed strange that someone would create not a castle or a futuristic city, but a smutty bar with tattered movie posters on the exposed brick walls and a floor where one might find hypodermics lying in the corners.

I kept in touch with Aimee in the ensuing months, watching her meteoric rise as an in-world celebrity. Fame came first through her founding of *Preen*, a line of avatar fashions anchored by her persona as an outrageously brash, flirty, vaguely tipsy ballerina with blue butterfly wings (the avatar as brand). Aimee Weber was one of the first to innovate this new kind of Net-driven entrepreneurship.

With the Aimee Weber identity, she invested her designs with a cultural sensibility and set of experiences based on her activities in Second Life. Wear her clothes, come to parties she hosts and attends, and hang with her and other Resident elite. In Second Life, the *Preen* line could actually deliver more fully on the promises real-world fashion companies make in ads that depict their products as tickets to the dream life of youth, beauty, and exotic locales. *Preen* advertising was brashly sexy with a third-wave feminist edge, with Photoshopped screen shots depicting cute *Preen*-wearing avatars doing disreputable things.

It was enough to launch her to the top tier of Second Life content creators; it was also enough to earn her a real income. At its peak, she tells me, the *Preen* line was earning her the Linden Dollar equivalent of $3,000 to $4,000 a month.

Her facility with the creation tools moved her from fashion to 3-D property development. She built the island of "Midnight City," a virtual New York City with textures and lighting that rivaled the best of contemporary video games, and on the strength of those creations, began to take on real-world clients.

Because by late 2005 or early 2006, real-world companies were beginning to express interest in "immersive advertising" of their products in SL. In that first flush of excitement, Aimee created a commission from Warner Brothers to create a "listening box" made up to resemble a New York City loft, where avatar friends could hang out and listen to the latest album of Warner artist Regina Spektor. American Apparel's CEO heard so much buzz about Aimee Weber that he sought her out to create the first virtual branch of a real-world retail chain.

These and other projects were arranged and negotiated through Second Life. Aimee didn't speak to her clients by phone, let alone meet with them in person. Executives from established companies had to create an avatar for themselves and take the trip to Midnight City to meet her. Avatar as brand had become avatar as entrepreneur.

But then, no one who knew Aimee Weber in Second Life had ever met her in person. Some theorized she was actually a gender-bending man (which, they thought, would explain her sexually provocative style). Another hypothesis suggested that Aimee was not an individual, but a group. How could one person engage in such extensive 3-D building and fashion design, while also keeping up with the prodigious amount of writing she contributed to three different Second Life blogs?

So it was with some relief and not a bit of surprise when, after some coaxing, she agreed to meet me.

It was in Manhattan during the late summer of 2006, on a day when the last waves of humidity were still lingering on the streets; she picked the place, and to give things a nice narrative circularity, she chose the actual Bellevue Bar in Hell's Kitchen. The Bellevue's heyday as decadent and seedy hangout had already passed, and it took me a while to find it. Spruced up and renamed, it was now the kind of place where executives at nearby design studios could take their corporate clients for a business drink.

So that's where I finally met Aimee Weber in person, and it took awhile to get used to calling her by her real name, Alyssa LaRoche. (In fact, we just referred to each other by our avatar names, a common practice among Residents.) A brunette in her mid-twenties with a creamy complexion and large brown eyes, she bore a distinct resemblance to Natalie Portman. Tutu and combat boots remained at home (she insists they do exist in her closet); instead, she wore a demure white blouse and blue jeans. And over a pint of draft, in a bubbly and girlish voice, she told me how Aimee came to be.

Her avatar is more or less her, LaRoche explained. After graduating in the late nineties from Columbia/Barnard, where she double-majored in computer science and English, she went straight into the peak of the dot-com boom as a consultant with Bering Point, a branch of financial services giant KP.M.G. She'd often present her analysis of the Internet economy to Fortune 100 clients. "That's the main thing Ivy League colleges train you in," she muses now. "It teaches you how to have confidence when you have no reason for it." By night, she ran with the Manhattan club kid scene, often in the punk ballerina garb that was popular at the time (including that pair of butterfly wings on her back, on occasion), with wild late night partying at Meatpacking District clubs.

Until, that is, she got into a serious scrape she'd rather not describe on record. The nightmare incident made her a stay-at-home hermit, while the boom's bursting bubble conspired to keep her there. "In large groups I start to freak out a little," she tells me. So Aimee Weber is a safe incarnation of the life she lived in those downtown halcyon days.

By the time we met, she'd all but abandoned the *Preen* fashion line, for she was already making the transition to full-time metaverse developer for a variety of clients, both corporate and nonprofit/educational. She misses the celebrity of being Aimee, saying, "My time is being taken up more with business work."

She was steeling herself for the inevitable time when clients would insist on an in-person meeting. "I guess I know it's coming," she sighed, resigned. (And it did. Several months after our interview, the unlikeliest of clients, a department of the United Nations, asked for a real-world sit-down. So LaRoche made the trip to the UN building, to start a commission on creating a poverty awareness campaign in Second Life.)

Her therapist is fascinated by her life as Aimee. "Midway she thought it could be destructive, as it cut out a lot of my so-called 'real' life," LaRoche told me. While still mystified, the therapist now thinks it's a perfect place for her to be, a place that, matched with in-person counseling, has created a safe environment where she can develop both emotionally and economically (Mirrored Flourishing, sanctioned by a licensed psychologist). Since it draws on her skills as a 3-D graphic artist and offers a creative outlet for the literary flair that made her an English major, LaRoche reasons, "In a lot of ways you couldn't write up a more perfect job description for me."

But it was her social anxiety that had first brought her to it. Because of that and her troubled history, her background and work experience had been laying dormant while she kept indoors and underemployed. They only flowered in this medium. And in that respect, she wasn't unlike all the other thousands of SL content creators who were otherwise cut off from business by some mental or physical impediment, or mere distance from the world's major centers of commerce. (Many of SL's top fashion designers are based in the South or the Midwest. Nephilaine Protagonist, perhaps the most successful of all, creates goth-inflected chic not in the East Village or the Mission District, but on a farm in Georgia.) In earlier years, eBay had created entrepreneurships in the collecting and selling of antiques and other rare physical items. Now, Second Life was creating an entrepreneurship in imagination.

So in the end, the girl with the butterfly wings incorporated herself. Aimee Weber Studios is now a company registered for business in the state of New Jersey.

Chapter 10

Investing in Utopia

A Rough Explorer's Guide for Corporations
and Organizations in the Metaverse

In January 2004, Linden Lab sold their first private island, in an intensely fought bidding war, for L$1,200. Losing the auction was a leather-clad vampire who wanted to build a castle with his friends. The winner was an avatar named Fizik Baskerville, and after taking possession, he announced his intentions in the community forums: "We are a London- and Chicago-based Innovation and Branding agency."

The company had the unlikely name Rivers Run Red, and using buzzwords like "revenue streams" and "real-world anchor points," Baskerville began describing the plans he and his colleagues had in mind. "We are commercial-based, but we are fans and active participants. We will be supporting a charity and promoting good causes. We will need help."

The next day, his island was overrun with protesters waving signs emblazoned with the words "Island Boycott." And so the first commercial purchase of virtual land led right to Second Life's first virtual antiglobalization protest. For the next couple of years, this flurry of dissent defined the terms of the debate and the community's perspective on real-world companies entering Second Life. They were unwanted and exploitative, was the general view, and once they started jumping into the metaverse, they'd clutter the world with billboards for real brands and put grassroots content creators out of business by offering professionally polished versions of clothing, cars, and more.

In the earliest years, Linden Lab itself evinced ambivalence about the presence of real-world corporations. In a January 2005 interview, for example, Philip Rosedale rejected them outright when it came to the sale of "sponsored links" in the user interface. Linden's plan was to auction these off to Residents who wanted to promote their virtual-world business.

But what's to stop a company like The Gap, I asked him, from buying sponsorships, too?

"No, we will not allow real-world advertising there," Rosedale told me then. "I can't see how selling jeans in those spots could possibly help Second Life. We reserve the right in the SL Terms of Service to not allow real-life advertising. I would certainly invoke that right to keep those listings directly beneficial to SL resident content."

By 2006, however, there was a distinct shift in perspective. Part of this came out of a board decision, Cory Ondrejka remembers, to take a "customer-agnostic" attitude and to let the community decide the value of real-world companies, if any. Now when speaking on the subject, while not quite advocating a corporate presence outright, Rosedale was decidedly accepting. And when presented with the concern that corporations would overwhelm the world with their assets and brands, driving out grassroots content creators, he was curiously unperturbed.

"That is a fear which comes from the real world that is not likely to be borne out in Second Life," he told *The Economist* in September 2006. His reasoning was characteristically ontological. In a world without scarcity, he argued, real-world companies would have no competitive advantage. However humble their resources offline, content creators could create a high-quality item, then mass produce it without first needing a factory, by simply clicking Allow Copy in the building interface. Seen that way, he concluded, Linden Lab could treat an international car company and "an 80-year-old woman from India" as equals. For the first time, he believed, they would be. This might seem paradoxical, for how could individuals compete with large corporations with vast resources to draw from, in both labor and capital?

So with little concerted resistance, companies begin trickling in throughout 2006—MTV to shoot a fashion video, Coke to promote a live music concert (it's possible to stream Internet audio into Second Life), followed hard by American Apparel to open a retail shop, Warner Brothers' artist Regina Spektor to market her music via a virtual listening booth built to resemble a SoHo loft, and more. Since Linden Lab lacked the equipment or even the interest to provide the content for these clients, another unique Web 2.0–era firm came forward to fill that demand: the metaverse development company. These companies were to Second Life worlds what Web developers were to the dot-com boom, for instead of creating Web pages, they built in 3-D. (And in much the same way that the first Internet bubble suddenly elevated art geeks into highly paid Web developers, these were largely comprised of underemployed students and stay-at-home moms who joined Second Life early on, gaining years of experience with the building and scripting tools, who were now being paid to provide it for Fortune 500 clients.)

First out of the gate with the largest corporate clients, a "meta-verse big three" emerged: Rivers Run Run, the British branding agency that endured initial scorn with its island purchase; then The Electric Sheep Company, led by futurists and technologists long immersed in Second Life; followed by Millions of Us, founded by several former Linden Lab staffers who saw more opportunity and potential in the "private sector" of their former employer's platform. (Disclosure: My Second Life blog briefly had a sponsoring partnership with Rivers in 2006 and maintains one with Millions.) By the end of the year, *BusinessWeek* conducted surveys of the pay-to-play these firms were billing companies like Reuters, Dell, and Cisco to set up a presence in Second Life. The numbers were astonishing. Invoices ranged from the low five figures into the deep sixes. In aggregate, millions of dollars were spent in those early boom times.

As of this writing, in mid-2007, here is the impact all that investment has had on the community and culture of Second Life:

Next to none.

On any given night, one need only glance at the list of Popular Places in the SL interface. These are the locales the most Residents are visiting, or where the most Residents are staying the longest. And despite the presence of so many real-world companies and organizations with deep pockets, nearly every single one of the most Popular Places is grassroots and Resident-run. An even quicker glance at the several hundred corporate sites (for that is all you would need) reveals beautiful storefronts, ornate high-rise towers, helpful billboards—and a couple of handfuls of visitors.

Across the grid, the world teems with game parlors and night-clubs shuddering with the lag of so many people clamoring to get in; sandboxes roil with thousands of Residents, building whole cities of content that climb overnight into the sky. The internal economy remains strong, for the Linden Dollar equivalent of hundreds of millions of dollars changes hands every day, Residents paying each other for goods and services that only exist virtually. In early 2007, Tristan Louis, a programmer with financial giant HSBC, crunched the in-world economic numbers published by Linden and came back with the astounding results that Residents were spending, on average, the U.S. dollar equivalent of $50 to $60 in Linden Dollars per week.

But despite all this activity, for the most part on most nights, the company-sponsored sites remained ghost towns of unrequited corporate desire.

It was an outcome that few had predicted. The community of users didn't rise up in open revolt against the corporations; neither did they leave the world in disgust. Instead, the companies came in and for the most part were simply ignored. (Ironically, some media reports implied that these empty marketing regions suggested Linden Lab itself was failing, but that was a serious misreading: in mid-2007, less than 5 percent of SL's virtual land-owners, Linden's main revenue stream, were real-world companies by my count.)

Rosedale had been proven right: Forced to compete on equal terms with average users, bereft of their economies of scale, corporations time and again lost out to scrappy individuals whose only capital was a broadband-powered PC, creativity, and a steaming turbine of self-motivation. And in this, Second Life appears to have woven itself into another Internet trajectory. The MP3 presaged the equalization of music, and a point where bands no longer needed record labels to distribute their content; video sharing sites like YouTube presaged the equalization of TV and film, and a point where talented filmmakers and videographers no longer needed the studios and cable networks to distribute their material. In a similar way and for similar reasons, content creation in Second Life might presage an equalization of nearly everything else that can be represented in 3-D form: industrial design, fashion, architecture, engineering, and beyond.

Marketing in the Metaverse:
A Lesson in Three Parts

In March 2007, a Hamburg-based research firm published the first extensive survey of Resident attitudes toward real-world marketing in Second Life. It had been a long time in coming; the British branding agency Rivers Run Red established a forward operating base in early 2004, and in succeeding years, a miniature dot-com boom has attracted a slew of big-name companies and established brands. Up until late 2006, few asked hard questions about what these companies were gaining for all that effort and cash (other than any publicity hit from the announcement).

The early results from Komjuniti were not encouraging: 72 percent of their two hundred respondents said they were disappointed with real-world company activities in Second Life; just over 40 percent considered these efforts a one-off not likely to last; while fully a third weren't even aware the companies were there to begin with.

As bleak as these numbers may seem, it's worth noting that they aren't actually too far off from reactions to traditional Internet advertising. Four years after Net-based advertising had reached full fury, for example, Yankelovich Partners conducted a 2004 study and found that 60 percent of consumers had a significantly more negative opinion of marketing and advertising on the Web now than a few years earlier, while 65 percent described themselves as feeling constantly bombarded by ads online. In a relatively similar space of time, in other words, advertisers and brand promoters in Second Life have managed to alienate their potential customers only slightly more than their established brethren.

More worrying, however, are another pair of numbers: While 41 percent of respondents in the Yankelovich study said that Internet advertising had at least some relevance to them, a mere 7 percent of respondents in the Komjuniti study said that the SL-based promotion would have a positive impact on their future buying behavior.

Why has the failure been so thorough? Not necessarily for lack of desire because the Komjuniti participants also report "they would like to be able to interact more with the brands represented" in SL; metaverse versions of established hotels and retail brands garner the most positive reaction.

As to the underwhelming results, I can suggest three factors not covered in Komjuniti's analysis.

Teleporting Is to SL Advertising What the Channel Clicker Is to TV Ads

The standard means of travel in SL is point-to-point teleportation, near-instantaneous transit from one x,y,z location to another. This was the mode for Second Life's first couple of years, but for a couple of years after that, teleportation was re-routed through "telehubs" located throughout the world. Instead of teleporting directly to the desired location, Residents would be 'ported to the nearest telehub and would have to walk or fly the remaining distance, usually several hundred yards. This was Linden's attempt to introduce a kind of smart city planning to the world, in the same way that subway stops in New York City or London become a locus of commerce and cultural activity in their neighborhood. After a time, the company reversed itself, did away with telehubs, and reinstated point-to-point.

In retrospect, this was a move that inadvertently created a disincentive to corporate advertising in the traditional sense. P2P teleporting rendered billboards and most other location-based advertising useless, and in any case, most SL marketers buy and develop on private virtual islands, where they can fully control the branding experience. (Building on the mainland meant dealing with neighbors offering ugly or near-obscene content.) Due to server architecture, however, these islands are accessible only by teleportation, making it the ultimate opt-in experience, giving marketers the unique challenge of getting Residents to voluntarily dive into their ad and stay long enough for meaningful brand immersion. So it was not all that surprising that marketers largely floundered in Second Life in the first year of their forays: The process was like trying to create ads in a 3-D Tivo.

Live or Die by Green Dots

Residents often navigate the world through a dynamic map available in the default user interface; in it, every avatar in-world is represented by a green dot, and this feature has become a quick way for getting a visual read on where Residents are in the world and what they're doing. (Posted events are dynamically displayed as well.) In various locales and islands, green dots congregate in large numbers, and new users' understandable inference is that if lots of people are going to these places, something interesting must be going on there. And so any noticeable clump of green dots attracts more dots, and as those grow, more follow—a feedback loop colloquially known as the green dot effect. Second Life's most successful entrepreneurs (who've proven far more agile and inventive than most of their real-world counterparts) sustain this flurry of dots by holding constant events, giveaways, and games, and even go so far as to pay Residents to visit with camping chairs. Amazingly, corporate marketers were slow to replicate these homegrown strategies. (Surely several company interns couldn't host regular activities at their company's SL site? Sure beats photocopying and bagel runs.)

A Failure of Imagination

To play in Second Life, corporations must first come to a humbling realization: In the context of the fantastic, their brands as they exist in the real world are boring, banal, and unimaginative. Car companies are trying to compete with college kids who turn a virtual automotive showroom into a 24/7 hip-hop dance party or create lovingly designed muscle cars that fly.

Fashion companies have it hardest, for a thriving homegrown industry of avatar clothing design (free of development costs and overseas mass production) already exists, largely dominated by housewives with astounding untapped talent and copious free time. And since the designers are well-known, popular personalities (whose avatars become their brand) in Second Life, they enjoy (and frankly deserve) the home-team advantage. In this world, these potential consumers not only have the power to ignore companies, but also to surpass them. And by expecting their customers to be passive content receptacles, as they'd treated them for decades, corporations now find themselves increasingly irrelevant in this memory palace of pure invention.

Despite the foregoing, there are still numerous opportunities for real-world organizations and corporate interests in the user-created metaverse, and as in the first Web boom, a number of worthwhile applications are emerging from the slew of failures. Through 2007, my blog's demographer noted that the top ten marketing sites were attracting 5 to 10 percent of total visits throughout the world. But in all likelihood, the next wave of metrics will measure results using these categories:

Early Adopter/Content Creator Appeal

By its very nature, Second Life often draws the Net's most active and influential user type. Already attracted to the user-generated aspects of Second Life, they are likely to be active users of Web 2.0 platforms as well, from blogs to social networks to video and image sharing sites. (Indeed, based on internal polling, nearly half of my own SL blog's readers publish a blog themselves.) So even if few Residents will be engaged by a given corporate effort in Second Life, those who are will exert a disproportionate, networked influence that would remain otherwise untapped. This is the long tail of SL engagement (in Chris Anderson's sense of the term).

The Sustained Interactive Experience

In 2003, Professor Ann Schlosser from the University of Washington ran a fascinating study in which she described the features of a digital camera to two subject groups through two media channels: on the one hand, static images or video, and on the other, an interactive, virtual-world simulation of the camera. By and large, the participants who learned about the camera virtually retained far more memory of its features, and a much greater interest in purchasing it. As it turned out, the interactivity worked almost too well: The participants remembered features of the camera that didn't even exist. In Professor Schlosser's speculation (as she wrote in the study's summary), "The ease of generating vivid mental images may create later confusion regarding whether a retrieved mental image was perceived or imagined, thereby leading to more false memories." (Or to consider it another way, the simulation seemed to have fired up the users' own creative faculties.)

If Schlosser's study can be applied to a wider virtual world, this is in itself a case for exploring the communicative potential of a place like Second Life for marketing, education, and other purposes. The immersive structure of the medium has another advantage: Unlike flat Web advertisements, which are seen on the periphery of one's attention, a 3-D world provides a brand experience that is more extended and more vivid. (Assuming, as mentioned above, the Resident doesn't just immediately teleport away.)

Rapid Prototyping and R&D

For all the emphasis on marketing to Second Life users, which still remains unproven, the ability to rapidly prototype content in a shared space is already returning compelling results. In 2006, the aforementioned Rivers Run Red was using Second Life to create marketing not for the metaverse, but for the real world, re-creating assets and imagery for the film version of *The Hitchhikers' Guide to the Galaxy* on behalf of their client, the Walt Disney Corporation. The firm created an SL version of Marvin, Hitchhiker's melancholy robot, and used it in mock-ups in various advertising contexts—print, video, and interactive; since this was done in an online world, clients and filmmakers could watch the process via their avatars from California and England and points beyond, and suggest changes and additions that could be made on the fly (a process that would otherwise require air travel, or at minimum, several arduous rounds of producing and printing high-res images and transmitting by fax or e-mail). Other examples abound: architects creating scale models of their designs that can be explored in first person; corporate trainers using SL as a 3-D whiteboard; scientists and technologists modeling complex systems in a shared space. While marketing will always depend on the capriciousness of Residents, the most reliable long-term value of Second Life for corporations is really just the same value all Residents enjoy: real-time content creation.

After my contract as Linden Lab's embedded journalist ended in early 2006, and it came time to create a new business card, I found myself in the uniquely odd position of adding "Metaverse Consultant" as a title. By then, advertising agencies and other firms were circling the world, desperate for insight on this place that was generating tremendous media attention. I'm not a marketer, however, so when approached, I've based my advice on observations I've gleaned from on-the-ground reporting. Most times, this meant simply describing, as best I could, how the SL economy and culture functioned, and how the native content creators had learned to thrive.

Create a Community

To refer to the Second Life "community" is actually to refer to the intersection of numerous smaller communities, many of which intersect, but others not at all. Formed primarily around personal interests (regional groups also exist, but are less common), these associations are key to active, regular membership in Second Life. (The group Instant Message channel is an indispensable resource of voices, a stream of collective consciousness from which veteran Residents constantly draw.) For these reasons, the best entry point for outside companies may be through brands and products that already attract a community—most obviously, around popular culture and recurring narratives. The first relatively successful corporate-funded presence in Second Life was built around Showtime's popular lipstick lesbian series, *The L Word*. Not only did the site feature re-created locations from the show, where fans could congregate and socialize, but using the capacity to stream Quicktime video into Second Life, the owners of the *L Word* island would host regular episode viewing sessions—a kind of virtual living room, gathering together around the viewing screen Residents from everywhere in the world.

Embrace the Fantastic

The worst mistake marketers make is to assume Second Life is a social game, or a mirror image of their target demographic's tastes, with imagery and totems already perceived as the most desirable in other contexts—in other words, to turn their branded location into a stylish shopping mall, or a standard music video. While it's true that malls and nightclubs are quite popular in Second Life, some of the most successful grassroots locales evoke in the full spectrum of possibility. Suffugium, a dystopian "noir punk" city of the retro future, for example, has a shopping area—surrounded on all sides by authoritarian propaganda and hovering police drones, which occasionally hit customers with scanner rays. The island of Nakama is a shopping mall made to resemble several styles of Japanese *anime*. And while a sizable segment of the active Residents have done up their avatars to resemble MTV celebrities, the dance floors are also teeming with warbots, vampires, and furry animals fully versed in hip-hop moves. This is the essential eclecticism of the SL experience, the Bebop Reality that makes up one of its main themes, and the smart marketer will imagine their brands not as they are, in the material world, but as they can be in this freeform play space.

Leverage Metaverse Brands

As suggested above, the world of Second Life is already bristling with established brands—it's just that they exist only in SL, strongly associated with top content creators in virtual fashion, aerospace, architecture, tattoos, dance choreography, and combat technology, to name but a few fields. The best known of them have earned their place and their name, and new content released through their brands engenders a surge of authentic buzz through the community. The same cannot be said of real-world brands, and so the solution has always seemed obvious to me: Instead of imposing them on the world, why not take these everyday brands, seek out the most famed content creators, and hire them to merge the brands together into a product release that exists only in Second Life?

This should not seem like such a strange suggestion, for numerous real-world industries are already familiar with virtual content creation, of a kind: Fashion companies regularly create fantastic, hyper-stylized designs meant only for the runway, as a way of promoting scaled-back versions that they've mass produced; the automotive industry annually showcases a number of concept cars that are fantastic, fetishistic, and not for sale, since their main purpose is to show off the talent of their engineers. In Second Life, however, the masters of content are often college kids and stay-at-home mothers. Faced with such talented competition, smart marketers will concede defeat and hire these supremely talented avatars to create concept designs and prototypes that reimagine their brands in a world of infinite possibility.

Leverage the Microcurrency

As mentioned in Chapter 4, many of the most successful content creators make use of camping chairs, a scripted piece of furniture that pays a Resident for sitting in it in proportion to the duration of the sit. This is most often done to artificially drive up a site's foot traffic (however seated it may be), and it is controversial in the community for that very reason. The salient strangeness here is why some Residents would remain inactive in a chair for fifteen to thirty minutes in order to earn the Linden Dollar equivalent of a quarter, sometimes less.

This isn't even a matter of being short on cash. I vividly recall a Linden staffer reporting back on the tour of Second Life she gave to a leading Web 2.0 executive. Shortly after the tour, she reported, utterly perplexed, a high-paid executive was sitting in a camping chair to raise Linden Dollars. The reason for this phenomenon brings us back to the "Magic Circle" aspect of SL, for that most gamelike quality of the world that evidently hasn't changed: Despite the ability to easily purchase Linden Dollars with cash and credit, the currency retains an ethereal quality; they're seen as having special value over and above their real-world worth. With that in mind, it's important not to discount the value of Linden Dollar handouts and prizes as a way of insuring attention.

Learn from the Veterans (or Hire Them)

When all else fails, there are thousands of longtime successful Residents who have already learned the subtleties of marketing in the metaverse through and through, and have even developed patented approaches to running their businesses. Most often they do not have MBAs, if they have even gone to college at all. But here again, the leveling effect of Mirrored Flourishing makes their insights far more valuable. Which is why I never get tired of telling the story of Jenna Fairplay. "There's a single mother of two who got her family off welfare by running one of Second Life's most popular nightclubs," I'll begin. "If you want to succeed in the world, don't just talk to the metaverse developers; talk to people like her."

"Jenna Fairplay and Maslow's Hierarchy of Booty"—2004

"They look like ants from here," Jenna Fairplay says, chuckling. The statuesque brunette in jewel-encrusted, spiked shoulder pads and a black bikini is standing with me in the private VIP suite of her pyramid-shaped nightclub, watching her clientele through a floor that's translucent from this side. "Just lets me see if someone is being bad." She laughs again. "They don't know I see all."

"Well," I point out, "they will now!"

"I'm clever; I'll find other means," she replies, unperturbed.

For the longest time, Jenna's nightclub, The Edge, has been among the most popular spots in Second Life, so I was expecting that our interview would be all about how her phalanx of casino games, live DJs, and half-naked pole dancers had transformed her into the ruling impresario of the in-world club scene. I wasn't quite expecting her to tell me that a Jewish Russian immigrant psychologist who taught at Brandeis was the one who'd taken her to the top.

"Well," she explains, "I go by Maslow's Hierarchy." In Abraham Maslow's model, human need is shaped like Jenna's pyramid nightclub, with the base representing the fundamental requirements for survival; the second layer, safety and security; and the pyramid's apex, self-actualization.

"I didn't know Maslow had booty in his hierarchy," I say.

"Yes," Fairplay says earnestly, "booty is a very, very basic need." She laughs. "People come into Second Life and need to find their basic needs, before they want to grow. Safety and food are needs in real life—belonging and booty are needs in Second Life."

Which is why, she says, The Edge has done so well in such a short time. "I think it's how we make anyone feel welcomed," Fairplay continues. "People come into the game and they are labeled 'the noob,' regardless of their real-life skills. People need to feel welcomed, find a place to belong and want to then do more."

"Topless dancers probably help in that regard."

"Oh no no no," she answers quickly. "I don't require any of that. That's the thing many assume: It's a club [with] sex dancers, escorts. I pay the dancers, yes, but that's all to dance. They are free to do what they want."

But back to Maslow's hierarchy. "It's that," she says, "and what I call the Great Big Circle of Stuff. People come into the game, and they aren't gonna run to the sandbox, or run to a skill class. They want to find a place. Form relationships. Have some aspect of real life in-game that they can connect to. Clubs are the first step [for] some who don't go to them [in real life] anymore, or [have] never been to one. It allows that social life they never had.

"Once they feel a sense of belonging," Fairplay goes on, "they then try new things, from making their own furniture for their house, to figuring out how the particle [system] works, so they can have those cool dance sticks. And then it goes on from there to higher levels and higher skills."

In this insight, Jenna Fairplay had created a structure of advancement atop the empty slate Linden Lab had provided. Still, I sensed some missing steps in her transcendence ladder.

"Doesn't that mean they skip the first few rungs of the Maslow ladder? Where's shelter and food and protection?"

"Shelter, though, is security," she replies. "To some, security comes in the form of self-esteem. In Second Life, you can be anything, look like anything. So that in turn helps their esteem, which makes them feel secure.

"Then you got the Great Big Circle of Stuff. Social players are in part the majority of the game and a necessity. Without them there are no clubs, malls, vendors, etc. Social players are the ones who want to enjoy being able to shop, 'cause to them, that is something they don't get in real life, or [is] fun to them . . ."

And from all this, Jenna Fairplay built for herself a club that came to dominate in-world foot traffic within three months.

And as The Edge thrived, the nursing student struggling to support two kids found herself the employer of some three hundred dancers, managers, and DJs attending a daily clientele well above a thousand—and clearing an average of $5,000 per month. And so Jenna Fairplay progressed a step or two up Maslow's hierarchy, and through the principle of Mirrored Flourishing, did so in both worlds. "You go through phases," she offers modestly. "I guess I transitioned well."

In the summer of 2007, I teleported to a new island, where a beach party of dancers, surfers, and sunbathers had been amassing with such regularity, the place had reached the top-twenty popular site list. Most of the partying went on without the keyboard clatter of chat, making it a surreal tableau, like an MTV summer special for deaf mutes broadcast in slow motion.

Peering further, I discerned why: Most of the partyers were actually in camping chairs, customized to fit the scene. They were getting paid, that is, to have their avatars zombified into surfers, dancers, et cetera. And glancing up, I saw their sponsor, evidenced by a white and glassy corporate building near the beach, fixed with the neon pink "T" of T Online—the Internet subsidiary of European telecom giant Deutsch Telekom. And that's when I realized I was looking at a questionable breakthrough: A major real-world corporation was now *paying* Residents of Second Life to visit their location. Steadily (and in this case, to dubious effect), they were learning the tricks of the metaverse trade.

For while it's true that "homegrown" content still predominates in popularity, even into mid-2007, aggregate traffic to real-world promotional sites had, at the uppermost level, become substantial. In a typical June week, about 400,000 Residents logged. By then, as I mentioned, my Second Life blog's demographer was measuring visits to the top corporate sites, and by her count, the five most popular were generating anywhere from roughly twelve hundred to ten thousand visits. Factored by visitors, it was a .8 to 2 percent click-through rate, so to speak. The typical click-through rate for a traditional banner ad on the Web is, by contrast, less than 1 percent.

Commercial sites in Second Life began opening in earnest around mid-2006, and most were failures (aside from the publicity hit from their launch); roughly a year later, at least a handful were seeing some return on investment. It's important to consider this in relation to the growth of the broader Internet. The Net reached the mainstream public in the early nineties, and at first was dismissed as an irrelevant plaything of hobbyist geeks; by the mid-nineties and the launch of commercial Web browsers, corporations were scrambling to stake out a presence there; by 2000, they had wasted hundreds of millions on Web sites that provided too little value to their too few visitors. (They were either bland and noninteractive or stylish but insubstantial.) By 2005, those several that *had* delivered sustained, substantial usefulness (Amazon, Yahoo, eBay, et cetera) dominated. As a platform for commerce, Second Life is repeating the Internet's indulgent failures, and at the moment, there's at least some hope it will repeat its successes.

Chapter 11

Law Is Code

Crime and Punishment in the Net's 3-D Future

In early 2007, a French political party opened up a modest, single-story headquarters in Second Life, for their country's upcoming presidential campaign. This move was not in itself strange, for by then, the world had already been visited by a Virginia governor and presidential hopeful and a longtime member of the U.S. Congress, not to mention members of the Dutch parliament and others.

But this particular party was the Front National of Jean-Marie Le Pen, a noxious figure whose call to exile non-European immigrants from France and dismissal of Nazi gas chambers as a mere "detail of history" placed him several notches to the right of Pat Buchanan. Unlike Buchanan (who got but half of 1 percent in the 2000 U.S. presidential election), Front National garnered 18 percent of the French vote in 2002 and forced a runoff with then-president Jacques Chirac. In subsequent years, mounting strife and riots associated with France's Muslim immigrant community threatened to bring more adherents to the flame-shaped banner of Front National. When the FN arrived in-world, an official press release transmitted to numerous SL blogs boasted that it was "the first political party in France and in Europe to open an official and permanent representation in Second Life"—evidently a move to position themselves as a technologically savvy, forward-thinking party of a new Europe (their version of a new Europe, at any rate).

And this was the political party that put up a shingle in the center of Porcupine, an island shopping mall, of all places. Within weeks, it had attracted at least two anti-FN protest groups, one of which bought land adjacent to their headquarters. Soon enough, most of the Front's neighbors were flying giant banners depicting Le Pen with a Hitler mustache. (For their part, Front National members—mostly muscular young white men dressed in T-shirts with the FN logo—stood inside their headquarters, impassively watching the outrage build outside.)

It didn't stop there, however. Very quickly, protest devolved into outright battle. And after decades of video games in which players pretended to be World War II soldiers fighting fascists, a motley, informal ad hoc coalition of Residents declared open warfare on actual members of the modern-day Front National. Days after peaceful protest, the sky over Porcupine was roiling with multicolored explosions and constant gunfire.

The fury of so many munitions airborne slowed the server to a crawl, so the battle was a ponderous and dreamlike conflict of machine guns, sirens, police cars—and, fitting to Bebop Reality's rules of engagement as prescribed by Bebop Reality, even more exotic armament: "rez cages" (which can trap an unsuspecting avatar), flickering holograms of marijuana leaves and kids' TV characters, and in the chat log, cursing back and forth across the front line, mostly in French.

All this, of course, unfolded during European prime time, so it was four A.M. for me when I managed to wake up to a protester who was strafing the FN building with a chain gun.

"Can I ask," I began, "why you are shooting?"

"Because I hate Front National," the heavily weaponized anti-fascist told me.

"If you use violence, doesn't that reduce you to their level?"

"I don't know," he answered after awhile. "I don't care. FN equals violence."

Having offered that axiom, he returned his aim on the enemy and unleashed another barrage. Another innovative insurrectionist created pig grenades, fixed them to a flying saucer, and sent several whirling into Front National headquarters, where they'd explode in a starburst of porcine shrapnel.

So, while America slept, the battle against extremism raged on thus in Europe. (And in a final irony, much of this went on during Martin Luther King Jr. day, which Linden Lab celebrated by literally insetting a digitized image of the reverend's face in Second Life's sun, inviting you to wonder what he'd make of this racially charged fracas in a world he never could have imagined.)

Since Porcupine is not a damage-enabled area, all of this violence actually had as much stopping power as pointing one's finger at the computer screen and saying, "Bang bang." (And as mentioned in the "War of the Jessie Wall" from Chapter 7, death in Second Life's free-fire zones is just a matter of temporary reincarnation.) But with so much weaponry in play, the server lag was bad enough to cripple anyone's use of the area, or even crash Residents out of the world.

In effect, then, this was a Denial of Service attack, a recurring nightmare for Web site system administrators, who often find their site brought down by an automated program that sends constant page requests at it. (Imagine a madman robotically clicking Refresh on his browser a million times, until the overtaxed hosting servers collapse.) These attacks are generally employed by hackers who want to bring down corporate, nonprofit, or government Web sites for political or ideological motives (or just as often, because they're young and bored). From a technological standpoint, the assault on Front National's building was similar, only personalized, immersive, and recast into the conceits of video gaming.

At a certain level, you could argue that something positive came out of this, for it turned political protest into a game, and gamers into activists. (One suspects the creator of the pig grenade and various machine-gun wielders didn't express much opinion about Le Pen or his politics up to then—until, that is, the group invaded their territory.)

But the result was just as concrete—a genuine political party that had invested resources, money, and labor into creating an information center had their communication channel choked by antagonists. Granted, it was a party of extremists against which opposition is understandable (and in this case, enjoyable in a juvenile way). But what if the antagonists had reversed roles, and it was the extremists who were assaulting the headquarters of a mainstream party? Which is just what happened in this particular case: The very week when Front National was being driven from the land of Porcupine (they simply rebuilt at another site), the center-left campaign of Ségolène Royal as the Socialist Party's presidential candidate created a Second Life headquarters of their own, and according to some reports, they were immediately set upon by far-right avatar thugs. Months later, Reuters reported still more firefights between the virtual headquarters of Spain's two leading political parties.

Seen at a remove, this should all seem inevitable because the Internet at large is well riven by splinters of hate, with quasi-violent extremist Web sites and blogs reachable through a single search—many offering immediate access to semiprivate sites and online forums where outright terrorists and their supporters rally each other to commit actual violence.

Few of us give this reality much more than a resigned shrug, and we simply ignore these sites entirely. But judging by the vehemence that greeted Front International, when the same content is embodied and depicted in a virtual world, somehow the stakes are changed. Residents feel intruded upon, feel invaded, feel as if this hate is no longer an odd abstraction somewhere out there in the unaccountable anonymity of the Internet.

This is why I suspect conflicts like this will become the norm, and legal experts will need to devote more and more resources to free expression in the metaverse. In the United States, we're fairly certain how the First Amendment applies to Web publications, and we more or less have an understanding that free press rights will be crimped around the edges when they reach other borders. (Consider laws against Nazi insignias in Europe, or Middle Eastern codes against sexual content that seems mild by Western eyes.)

It is probably not enough to say that Linden Lab, being a privately held company, can set the rules of expression. Certainly not from the perspective of the informal social contract that, as we saw in the 2003 Tax Revolt and the 2006 CopyBot Boycott, established the rules upon which a healthy user-creation community depends. As it happens, the real Front National party would likely run afoul of Linden Lab's Community Standards, which explicitly prohibit "use of derogatory or demeaning language or images in reference to another Resident's race, ethnicity, gender, religion, or sexual orientation." While Front National may have run counter to those standards in real-life France, it's uncertain whether their chapter had ever done so in Second Life. But the SL community was sufficiently offended by the real-world analog, and that association redounded to its metaverse component. Unsurprisingly, insurrection and pig explosions ensued.

Social ructions like these are not simply political, it should be added, for over the years, just about every Internet-based subculture has established at least a modest beachhead in Second Life, with the more extreme fringes inhabited by groups that could easily disturb the most liberal standards of obscenity. These would include everything from the Goreans (a sci-fi culture featuring voluntary female slaves, who in Second Life own entire continents) to edge play (simulated rape, bestiality, and even stranger erotic grotesqueries) and at the farthest edge, "age play," adults role-playing children while others pretend to be their parents or guardians, occasionally leading to avatar-based simulated pedophilia. Any or all of this is bound to offend most Residents, many of whom are not appeased by assurances that these are consenting adults role-playing in 3-D computer animation.

As a result, largely driven there by vigilantes, many of SL's most controversial sexual subcultures keep to themselves. And after years of forbidding such activity only in public areas, Linden Lab finally reversed its hands-off policy in early June 2007 and explicitly forbade sexual age play everywhere in-world. Why the sudden sharp course correction? Second Life analysts suggested it was a panicked response to a German tabloid exposé that uncovered a number of actual pedophiles within SL's age play subculture, who were exchanging digital photos of real child porn; others speculated it was part of a general cleansing to make the world more palatable to a mass audience. More likely (in my view), it was simply a matter of geographic location. At the time, Linden Lab was planning to co-locate Second Life servers in Europe; doing this would vastly improve the experience for the world's many EU citizens—and it also meant complying with laws of the host nations. And in Germany (where SL has some of the most active users), even *virtual* depictions of child pornography are illegal.

All of this strikes me as a reversal of the "code is law" axiom of Stanford law professor Lawrence Lessig, who wrote a ground-breaking book of the same name. Roughly summarized, to say "code is law" is to say that the Internet's architecture defines what is permissible, no matter what the State says. Create a non-encrypted audio file that allows Net users to swap copyrighted music free, for instance, and that is what they will do by the millions, regardless of what the government-recognized rights holder asserts.

But my observations suggest that this principle changes in a place where code (the Second Life server network in this case) can remain viable only while a social contract is kept in place. As landowners, the neighbors of Front National had all the hard-coded tools at their disposal needed to ignore the headquarters. They could have cut FN off from view by building large walls or billboards and banned all its members from their land, to make sure they'd never stray into their territory. Instead, the physical proximity and the mere *fact* of their presence were too intolerable for code to conquer.

And what happens when ideology extends beyond extreme rhetoric into the politics of violent action? The Internet is already an essential recruiting, communication, and logistical tool for Al Qaeda and its ideological adherents. Many national security experts have argued that Al Qaeda, bereft of a stable geographic base of operations in Afghanistan following America's post–9/11 invasion, is best understood as a virtual, Internet-based network. Already this has transformed the Web into a subterranean battle-ground of shifting identities and false fronts, terrorists and coun-terterrorists fighting for territory and control of the battle space that is the Net. It seems inevitable, then, that terrorists will be

attracted to worlds like Second Life as their next haven and safe
harbor. (Entirely feasible applications of villainy include "dry
run" simulated attacks in environments they custom build; laundering money through Linden Dollars; and most advantageously,
perhaps, communicating anonymously as avatars in a way that
would be very difficult for officials to track.)

I had a rare chance to put that dilemma to a Resident in a
unique position to offer his opinion. In late 2006, Judge Richard
Posner, the extraordinarily influential polymath member of the
Seventh Circuit Court of Appeals, visited Second Life to promote
Not a Suicide Pact, his analysis of law in an era of apocalyptic terrorism. When he was not befriending a six-foot raccoon ("I like
your tail," the judge told him) or enduring an impromptu rain
of fireballs, he took questions, and so I asked him about the Al
Qaeda scenario and where he thought the law stood.

"There is I believe no legal impediment to an FBI special agent
enrolling in Second Life under an avatar that would not identify
him as an agent," Posner opined. "The general rule is that if a
building or other area is open to the public, anyone can enter if
he adheres to the rules of the owner, but the owner cannot bar
an investigator who does not resort to coercion or other distinctive police methods of investigation." He went on to offer a tacit
acknowledgment that the conflict could make its way into the
metaverse. "The Internet offers opportunities both for terrorists
and counterterrorism," he observed. "So it's an arms race between
the opposing forces, both seeking maximum advantage from the
digital revolution."

Then again, Linden Lab the company might disagree with
the assumption that its online service is analogous to a privately
owned, publicly accessible building. So, too, might the SL community were they to learn that the rusty robot or voluptuous
dominatrix they've befriended was actually a Federal investigator

under cover, searching for jihadists. (Or, just as likely, suspected money launderers. A June 2007 Linden database report indicated that the most active SL users by country were based not in the United States or the European Union but . . . the Cayman Islands.) What if the agent's trail led him to a private estate restricted by its owner to all residents? To whom would he serve the search warrant—the company or the individual owner? And how would he convince a judge to draft it? I raise these points and, invoking a writer's privilege, scamper away, leaving the issues they evoke unanswered, where they wait for legal minds to tackle them.

And if the community resisted the intrusion of law enforcement, how would they react when rumor got around that there was, say, a semiprivate island where a destructible scale model of a famous European landmark was owned and run by an eccentric and antisocial group of dedicated ideologues?

Questions like these converge in the story of Better World island. Recall that Osama bin Laden himself has warned the West numerous times not to intercede in Sudan, with its government run by the strict traditions of Muslim *sharia* law—and therefore, in Islamists' eyes, inviolable territory. What if the attacks on Better World were motivated not by racism, but by forces even more malign?

"Guarding Darfur"—Spring 2006

Second Life has its own Darfur, so it's sad (though not surprising) that it also has its own wild bands of marauders, preying on the innocent.

Activists recently built a virtual world information site on an island called Better World. Funded by the Omidyar Network (an investor in nonprofit initiatives created by eBay founder Pierre Omidyar), it was meant to raise awareness of the ongoing ethnic cleansing in Sudan. Called Camp Darfur, it featured the re-creation of a refugee tent city with a tiny bonfires and large display photos of the real camps, where the blue UN humanitarian tents seem to go on for miles.

Shortly after it was unveiled, however, the place was sacked. The first invader discovered that the camp's creators had not fully locked down their property and used that opportunity to raze the place to the ground, strewing tents and images of refugees everywhere. According to Zeke Poutine, officer in the "Not On Our Watch" Darfur activist group that built the site for Better World, the invader shouted racial slurs while he trashed it.

The camp was rebuilt, but copycat attacks by others followed.

But if Camp Darfur has its antagonists, it has its guardians, too. For shortly after the raids began, a Better World visitor who'd learned a lot about Sudan's genocide from the camp called a group of friends to the island to offer their protection. Which is why Camp Darfur fell under the vigilant eye of the Green Lantern Core, a band of superheroes who patrol Second Life wearing masks and tights, and the magic lamps that give them their name.

I met Poutine and some members of the Core at Camp Darfur on a day in 2006, when most members of "Not On Our Watch" were already in Washington, D.C. for the nation's largest march against genocide. When I arrived, she was already talking with KallfuNahuel Matador, a bald, broad-shouldered Core member who guards the camp.

A mysterious visitor had just attacked Poutine with a "push gun" that flung her across the island. "He said he didn't know the weapon would work," Poutine said.

Matador grunted, unconvinced. Poutine still wasn't sure the attacks on Camp Darfur were politically motivated. "Who knows? Some people just do stuff because they can," she mused. "'Cause they have issues? 'Cause they don't like Africans?"

"It's a hate crime," Matador insisted.

The Green Lantern Core was created to build devices and scenarios inspired by the classic comic book; it then evolved into a role-playing group, with members pretending to "patrol" sectors of Second Life. This began as fun, but as it went on, they found themselves monitoring actual violations of Community Standards and Terms of Service prescribed by Linden Lab.

"The role-play aspect kinda fell to the wayside," Matador acknowledged. "Certainly it started as a group of fans of a comic book, but it's grown and is growing into something more."

When the attacks on Better World's Camp Darfur first began, the Green Lantern Core helped them secure the island. Their lead officer built a security script that scanned the identity of all avatars who visited and showed the Better World owners how to read it. Jeremy patrolled the island in the morning and Matador at other times, as did other Core members.

In this, one sees a trend for the future of Second Life—as the world grows ever larger, the sheer population size will make it impossible for Linden staff to meaningfully regulate it. Into this gap will rise neighborhood watch groups and private security forces, acting as the first line of defense while citizens wait for the company to arrive (if they do at all). And in the near future, these violations won't just be within the framework of SL, but real-world crimes—reports of money laundering, accusations of fraud where thousands of dollars are stolen, or worse. And then superheroes will truly be guarding that thin blue line.

"How does it feel to be devoting so much effort to protecting a virtual information site about genocide when the actual one is still going on?" I asked Matador.

The bald giant was silent for a long time.

"Well," he finally began, "I can only do so much in real life, and I suppose only so much in SL as well. But I think every little bit counts." He says that the Core often spots suspicious characters lurking in Camp Darfur—and when they see the Green Lantern Core approaching to investigate, the invaders now flee.

"And when we're here," Matador added, "we don't just fly around but talk to visitors . . . I can be a part of raising awareness." (As it happened, the Core didn't end their duties at Darfur. When the fifth anniversary of 9/11 loomed, a ceremony was planned around the memorial someone had built, a scale model of the World Trade Center in lit crystal. But rumors were spreading that someone was planning to crash the service—by slamming a jet plane into the towers. Which is why, on that day in September, the Twin Tower memorial was guarded on all sides by the Green Lantern Core.)

Days after meeting Poutine and the Green Lanterns, I briefly attended the San Francisco rally for Darfur, held in Presidio Park beneath the Golden Gate Bridge, under a sky that was a vast and perfect blue. A helpful lady was in the crowd passing out information sheets, which explained how to send a letter to the Sudanese embassy so you could ask them to call off the janjaweed. The sheet also had the e-mail address of the embassy's chargé d'affaires, so if walking to the post office was inconvenient, you could always ping him about the massacre from your workstation. It's not a slight to these efforts to note how futile they often seem, set against the oceans of horror roiling a hemisphere away. All else being equal, what can one person do that's more substantial than firing off an e-mail—or for that matter, putting on a superhero avatar and guarding the grounds of a virtual world information site?

In a better world, there'd be no need for protest. In a better world, after short deliberation, international leaders would send their elite soldiers with a mandate and an arsenal, and for the first time in their bloody careers, the butchers of women and children would be the ones who felt afraid, knowing that the arbiters of rough justice had gotten their guns and were coming for them. In a better world, all this would happen so quickly, there wouldn't even be time to create the simulation of a refugee camp in Second Life. Let alone find it necessary to protect it.

The Core's lanterns don't just emanate emerald light, but on command, also play an audio sample from the old television show—the Green Lantern reciting his oath to a crescendo of trumpets. The Core members fly up to the Camp Darfur entrance to demonstrate for me. And though it would probably seem silly in any other place, up there, above the ragged tents and the scenes of despair and the faces of the endangered, the oath seems like something thrilling and real:

> *In brightest day*
> *In blackest night*
> *No evil shall escape my sight*
> *Let those who worship evil's might*
> *Beware my power*
> *Green Lantern's Light!*

Chapter 12

Building a Better World

In early 2007, nearly four years after Second Life began, Linden Lab announced that the company would finally build voice software into its architecture. Up until then, most in-world conversations were conducted through text chat, with the only audio cue the clattering of a keyboard, accompanied by avatars pantomiming a typing motion as they talked. With the new technology and a microphone headset, the Linden staff enthused, those days were over; from now on, instant communication would no longer depend on raw secretarial skill, and interactions would accelerate to the speed of the human voice.

But the aggregate response was tepid, leaning toward the negative. Many in the community wondered why this feature was being added at all, since there was hardly a democratic clamor for it. In a casual pre-launch survey, Residents overwhelmingly declared that voice chat would not be broadly adopted; in a follow-up poll, nearly 70 percent of respondents said they used voice rarely or never.

This reaction would seem strange because the advantages of voice technology (or VOIP, for "voice over Internet protocol") were so obvious. It was already standard in most other online worlds; it was practically mandatory for playing World of Warcraft, for example, and a longtime feature in There, Second Life's closest competitor. Real-world businesses and other organizations were particularly excited by the new potentials VOIP could bring. So why didn't a majority embrace the announcement?

Some of the more obvious reasons were stated up front, from the technical (won't this cause even more server lag?) to the social (won't VOIP "out" people who role-play in a different gender?). But an often unstated motivation was more complex and difficult to express: Voice would not only threaten to expose real-life gender and offer hints at other identifying details (accent, diction, and so on); the concern was deeper than that, and here again is another case of software shaping not just experience, but social structure. From a business perspective, Second Life's lack of VOIP was a serious deficiency. But the lack of voice had also created a cultural hierarchy defined in large part by the written word— and in the process, had advantaged diverse groups of people who had never before flourished in a group setting.

This was perhaps most evident in Residents with Asperger's, a mild form of autism colloquially known as "geek syndrome," since it disproportionately inflicts people proficient in mathematics, engineering, and high tech. In early 2004, a Boston mental health nonprofit called BrainTalk Communities opened up Brigadoon, a private Second Life island, as a secluded virtual therapy retreat. Using avatars as instructional reference, the project aimed to teach people with Asperger's to learn the social rules of personal space, person-to-person communication, and all the other real-world interactions that demand a tango of unwritten cues and gestures that most of us subconsciously absorb by adulthood, but to someone with Asperger's seem like so much incoherent babble. The project was fascinating in itself, but after visiting Brigadoon, I began noticing a marvelous thing: There already seemed to be a disproportionate number of regular Residents with Asperger's, and what's more, many of them were flourishing socially.

This came to me most clearly in an interview with Tateru Nino, a contributor to my blog who I first met as a Mentor, part of a volunteer group who help new users. Dressed in a Victorian gown of crushed blue velvet, with a wry wit and an arsenal of endearments, she was something like a hip Mary Poppins, gracefully and gently guiding émigrés through the complexities of Second Life. She was so beloved, some Residents had even built a shrine in her honor.

Which would likely be strange to people who knew the person behind the avatar, she told me, for by her estimate, Nino has all of four "flesh friends" (as she puts it), two of whom she sees only once a year. "I soak up knowledge," she explained, "but I can't remember if I had breakfast. Most memories before ten years ago are just a gray haze. Nothing there. People are unable to interpret my emotional states accurately, if at all. The more people talk to me in person, the less they like it. Because I'm usually facing in the opposite direction."

Despite all this, she had quickly become a leader and a beloved persona, but as it turned out, this Mirrored Flourishing was precisely because of Second Life's systemic limitations—i.e. its dependence on text-based chat.

"People . . . think differently when they have to serialize their thoughts into text," Nino speculated. "Maybe they think a little more like me. Certainly all the confusing body cues and tone cues don't mean so much here." It was why she and others like her had at an advantage in this world. "For twenty years I've worked to come to terms with who I am. SL showed me I was not that person."

The other danger of VOIP, of course, is a balkanization based on language, for while a large segment of users from the developed world are at least nominally functional writing and reading English, an online world where communication is defined by the spoken word would surely transform into a virtual Tower of Babel. This outcome would not be so worrying to traditional MMOs. World of Warcraft, for example, operates through thousands of copies separated according to global region, with Europeans shunted to servers based in the European Union, Asians to servers in their region, and so on, creating de facto segregation based on national origin and language. Second Life, by contrast, exists on a single network of servers, so Residents interact with each other in the same space, no matter what their origin point.

Here again is where architecture defines social good. Shortly after President Bush's reelection, when international anti-American sentiment was peaking, I conducted a survey of Residents. At the time, just under 25 percent of subscribers were non-American (at this writing, those numbers have reversed, with nearly 75 percent of Residents based outside the United States). I was curious to know whether the in-world experience of the international users in a place that was then still predominantly American had any discernible impact on their perception of Americans as a group.

"After spending so much time with Americans in Second Life," the survey question began, "my general opinion of Americans [has become] . . . ," with answer options ranging from "much more favorable" to "much more negative."

The results were pretty striking: While 60 percent of those polled said Second Life hadn't changed their opinion of Americans much either way, 16 percent said their opinion had become somewhat more favorable, and 11 percent chose much more favorable—this versus 12 percent who said their opinion of Americans was now somewhat or much more negative. In aggregate, then, this represented about a 15 percent overall change for the positive. (It was based on an entirely unscientific sampling, to be sure, though operating with a similar hypothesis in another online world, researchers at the University of Southern California's Center on Public Diplomacy found similar results.) More study is probably needed, but avatar proximity and an immersive sense of shared space are evidently activating factors to a phenomenon that quite literally seems to improve global relations.

These are architectural elements on a macro level and over the long term, but some of the more profound changes are immediate, and more intimate. A Linden Lab staffer once told me about getting to know a uniquely gregarious Resident who didn't explore, didn't create, and instead preferred loitering in his usual place and talking with avatars who happened to pass by. This seemed odd, until the Linden staffer found out why: In real life, this Resident was severely paralyzed and to chat, *typed with his feet*. But the engagement isn't limited to socialization, as important as that is, for the internal creation tools and economic system also open up new avenues otherwise closed. And here, another anecdote: A New England advertising executive struck up a business relationship with a well-known talent promoter in Second Life to book gigs on a client's in-world sites. (Since it's possible to stream Internet audio in-world, many Resident musicians have established themselves as avatar-based performers.) And since they met as avatars, it was awhile before the ad executive learned that this stylish player in the virtual music industry was confined to a wheelchair and an air mask. "It's hard not to get choked up by things like that," the ad man told me, and proved those words by doing so as he said them.

The number of disabled Residents is difficult to quantify—and considering all those who've carved out an alternate identity they wish to maintain separate from their real-world condition, will never be fully tallied. Anecdotally, I'd estimate 5 to 15 percent of the active population have an infirmity that would prevent their full and active participation in the material world. Online worlds become their bridge to the broader community of the able-bodied.

In the first several years of its existence, a steady number of real-world nonprofits were launching a presence in Second Life and holding regular events. Lectures and art showings were hosted by Creative Commons, the 3-D genocide awareness site created by the Omidyar Network, yearly fundraisers for the American Cancer Society that raised tens of thousands of dollars (and in 2007, amounts well into the six figures). But despite their undisputable value, what strikes me is the inherent social benefits that naturally emerge from the medium itself. Not just in text, or the interaction of avatars, but also in the essential rendition of data and interpersonal communication as represented in a simulated 3-D space. Especially for those confined in the prison of their own bodies.

"The Nine Souls of Wilde Cunningham"
—Summer 2003

When Wilde Cunningham get their Second Life sea legs, they'd like to build a house. They'd also like to build a castle, though not as much as a house, and to a lesser degree, they'd also like to run a store. (More on why I'm employing the plural in a moment.) They all seem to like creating note cards, however, and also love waterfalls. Some of Wilde wants to influence the world positively, while at the same time, another part wants to fly a helicopter and get some guns. Another portion of Wilde would like to be a woman; still another, to make money and publish the first part of their life story. More Wilde desires: to communicate their thoughts with ease and to be honest about their challenges.

I finally met Wilde Cunningham after days of residents enthusing to me about them, and truth be told, if I hadn't known their story beforehand, I'd probably never notice them. Because at the moment, Wilde is a startling avatar, with a bulky body and orange skin, and red hair jutting in every direction from a balding head.

But there's a very good reason for Wilde's appearance, and also for their name.

"We decided on our name because we have a group at our program which we had to name, some time ago," Wilde Cunningham tell me. "We took ideas, and then voted on them, and named ourselves 'the Wildes' back then. We have had this name for two years." They laugh. "Just too Wilde to be normal."

I smile, and they continue: "How did we decide on what we would look like, and our gender? We formed the man avatar first, because that day, we had more men in the group. We always wanted a female one, but we haven't taken the time to create her yet. Mary and Johanna would like that very much. We decided on how Wilde would look first by starting with skin colors. We have both black and white in our real-life group, and didn't want to have those because neither is better than the other. So we picked orange."

The people of Wilde Cunningham are severely disabled physically (but not at all mentally), and all but one of them are confined to a wheelchair. They owe their Second Life presence (though not their essence) to lilone Sandgrain. In her first life, she works with the people of Wilde at a care center in Massachusetts. She's come to know them all: assertive John, big-hearted Mary, Micah the joker, shy Nicole, and many more.

Sandgrain uploads a photograph of an old African-American woman with kind eyes and on her face, a shocking deformity. "See this woman. This is the Mary I know and love . . . When she speaks, no one can understand. Even me at times. She's lived all her life this way. Children cry and run from her—when her heart is golden." She goes on, uploading more photos, men and women of all ages and sizes, some expressions sad, some resigned, some twisted by paralysis, where only the eyes are alive.

In early December, I got to chat with them in person, near the gift shop Sandgrain helped build for them in the snowy region of Bretton. Holiday music is streaming over their property—a Bing Crosby song, a Snoop Dogg Christmas rap, and so on. "We have been looking forward to meeting you," they tell me. "As you can see, our typing is even very slow. Sorry."

I ask them how they decide what to say.

"Well," they reply, "members of Wilde, together with lilone, toss out ideas and everyone chimes in when they agree, or choose not to answer, which is also okay. Mostly we vote and take group census on things."

When Sandgrain told them about this online world she had discovered, her group clamored to visit for themselves, but doing that wasn't immediately possible. The care center had its own various concerns. ("Lots of red tape and circles," she groans.) Then came the serious hardware upgrades needed on the center's ancient computer. And after that, there was the problem of using an interface.

"Micah and Charlene could use the mouse," Sandgrain explains. "John and Nicole could, but wouldn't alone. Micah can't read. Charlene has one hand, but can read." She shrugs. Their solution was for Sandgrain to effectively become their interface: She sits at the keyboard, with the Wilde group gathered in a semicircle in the center's cramped computer room, peering over her shoulder and into the monitor at the world inside.

Their time in-world is short, and with minutes left before they need to log off, I ask them if they want to fly with me somewhere, for awhile. So after a few false starts, Wilde Cunningham and I take to the air, leaving behind the gift shop where they display their creative wares; the holiday music stream drifts away behind us. I've only been in-world with them for just over half an hour, but their sessions in the care center are regimented, so they'll have to leave in ten minutes or so. "[W]e get about forty-five minutes of playing time per session," they tell me. "We are full of desires of things to do, but all in good time."

I take them to the Field of Dreams, a meadow of flowers that change color on command, set beside a crystal lake. Somewhere on the East Coast, many pairs of eyes are squinting.

"We can't see it very well," they say, "but from what we can see, it's lovely. We will create a landmark here."

"What's the group's favorite flower color?"

There's a brief pause for deliberation. "Most of the group likes roses." And the field around begins to bloom a deep red.

I ask them what the experience of flying is like for the group.

"Flying is like watching TV," they reply in midair. "It's cool we can do it, but we are still a little removed from it."

"How about just walking around in Second Life? That's something you can't do in real life."

There's a brief offline discussion. "A few were fast to say yes," they finally reply. "Most of us thought, while it's nice, it's still a little removed from us, as we watch it instead of do it. But it's nice to be able to do what others can do. (John chimes in loudly here. So does the room. It gives us an equal playing field.)"

In Neal Stephenson's *Snowcrash*, the hero is helped out at one point by a brutally disabled man without legs or arms, who still manages to run a successful technology company from inside his virtual office in the Metaverse. (In the real world, he also drives an automated van that carries his body, via remote control, from his office.) He actually *pities* Stephenson's hero, still tied as he is to his body and its constant needs.

In Wilde's case, however, the exploration conducted so far is largely in the social realm. "The community is so moved by them, Hamlet," lilone Sandgrain tells me. I say I'm not surprised, to which she responds, "I'm stunned, and overwhelmed even. In real life, it would never happen that way. Couldn't get past the real-life aspects. Here people ooze over them. Say how they touch them, make them better people for knowing them. Person after person after person."

"Well," I observe slowly, "it does make people uncomfortable, even against their best intentions. Being with a disabled person in real life, I mean."

"Yes," she replies. "They know that, too. That's been a harsh reality all their days. Having so much to offer, give, and share. And not being able. Who has the time anymore? To go beyond themselves."

Some of that energy has even allowed a few of them to manage an in-world activity that most take for granted. "Weeeell," Wilde drawls, when I ask, "Micah's our group flirter. He flirts as often as he can. But. Due to our time constraints and our day program formatting, forming romantic relationships online is not why we are playing."

After my initial meeting with Wilde Cunningham, I discover they've left a note card in my inventory:

"The following was not covered in your questioning line but Wilde would like included (with loud and strong group approval) the following:

"As you've been kind to us, in spite of our challenges, so be kind to others in spite of their flaws. Every soul has its disabilities. When you run into someone who makes you feel uncomfortable, remember the golden rule."

Virtual reality enjoyed an intense but brief cultural vogue in the early nineties but fell short of its promise, mostly due to cost and the technical infeasibility of creating high-definition simulations. Ten years later, that problem has flipped, for now the technology exists and the costs are relatively affordable. In the end, however, virtual reality still requires creating a room with massive projection screens and a high-end software package that can generate images on them. Now there are caves in regular use across the world for every conceivable purpose. The military trains paratroopers in a jump simulator; a ten-foot cube based in a Midwestern university immersively re-creates any number of environmental phenomena; there's even a cave to combat glossophobia, the fear of speaking at public events, by placing the afflicted before an animated (and notably rude) audience. More recently, U.S. Army doctors have begun experimenting with caves that re-create horrific combat situations as therapy for soldiers suffering from post-traumatic stress disorder.

The salient and ironic hitch to all these projects is that in order for someone be in virtual reality, he or she needs to physically be in a very specific place—that is, in a room that holds the cave. Assuming the person can even gain access (which is almost always closed to the broader public).

Very early on in Linden Lab's history, the company had to decide whether they would continue working on VR hardware technology or devote their resources to creating the software that would provide the 3-D platform for it. Company founders remem-

ber opting for the latter because the virtual world was more compelling and potentially transformative; they also remember that
software tends to earn ten times the revenue of hardware. But
as is often the case, choosing to build the world inadvertently
opened up another avenue of VR and all the potential it had; it
was lower definition, but set on a platform where anyone on the
Internet could conceivably experience it.

"A Lever to Move the Mind"—September 2004

The fear of wrong things begins as a spidery prickle on the back
of your neck. You feel a sweet chill as it begins to skitter up your
skull, then becomes a soft, sickly expanding pressure in your
chest. This isn't the kind of fear you feel from a horror-themed
video game; it's not like the jack-in-the-box shock you get, for
example, when an animated ghoul pops its head out from behind
a dark corner. This is a cloying, helpless, desperate panic, and it's
no fun at all.

The Virtual Hallucinations building that just arrived on the
region of Sedig's is a project sponsored by UC Davis's medical
department. The brainchild of Nash Baldwin—"Nash," named
after John Nash of *A Beautiful Mind*, for reasons that will soon
become obvious—the building contains a closely researched re-
creation of visual and aural hallucinations based on interviews
with real schizophrenics. Baldwin transplanted the simulation
from a restricted private island to give residents a chance to try it
out, and to collect their feedback afterward. And as I first watched
residents enter the doors yesterday, I wondered whether they'd
feel the same kind of terror I did last month, in a brief preview.

Fred Extraordinaire, a tall Goth with red hair, emerges from
the building and pronounces himself "sickened."

He pauses, as if to collect his thoughts. "I don't like the feel of
asylums."

But the sickness doesn't come from the realism of the graphics, which are, as Baldwin would be the first to admit, rudimentary. The interior of the building is a re-creation of a real hospital ward—for that is typically where schizophrenics will be, when their worst episodes hit. Baldwin, who has a master's degree in computer sciences and a medical degree, but not much in the way of 3-D rendering skills, ended up building the place himself.

Not that this matters so much when it comes to the actual experience. At the entrance, a note cautions, "If you have a history of mental illness, particularly a psychotic disorder, you may not want to tour this facility," and it's not an idle warning. As nondescript and rough-hewn as it is, something about the hospital changes when you enter. And, as it happens, so do you.

> *Kill yourself!*
> *Do it! Do it now!*
> *Dead! Dead!*
> *You're nothing—you don't even exist.*

It's the voices in your head that devastate you. Baldwin has built an audio attachment, so you hear these several voices in stereo, as if they're speaking directly into your ears. And again, these aren't the voices you'd hear in a horror movie—no gravel-throated demonic roars. They're conversational, almost cheerful, and they never let up.

The concept of creating a visual re-creation of a purely internal experience originated with Baldwin's colleague Dr. Peter Yellowlees, an Australian psychiatrist who often treated his patients in the outback remotely, via video conferencing. This inspired his idea to visualize the hallucinations associated with schizophrenia, a mental illness that afflicts some 1 percent of the population (it strikes mostly people in their teens and twenties). To determine what they hallucinated, Yellowlees compiled interviews with his patients to draw out specifics. What kind of voices did they hear? How many voices? Like a police sketch artist of the mind, an artist drew out the visual descriptions, and Dr. Yellowlees integrated the results into a computer mockup. The first attempt was produced on a Silicon Graphics machine and took nine months to build from scratch. By contrast, Baldwin put his Second Life version together in some three weeks.

> *You're nothing—you don't even exist.*
> *Join us in the world of the dead.*

In Baldwin's hospital ward, things change as you approach them, but the shift is subtle. A poster suddenly shifts to contain obscenities; a single word in a newspaper headline suddenly becomes the only word you see. A bookshelf seems to hold nothing but volumes about fascism. A bathroom mirror that is supposed to contain your reflection becomes, when you come closer, a bloody death mask.

"You may notice," Baldwin observes with typical understatement, "it's difficult to concentrate in this environment. Imagine if you had schizophrenia."

> *You're not sick, you're not really unwell.*
> *You know this is not the real world—you're dead.*
> *Join us in the world of the dead.*

Other shifts are less subtle. The floor falls away into sky when you start to walk on it. A gun suddenly appears on a table and a spotlight is cast on it, while a voice keeps commanding you to pick it up and kill yourself. (This is based on the testimony of a schizophrenic who was arrested after he tried to snatch the pistol from a police officer's holster.) A stereo broadcasts a radio news program—which, if you listen to it for more than a few seconds, begins speaking directly to you.

"Is there any therapeutic use for this?" Baldwin asks rhetorically. "We have no idea, it hasn't been tried . . . it's worth a shot." He's pondering the idea of putting nonschizophrenics through the experience, while they're hooked up to an MRI system, to see if hallucinations affect the same areas of the brain as they do in a schizophrenic during an episode. (At minimum, its effectiveness as an educational tool was established by a short survey waiting for visitors at the hospital exit. Nearly 70 percent of those who took it said the simulation had improved their understanding of the illness.)

Another application Baldwin foresees is more immediate, hands-on, and empathic.

"When someone in your family is diagnosed with schizophrenia, you try to find out what it's like." And now, "we can pretty quickly mock it up and we can put the patient's family [through] it."

Some Second Life Residents who've taken the tour had similar insights. "It had a personal side for me," Ginger Murdoch tells me later, "as my first husband was schizophrenic, and it allowed me a glimpse into his world."

Another Resident happens to be a graduate student training to be a therapist. "I have seen patients start yelling in the middle of a group session," Helga Kerensky tells me, "and I would be clueless as to what set the person off. You know when this happens that it is most likely a hallucination—but you expect that they are seeing something very threatening, the type of things seen in slasher movies. These hallucinations are terrifying in a more Hitchcock sort of way." Conveying their subtle horror is important, she says, because a schizophrenic "may not gain as much sympathy and understanding for saying 'The paper said I am dead' as they would if they said 'A man was coming at me with a knife.'" Now it's possible to see how wracking a newspaper headline can actually be.

"It genuinely kept me up at night like two days afterward," I tell Baldwin later. "I'm not lying."

"Well," he replies, grinning, "you're one of those artistic types. Not such a strong grasp on reality anyhow."

But just how much investment of time and resources should be put in online worlds to effect social good? The question recurs with every new nonprofit, government body, or educational institution that takes up residence in Second Life, and ultimately, it isn't different from the question being posed about the endless arrival of corporations to the world. What's the return on investment in the metaverse?

The topic was raised during a real-world conference where I mentioned the Camp Darfur genocide awareness site in Second Life as an agent of social change. Ethan Zuckerman was in the audience, and Harvard's renowned online democracy activist took great umbrage at the project. As he'd later write on his blog, "The Web, now twelve years old, will help draw attention to people affected by these situations, improve reporting and give us voices from people on the ground . . . It's not that the metaverse doesn't matter. It's just not a very high priority yet."

His point was well taken, though it does make one wonder what role all those who aren't in a nongovernmental organization or the Marine Expeditionary Force can play (beyond contacting their congressional representatives and the media, and seeking other traditional avenues of redress). And while it's surely not a high priority in the vast scheme of things, I do want to make the case that virtual worlds like Second Life should at least be seen as a medium priority for effecting social and political progress—certainly in the next few years.

By mid-2007, the SL active monthly user base had reached 500,000 Residents, meaning that it was nearing the popularity of top political blogs; given current growth rates, that number will have doubled or tripled by 2008. Of course, unlike a blogger, most Residents aren't coming in-world to engage in politics. But the unique user-creation tools of SL make a kind of 3-D blogging possible—quickly responding to the day's events with images, audio, video, and builds, in a way that can be experienced by other Residents in the same space.

I saw this perhaps most vividly during the Katrina hurricane disaster of 2005, when distraught Residents uploaded shared photographs from New Orleans and other ravaged areas and created memorial candles for the victims, some of whom were SL members directly hit by the storm. At the time, I called this immersive blogging, to capture the quality of being surrounded by experience in a way that shifts you from passive watcher to embodied participant. See yourself as an avatar, see the graphical 3-D world around you as a true space—and see the people you're interacting with as people you know and can have a moral emotional investment in.

Unlike blogging and other Net-based interaction, however, the quality of a virtual world punctures the fourth wall, removing the barrier between medium and participant, and translates into a willingness to engage that mediums established before it do not usually encourage. I'm not an academic, so this is my inference based on anecdote. But I saw this phenomenon time and again in Katrina's wake, when Residents who didn't know each other personally before took great risks and made significant sacrifices to help other SL users who'd become the storm's refugees (some going so far as to buy bus tickets or even driving into the storm's disaster zone, to spirit people they'd only known up until then as vampires or other fantastic creatures to safety).

It was also evident in Camp Darfur, when role-playing heroes quickly morphed into something like the real thing in the effort to protect the site from vandalism. Where there were once mere gamers, there are now nascent activists, struggling to do something, anything, on an issue that many hadn't previously given much thought.

These cases are small and not necessarily typical, but they're the kind of things that make me think that something like a lever to move the civic-minded is developing here. My guess (and hope) is we'll see more of the phenomenon as the world expands, and as it expands, so, too, the will we see the glimmer of an influence on the real world.

Chapter 13

Convergence

An Internet-to-Online World Road Map for the Next Decade

In 2005, a group of Second Life's most dedicated residents launched the first real-world community convention in downtown New York, and Philip Rosedale gave the keynote speech. After a last-minute shopping spree, the organizers scrounged up clothes that roughly resembled what Rosedale's bizarrely dressed avatar wore, and gamely, he put them on. Which is why the chief executive officer of Linden Technologies gave his first public speech to a large group of Second Life's user community wearing a big-lip Rolling Stone T-shirt and a sequined codpiece.

In August 2007, for the third Second Life Community Convention, Rosedale also gave the keynote address in a costume of sorts, but this one was more muted. "Let me start with an apology," he began, after taking the stage. He opened his jacket to reveal a T-shirt that simply read "Missing Image"—the message users see when a graphic texture fails to resolve properly. "That's me in your way," he explained. "That's us as a company in the way of everybody manufacturing a future. And lately we're more visible because of all the problems." He was acknowledging what was happening with the world as the geometric growth rate throttled the system, while wayward upgrades consistently led to frequent downtimes.

Rosedale's message told a larger story: Now he wasn't addressing only a group of hero-worshipping fans of a niche hobbyist's product. Also in the audience were entrepreneurs and contractors, virtual land owners associated with Fortune 500 companies, NGOs, and government agencies around the world, all of whom depended on Second Life's stability for their livelihood. And like shareholders of a major corporation, they wanted fewer amusing anecdotes and philosophical musing (what Rosedale had mainly offered in previous talks), and more hard numbers and tangible metrics.

In SL itself, this shift was just as tangible. In the first couple of years, it was commonplace to find Linden staffers in-world playing with their subscribers. The programmers regularly challenged residents to laser tag and other games; Rosedale himself went in to build prototype content like chimes, or to improve the motion of his trees when pushed by the wind. Cory Ondrejka was perhaps the most puckish of the group: On a lark, for instance, he once turned his avatar into a Betty Boop–worthy cartoon sun with a grinning face, then hummed loudly while his development staff team, laughing behind him, floated just above a clueless new user like her pet sunbeam. And when a staffer came across a particularly amazing piece of resident-made content, the office would suddenly come to a standstill as the others gathered around to see it.

But in more recent years, most Linden staff would rarely go in-world unless they had a specific task, interacting with Residents only when necessary. The community noted this, and poignantly, many complained, as if they felt abandoned. But now when Rosedale or Ondrekja or Robin Harper did visit, they were usually besieged not by adoring worshipers but by protesters grousing over the latest technical glitch or policy change. They were no longer gods in their own world; they had mainly become its plumbers.

The last ten chapters have contained an invisible thread: "The Engines of Creation" suggested new ways of working online, with disparate collaborators who could succeed only in a place like this; "Avatar as Entrepreneur" restated this point, connecting that activity to genuine commerce. "Self-Made Mankind" and "Making Love" illustrated new and arguably valuable ways of playing with individual identity and desire through avatars, while "Investing in Utopia" and "Building a Better World" took the broader view that Second Life's social activity can have a positive economic and humanitarian impact on the larger society. "The Unwisdom of Crowds," "Burning Down the House," "Law Is Code," and "Building Walls, Defending Territory" were cautionary observations about the conflicts and policies that enhance these benefits—and sometimes threaten them. Throughout, I've tried to show how three reoccurring principles make all this possible: Bebop Reality, the playful improvisation of reality; an Impression Society, which values this creative improv, and the talented, great-souled people who play it best; and Mirrored Flourishing, which energizes the community with expectations that what they do in Second Life will directly benefit them in both realities. Taken together, they build an implicit case that user-created online worlds like Second Life will be integral to the future Internet.

But will Second Life be *the* central story to the Net's next generation?

Maybe, but that was not the original intent.

My first look at SL was in March of 2003. At the time, it seemed to me a compelling but decidedly obscure online game. When I suggested as much to Philip Rosedale, who gave me the demo, he basically agreed. "If I can get forty thousand subscribers," he told me then, "I'll be happy."

Reminded of that statement four years later, Rosedale laughs.

"We expected to have forty thousand people subscribing by the end of 2003," he says. "That was like our business plan, right? We missed that milestone. Now, we got past it, a lot." To do so, they'd endured a tax revolt and a round of layoffs, and changed the business model from monthly subscribers to land ownership. By May 2007, nearly ninety thousand Residents were paying Linden for land, nearly 300,000 were using Linden Dollars, and the company itself was turning a profit. But Rosedale's answer was about more than mere profitability; he was interested in talking about how large the population would grow, and on that score, he thought it had reached full escape velocity long ago.

"I knew it was game over in early 2005 sometime," he claims. "We used to go out and talk about it quietly; we'd laugh and we'd say, 'It's all over.' That network effect inherent in what we were doing was irreversible . . . It was a runaway train, it was headed down the hill now." I brought up the poor retention rates, because at the time we talked, by the company's own metrics, only 10 to 15 percent of people who tried out Second Life remained regular users. Rosedale remains unruffled. "The growth of the retained base and the growth of the content base was clearly a positive feedback runway in 2005," he claims. Those few who remained brought in others, and they, too, did the same; that momentum, he believed, was enough for SL to grow truly big.

I spent the first three years of Second Life's history privately expecting the world to implode under the gravity of its own contradictions by, say, the next week. Old enough to recall the promises of virtual reality and Net-based community that went largely unkept, still bruised by the first Internet boom's collapse, I never saw myself as the metaverse's naïve booster. For the longest time I watched for warning signs of its imminent shattering, often thinking that *this* was the thing would that bring it all crashing down: The tax revolt would destroy the core community and cause a critical mass of exiles; the CopyBot panic would erode the economy's foundation; the native user interface, complex and intimidating, would throttle the growth rate until it finally plateaued.

In every instance—and Second Life's death is prophesied by someone roughly once a month—the world kept rumbling along at such a pace that it was difficult, weeks later, to even remember what had provoked the doomsaying in the first place. Certainly not in the mainstream media, which never ceased covering it. Instead, coverage expanded in proportion to the population's growth rate. Much of the attention was hyperbolic, but a backlash failed to take. Perhaps the last gasp of meaningful outside skepticism was attempted in late 2006 by Clay Shirky, a New York University new media professor highly regarded in the Internet community. The valid core of his argument was that Second Life had a relatively small number of active users in relation to the millions who had tried it out and gave up after a single attempt. So, he argued, it wasn't really growing that much. At the time, the active user base (defined as Residents who goes in-world at least once a week, three months after account creation) was about 200,000; six months later, however, it had more than doubled, to about 500,000. And yet again, the world kept rolling on.

The growth of Second Life will determine whether it remains an important but relatively niche platform or evolves into an essential part of the Net's next generation. As I write this in July 2007, current velocity suggests that the number of active SL Residents will be well over a million in the beginning half of 2008.

Even assuming that Second Life growth then stalls, with some one million active users, it would still wind up a successful MMO. Given the world's current activity, the number of companies and institutions investing in it, the growth of EU users (who now out-strip American users), the expansion into Asian markets, and the continued expansion of broadband infrastructure, this outcome may actually be the *least* plausible scenario. Even then, we are still talking about a virtual world that has been fostered and sustained entirely through user-created content, made up of a million regular participants from around the world, existing in a diverse ecology of commercial, artistic, entertainment, technological, educational, and scientific pursuits, most of them homegrown, some of them financed by corporate and nonprofit concerns from around the globe.

The far more plausible scenario is that the existing growth rates will continue through 2008, meaning active user numbers rising to the several millions by the time the United States has a new president, and continuing beyond.

Randy Farmer, in many ways a founding father of virtual worlds, who also worked on Second Life as a contract developer early on, maintains his skepticism.

"The future depends on too many people and too many vari-ables," he tells me. "For example, at any time, the U.S. government could declare that the LindeX Exchange [the company's commerce trading service] violates the ban on online gambling (or declare it an illegal currency, since the U.S. dollar is the only legal currency here), which . . . could cause the collapse of the Linden Dollar and put Linden Lab out of business in a heartbeat. I'd never wish or predict that, but then again, who could have predicted the bizarre intellectual property and online laws they've passed in the last two decades?" Just as problematic to him is the high barrier of entry; he worries that the proposition of "[l]oading a large client, traveling a virtual geography with an awkward avatar, looking at a map to find and interact with people, and experimenting with a bunch of user-generated experiences of varying quality is just too heavyweight for people who are used to television, instant messaging and e-mail."

Where the world finally lands on this spectrum may depend on the success of Linden Lab's open source initiative. Announced at the beginning of 2007, the company made the code that runs the viewer freely available for outside programmers to develop and improve. Tangible results emerged by the close of 2007, and shortly thereafter, the company has promised to open source the server architecture, enabling people to add new connected, but independent, regions of the world to Second Life at will. ("SL cannot truly succeed," Linden Platform and Technology Development VP Joe Miller told a New York audience in March 2007, "as long as one company controls the grid.")

With that in mind, what follows are five possible scenarios in the coming years:

Second Life Plateaus
Second Life growth stalls and is not replaced in interest by another user-created metaverse. Open sourcing the servers does not improve the world's mass appeal.

Second Life Becomes the King of a Niche
The mass market appeal of Second Life stalls, but the total active user base remains large (three to five million) because it remains an important application for numerous real-world interests (architecture, education, games, et cetera).

There's a Fork in the Metaverse
The user base for online worlds remains divided into numerous, incompatible worlds according to interest/preference: So-

ny's Home, Multiverse, Croquet, Areae, traditional MMOs, and revamped Asian online worlds. Linden's open source initiative leads not to a more robust single world, but a Babel of different, incompatible mini-worlds without any sense of integration.

Second Life Becomes an Operating System

Internet guru Robert Scoble's prediction comes true, and Second Life becomes an integral part of computer operating systems in the same way that DirectX or Internet Explorer became integral to Windows. Companies begin developing applications to run in SL, and it becomes a standardized virtual reality markup language for the 3-D Web.

There's an Open Metaverse

As promised, Second Life open sources/licenses its server code, and in doing so becomes the industry standard for which other online worlds and Web applications create. In this scheme, SL becomes accessible to hundreds of millions of users and begins defining the shape of the Internet experience, in the same way Web browsers do now. At the same time, the metaphor of a virtual world is retained as a cultural and political principle, and in this scenario, comes closest to Stephenson's vision of the Metaverse. It's no longer relevant to refer to Second Life as a separate program, any more than it would make sense to confuse Internet Explorer the program with the Internet itself.

Let's run with the open-metaverse scenario past five years, into the decade beyond. The implications become too wide-ranging to fully comprehend, but at least five scenarios are also plausible.

The Metaverse, Googlized

By the time this book reaches print, Second Life will likely incorporate full capability to stream Web pages into the world, and interact within it—the Web browser no longer being just a 2-D interface on your screen, but another channel of data that can be streamed onto objects. In that way, the metaverse will begin to be indistinguishable from the broader Internet.

This is already occurring on a more limited basis, as I learned when Google searches for my real name first turned up my avatar, or sites associated with my avatar (a sobering realization, since a writer on high-tech issues survives only inasmuch as Google recognizes his existence; in that sense, my success was now dependent on my avatar, Hamlet Au).

This process is even transforming our collective cultural memory. Recently, a Google search of "Hamlet" returned over twenty million results—and in the top one hundred, situated among commentaries and references to Shakespeare's character, was a reference to my avatar.

That cognitive seduction will continue, I believe, until the sheer volume of user-created SL content overwhelms the aggregation of everyday objects and ideas. (Think of it as an emergent Google bomb, only metaverse-based.) Like the fanciful encyclopedia from Jorge Luis Borges's short story "Tlon, Uqbar, Orbis Tertius," the very act of documenting an alternate world will infect our own material reality with its values, its conflicts, and its folk tales. Shortly after that, the distinction between virtual and real will, from the search engine's point of view, become irrelevant.

To stem this tide of virtuality, search giants like Google may attempt to create a Chinese wall between the metaverse and the real (a slippery slope), or co-opt it as a partner or buyer.

The Metaverse, Externalized

In 2008, we're still not clear how much the personal computer will be the dominant Internet portal in the next decade, but it's surely inevitable that it will share the market with other hardware. Not just with PDAs and mobile phones (already the connector of choice in the developing world) but, most immediately, with game consoles. With the plunging cost of broadband and high-definition televisions, they will quickly become the Net access of choice for the gaming generation. In the near future, one of the leading consoles will certainly have a version of Second Life made for it, with the most obvious and organic choice currently the Nintendo Wii, with its wireless controller designed for 3-D interaction. (According to a 2007 projection from Merrill Lynch, Nintendo's console will be owned by some one in three U.S. households by 2011, and still greater numbers in Japan.)

Thanks to Linden's open source initiative, several developers have already created a Wii-to-SL interface. Initiatives to make Second Life compatible with cell phones were already underway by 2007, with others rumored to soon follow. (Limited compatibility, to be sure, but enough for basic interaction with SL by phone.)

The upshot in both cases is an online world brought to tens of millions more people, and one that exists pervasively, readily accessible throughout the home and on the streets outside. This step is all the more significant when you consider the GPS functionality of mobile phones, along with their video/audio/camera inputs, all of which make it possible to immediately import meaningful real-world data into the metaverse.

Another form of externalization will happen through the growing use of 3-D printers to create physical copies of objects in Second Life. Already prototyped by a number of energetic hackers in 2005, homegrown commercial applications began in 2006; corporate and institutional applications in prototyping and modeling are sure to follow.

The Metaverse, Globalized

By early 2007 (according to Linden Lab's publicly released data), the SL population lost its status as an American-dominated world, internationalizing to such a high degree that U.S. citizens, at least 80 percent of the Residents in the early years, fell to only 30 percent of the total polity. Strikingly, only French and German citizens had percentages in the double digits; ten more nations had single-digit residency, with the rest scattered in fractions from dozens of countries in both hemispheres. It's also striking that this distribution hadn't yet mapped proportionate to the world's total broadband penetration, but it's safe to assume that it gradually will, with South Korean membership growing dominant, followed by China (government regulation permitting) and the other countries of the Pacific Rim. By then, there will be enough outposts of broadband across the developing world to map Second Life onto the globe. And as the metaverse becomes ever more cosmopolitan, new cultural mores will evolve, creating a polyglot language of the most common tongues integrated with the unique lingua franca of Second Life. (At this writing, the economic implications are already unfolding, with at least four content creation studios developing for Second Life from China, Vietnam, India, and the Philippines.)

The Metaverse, Nationalized

By "nationalized," I do not mean that SL will be recognized as a country in a cyberlibertarian utopian sense, merely that official recognition of SL-based economic activity will come from all or some of the G20 countries in a way that acknowledges the world metaphor as part of the wording. This could mean, for example, explicitly recognizing Linden Dollars as a currency, or Residents as entities who may enter into a contract enforceable by traditional state mechanisms.

Given past history, this should happen within five years of this book's publication. E-mail became a pervasive communication channel in the mid-nineties; by 2001, the U.S. government had passed the Electronic Signatures in Global and National Commerce Act, validating e-mail–based agreements as legally binding. With that trajectory in mind, it's plausible that contracts entered into by avatars will also be recognized in a court of law. This will further encourage the flow of commerce between the metaverse and the traditional world.

In the likeliest scenario, this nationalization will come from that most essential of state activities: tax policy. In late 2006, a U.S. Congress subcommittee was seriously considering the question—"Right now we're at the preliminary stages of looking at the issue and what kind of public policy questions virtual economies raise —taxes, barter exchanges, property and wealth," Dan Miller, the senior economist for the House of Representatives' Joint Economic Committee, told Reuters. That same year, the Australian government announced that income from Second Life was thenceforth taxable. "The real-world value of a transaction may form part of your taxable income, even if it is in Linden dollars," the country's Tax Office announced.

And with taxation comes the demand for representation, especially as the number of active SL users is perceived as an important voting bloc (an impression already created by regular campaign appearances by real-world politicians in Second Life). Rights will be sought and freedoms demanded, and the U.S. Congress, eager to appear forward-thinking, may grant many of them.

The Metaverse, Monetized
SL currency is recognized as a near-universally transferable microcurrency for real-world goods and services in the larger Web. Dot-com startups clamored for a viable micropayment system

throughout the first Internet boom, to buy media content and other small-ticket items and to avoid the constant invocation of credit card registrations anytime a purchase was made. But no one system took off, thanks to the chicken–egg conundrum: People will take the time to register and buy into a microcurrency when it's already in common use, but it can't enter common use until people take the time to register and buy into it.

Through the backdoor of whimsy comes a viable alternative: Linden Dollars becoming the common currency for several million people through online play, and without quite intending it, creating a large informal barter network for whom the Linden Dollar is the gold standard—and beyond that, the primary currency online.

This economic evolution will hardly be confined to Second Life. All three of the latest video-game consoles—Xbox 360, Nintendo Wii, and Sony PS3—include microcurrency systems designed for purchasing games and other products from their online networks. But with tens of millions of players who find value in these virtual currencies, what's to stop them from using it for purchasing other goods and services from each other?

Consider QQ, the virtual currency of Tencent, China's largest instant messaging platform. Originally, Tencent sold QQ as a fun way for customers to purchase online games, greeting cards, and so on, but as the service became more popular, many started treating it as an alternative to the yuan, using it to bet in gambling games and (of course) purchase online sex. (For a wild time in Shenzen, you can now instant message a "QQ girl.") The expanding trade in QQ became so worrisome to Chinese officials that they began issuing warnings in 2006 against its unauthorized use. ("The QQ coin is challenging the status of the renminbi [yuan] as the only legitimate currency in China," the *Asia Times* quoted public prosecutor Yang Tao.)

The other problem with microcurrencies, of course, is that they have dubious staying power unless they are integrated with a retail system that boasts a wide swathe of purchasable goods and services. And here, the solution may already have been antici- pated by two of Linden Lab's primary investors: eBay founder Pierre Omidyar and Amazon founder Jeff Bezos.

Reading a Road Map

In early 2006, I was invited to help brainstorm a metaverse road map, a project of the Acceleration Studies Foundation, a nonprofit futurist group. Working with media folks in the same field (Mark Wallace of 3pointD.com, Eric Gruber of MTV, Johnny Swords of Second Cast, and Jerry Paffendorf, then with the Electronic Sheep Company), we were asked to come up with a statement that laid out the place of online worlds in ten years. It went something like this:

"Invisible, unobtrusive PDAs will be the cell phones of 2016, and they will access a datascape where information is presented in a variety of contexts—a future Internet where Google Earth merges with pervasive digital readouts to describe the entire world in terms of data. On your screen you will see a 3-D map of your city, overlaid with icons, revealing where the popula- tion is concentrated, know where the high-crime areas are, and more. The walled gardens of fantasy and narrative will become just one annex among many in the metaverse—instead of jump- ing between Second Life and World of Warcraft and your desk- top programs, imagine the operating system (as Robert Scoble predicted) as a 3-D space where you move from one reality to another. There will always be a place for MMOs and worlds where you have an alternate identity—you just won't need to log out, to go from one to the other. It will be an equal and parallel partner to the legacy mediums of popular culture—music, film, TV, celebrity. Just as MySpace launches music careers and promotes movies now, worlds like Second Life will do the same for traditional passive media. (And just like MySpace, the barrier to entry will be low, and unknown talent will have a chance to compete with the well-funded names.)

"Real-world companies will be incubated, developed, and in large part run in the metaverse, which will be the office space and whiteboard for employees across the world. This will engender a high degree of personal entrepreneurship—metaverse as the eBay of 2016. Developing nations will collectively share metaverse portals that will enable them to join the global economy. In this future, poorer nations will still be struggling for full access to the Internet. But just as international corporations ship high-end computers to India now so they can outsource technical labor, they'll ship 3-D–enabled computers with 3-D printers to the places in the globe that can still create the world's 'stuff'—not just information, but foodstuffs, manufactured goods, etc.

"The datascape, providing constantly updated knowledge about every corner of the world and accessible by all, will create total transparency over politics, the health of the globe's citizens, and the planet itself. The metaverse will provide a 3-D visualization with live satellite feeds, cell-phone video captures, etc., which show everyone in the metaverse the state of things everywhere— ensuring that governments don't ignore faraway troubles when they happen. You won't check Google News to read up on a coming storm in Southeast Asia—you'll RSS the hurricane itself."

That's an external forecast. For the internal view, I met Mitch Kapor at his Open Source Foundation office. It's a multilevel, wood-paneled and open-architectured building, with Asian art set on the walls and in display cases, a summation of Kapor's success in the computer industry. I asked him to describe the endpoint of what began in that 2001 board meeting with a digital snowman, twenty years down the road.

"Somebody—Linden, or if we fail to, other people, will take the virtual worlds concept and expand it to its full potential, and that's going to be as large and as important as the personal computer or the Web." Kapor has a raspy laugh and a Brooklynite's brio. "I'll say that without reservation—3-D, virtual world shared space. And it will become profoundly ordinary, that's the other thing . . . Does anyone think e-mail is cool anymore? No, if you're a young person, e-mail is so old school; you're [using cell phone messaging], you're doing IM. This idea of having an avatar and representing yourself and being a participant will, in ten to twenty years . . . be no big deal. It's how people use it, it's how it's going to be integrated into education, into business, into daily life as a social experience."

Kapor qualifies this somewhat. "I'm not clairvoyant," he allows, then goes on to make the case based on his three decades in high tech. "My skill set is around identifying disruptive technology with the possibility of becoming enormous global platforms. The fundamental thing is, at a deep level, it fits that pattern. It's empowering at multiple levels." But this wasn't a business pitch, for in the end, he saw the company he helped launch as just a cog in a larger metaverse. "Linden will own or control no proprietary technology on this. Well, that's the way you get the biggest possible pie; you get everybody in the world with an interest trying to innovate and figure out their place in it and build the value of the whole ecosystem."

I put the same question to Philip Rosedale from Linden Lab's office on San Francisco's Sansome Street, in a building quite literally across the street from where Filo Farnsworth invented television. It was March 2007, roughly eight years after the enterprise began in a warehouse on the disreputable side street of Linden, between a seedy chop shop and a fetish boutique. The previous year, the entire company was housed on a single floor of the building; by the time we talked, they had taken over most of the available square footage. (An adjunct was already operating in Mountain View, with branches in Boston, Seattle, and England imminent.)

"When you talk about the sort of twenty-year view," he says, "it becomes our world to a degree that is difficult to imagine today . . . [T]here are two ways of doing things—so there's a way to do financial transactions which is meet in a building in New York, and there's a way to do financial transactions which is meet in a space in Second Life. Once those two come into serious competition, there's only going to be one in the long term."

I ask Rosedale if he's willing to see that digital progression as part of human evolution, and whatever course humanity takes.

"Yes, without question. Because the leading edge of human evolution is culture and mind, and the trailing edge I suppose is our bodies." In the future that Rosedale would shape, he believes his grandchildren will perceive the real world as a kind of "museum or theater," with realms like Second Life the locus for work and much of our personal relationships. "In some sense I think we will see the entire physical world as being kind of left behind, and it will have this charming quality to us, like Williamsburg or something, you know?"

And while I see an appeal to all that, an equal part of me already feels nostalgia for all that can't be made digital, so I have to ask: "Do you want to live in this future?"

No hesitation: "Do I? Yeah. Because it's a future with better communication and higher fidelity between people. Totally, totally."

"But the real physical world kinda . . . slips into the background."

"I'm cool with that," Rosedale answers breezily. "I like the real physical world; I think it's still going to be fun, right. I don't know in twenty years if we're still going to have the experience of riding a motorcycle on a dirt road, so we'll go do that [in Second Life]."

And as Rosedale spun out his vision of Second Life ten and twenty years beyond, we began creeping up on a question I'd been meaning to pose since 2004, when his company was still in its infancy. It was a question so pressing that when I finally contracted to write this book, it was the very first question I knew I'd ask him.

It was based on a provocative comment Rosedale had made not during an interview, or a company gathering, or an investor's meeting. We were upstairs in the Hotel Utah Saloon, a famed San Francisco bar in the heart of the city's multimedia gulch, and we were talking about the future of this technology he had created that had, back then, a mere few thousand subscribers. Even then, he saw it as a potentially transformative software, but it seemed more profound to him than that.

At the peak of his speculations on SL's future, Rosedale had turned away to sip his pint and murmured something that had stayed with me ever since:

"All we have to do now is figure out how to escape death."

Now I finally had a chance to chase that aside down. Did he mean what I thought he did?

He laughs, and another grand regaling begins.

As it grows more complex, he told me, "there will be things in there in Second Life that will be able to think . . . [Whether] that means that we'll be able to like upload ourselves, I don't know about that." He meant uploading our very consciousness into SL, similar to what futurists like Ray Kurzweil imagined. "So it may be that to be having this conversation means that we are fundamentally mortal, and that would be unfortunate, but I think it's possible. So without being able to answer that 'Can we escape death?' question . . . I think that the most interesting of our progeny will be things that are pure computation. It'll be possible for constructs that we build in Second Life and things like it in a simulated space to actually think."

In Moore's Law, which engineers consider as absolute as a law of natural science, computing power doubles every two years. And in Rosedale's eyes, this law factored into a calculus of transcendence.

"It's only a decade away, the simulation engines," he argues. "The physical world is evolving at exactly zero; the laws of physics are not changing. The simulation granularity and realism and fidelity of Second Life is increasing at Moore's Law; or beyond it, given some software work on top of it."

But is cheating death a thing to be desired in itself?

"Me," he answers easily, "I'd love to live forever. I love it here, and in Second Life too. Absolutely. I think the idea that people are only supposed to live for a hundred years is really dumb."

The train of conversation takes him back to his childhood, and the first moment he was aware of his mortality, which he reckons occurred somewhere in Maryland, around kindergarten, standing near the woodpile and staring into the deep forest.

"I've been obsessed with the idea that we're mortal . . . [a]nd to be stuck in a skeleton," he laughs, "it's not a good outcome, not a good situation."

And so there it was, and seen in that light, all the components that had been built up until then were part of this goal that couldn't quite get spelled out in a business plan—a childhood wish to cheat death, by merging avatars to the biological aspects of our mind and living beyond the physical sphere as conscious data, streaming across a world of his devising inhabited by both the living and, presumably, the near-comatose dead.

Did immortality go even farther than that? I asked Philip if he believed in God, and when he answered, his eyes lit up.

"[A]ll the unbelievably amazing and forward-looking and magnificent aspects of our being are emergent, from small parts. That is a kind of religion in a way, but it does not require a sky hook, it does not require a God that started the ball rolling, or that is monitoring the progress of the experiment. That position is exactly why I'm passionate about Second Life because there doesn't need to be a God. Because Second Life can be as real, and beyond—it can be hyperreal, it can go beyond the real world."

So as it turned out, he saw his scientific humanism imbued in the world he was making, flowing from Rosedale to his programmers in the Sansome Street office, to the several thousand servers in the metal box a mile away, to the endless supernova of ones and zeroes twinkling out across the Internet, to the software that resolved binary data into a vivid tangibility of mountains and oceans and infinite variations of collaborative creation, depicting a place collectively experienced in homes and Internet cafés and corporate offices and artists' studios in a hundred nations, from the old new world of America, where it was first conceived, to Europe and Asia and Latin America and the globe beyond.

"[T]there are those who will say, 'No no no, Second Life can never be real,'" he continued, "'because . . . God has to breathe life into Second Life for it to be magical and real, like the real world.'"

Philip Rosedale vigorously shook his head. "And my answer to that is, No way. It's not necessary. It'll breathe by itself, if it's big enough. We're helping because we're going in as avatars. It's simply the fact that if the system is big enough and has enough complexity, it will emerge with all these properties. People will come from out of the dust."

But whatever the technology might ultimately do to our souls, or the world mind, those ruminations remain several decades down the road. Which should be a blessing, for we are far too young to even pose the questions those times will ask of us.

Personally, I prefer to see the streets closer ahead. Virtual worlds began, like this book, with the descriptions of images that mere words could create, so perhaps it's fitting to end with an extrapolation of the next five to twenty years, merging what the world is now with what it can be:

You are in a small cottage.

The cottage exists in both realities, but it began in the virtual one, prototyped by a Brazilian architect who launched his career as a steam-belching robot who created homes of fragile beauty from an NGO's Internet café in the slums of Vidigal. There, his talent brought him acclaim, and a college scholarship. Now he tailors his simple but whimsical buildings for real-world clients from his workstation in São Paolo, designing each to make optimal use of the terrain and the yearly weather conditions, which are perfectly simulated in the mirror world on his computer screen. The structure of your real cottage was sent from his server to the 3-D printer at your contractor's warehouse (as were all the wall and ceiling moldings). Any appliance or piece of furniture that exists in the real cottage first existed in its virtual version, where you and your family reviewed them in relation to the existing layout, and the way they looked when illuminated by the sunlight on every day in the simulated year. (You're particularly fond of the Grecian vase you bought at a time when the drachma was trading weakly against the Linden Dollar.)

There is a secret entrance to your cottage, but this one exists only in the virtual version and is off-limits to your children, for it is a direct portal into City of Lost Angels, a dark and sensual fantasy game where gun-toting seraphim and cybernetic vampires fight and sometimes make love in a post-apocalyptic metropolis. This is where you met your wife, though at the time, she was a sylph with titanium wings and an assault rifle, flirting with you as she flitted in between soot-matted skyscrapers, daring you to catch her. Later you learned she was an MFA student whose SL machinima had just been acquired by a Japanese animation studio (which subsequently launched her career). For you two, Lost Angels is both your neighborhood bar and your romantic getaway, and when either of you is physically away from the other on a business trip, this is where you go, to resume that midair chase.

There is a city to the west.

In the virtual Wall Street, every stock on the Dow and the Nasdaq is a skyscraper that grows or recedes based on its latest earning reports; global financial conditions are represented as a cityscape, which investors and analysts fly over as avatars, looking for trends, hovering over towers that have suddenly grown unexpectedly high.

In the virtual Washington, D.C., hundreds of thousands of voters are expectantly waiting for the parallel inauguration of the first senator to win his party's vote as an avatar. (It was only months into the campaign that the press revealed the person behind the avatar, and that he was a decorated law professor cut down by a tragic car accident, running his election by voice-activated computer from his bedside.) There are rumors that a virtual component of Al Qaeda will attempt a spectacular attack on the Capitol steps, destroying the senator's avatar while issuing a call to jihad. But if he has enemies, he also has protectors, for he is guarded by a voluptous redhead with a data-infused nightstick, the avatar of a Special Forces commando in his fifties who finally recovered from a decade of post-traumatic depression through an ultrarealistic simulation of the IED blast that killed his entire platoon—and despite his age, realized he could do a final service for his country.

There is an untamed wilderness to the east.

It is a mirror world of the entire Earth, including every mountain range and ocean, updated on a second-by-second basis with data from every satellite that orbits it. You and your family explore it in preparation for vacations to their real analogues, and for your daughter's geography class; when you visit, you see other explorers with more serious plans: scientists who run environmental models through it, for example, using it to show lawmakers and voters the consequences of their industrial policies in a direct and immersive way. Human rights activists have also set beacons on every community in the world, and when any report of social collapse or atrocity is filed, these glow bright red, and the abusers soon find an army of avatars standing in a circle around the innocent, acting as their witnesses and defenders.

There is a road to the northwest.

Are you ready to take it?

Afterword

Of all the phrases in this book, "As of this writing" is the one of those that permeates most. I began work on it in January 2007, completing it around mid-September of that year, which is when I'm typing these words now. True to its Bebop Reality nature, new riffs from users and the company alike keep changing the shape and progression of Second Life, and throughout the writing cycle, I've incorporated many of the more recent developments in the chapters you've already read. The rest I include here, as short dispatches that may or may not be significant when the book finally makes its appearance in material form.

The Frontier Days End: Virtual Casinos and Extreme Sex Made Illegal, Real-World Identification Introduced

In July 2007, with little warning, Linden Lab suddenly announced that gambling for Linden Dollars would no longer be permitted; within days, casinos were shuttered throughout the world (though Reuters' Second Life bureau reported that many of them simply went underground, accessible only by word of mouth). For a time, at least, aggregate spending of Linden Dollars dropped by half. Curiously, aggregate user activity or user growth did not noticeably slow, suggesting that excessive gambling appealed to only a relatively small percentage of the population.

The previous month, after years of ambivalent responses, the company had prohibited avatars from engaging in virtual pedophilia and "portrayals . . . of sexual violence including rape." (Before this, Linden staff had suggested such behavior was permissible, as long as it took place entirely in private.) Some residents interpreted these policy shifts as preparation to mainstream SL to the masses; the more plausible explanation, in my view, involves server location. During this time, Linden Lab was preparing to move SL servers into Europe and Asia, to improve performance for users in these regions. Doing this would also mean abiding by the laws of the nations where those servers were physically based, and in many countries, even virtual depictions of pedophilia and other extreme pornography are outlawed.

A month before *that*, in May 2007, Linden Lab announced a plan to introduce a third-party identity verification system so residents could independently validate their age, real name, and other crucial real-life details to other users. When I discussed the system with Philip Rosedale in September 2007, he emphasized the advantages for real-world companies and organizations that wanted to do business in SL; he expressed little worry that it would undermine the very meaning of his world—to have a "second life." Instead, he argued, residents would likely have two avatars, one for conducting real world–related transactions, a second for private anonymous activity. Redhead SL philosopher Gwyneth Llewellyn argued that another motive was at play: Linden Lab was contracting with the verification service Integrity to buy another level of legal protection should they be sued: "Integrity does not really provide 'just a verification service,'" she wrote on her blog. "Their core business is actually far more interesting: *they buy Linden Lab's liability* in case Linden Lab gets a lawsuit for letting minors to see 'inappropriate content.'" (It was also for this reason, Llewellyn further reasoned, that Linden abruptly prohibited gambling, since Integrity did not validate Internet casino sites.)

Taken together, this cascade of changes seems epochal—changing the world from a small, decadent frontier town into a state capital where families and legitimate businesses would feel safe.

When asked about this, Cory Ondrejka dismissed any such trend: "At any given point if our lawyers say, 'This [behavior] might be damaging to our ability to operate as a company,' we make the decisions we need to make." And he left it at that.

HBO Buys North American Television Rights to Second Life–Made Movie

For a long time, Tringo was the only prominent example of Linden Lab's IP rights policy for users jumping the barrier from virtual to real life. (Kermitt Quirk sold the rights to his SL-based popular casual game so it could become a Game Boy Advance title.) In September 2007, that precedent was far exceeded: Multimedia director Douglas Gayeton's *My Second Life: The Video Diaries of Molotov Alva*, a movie created entirely in Second Life, was bought by HBO, which also fast-tracked it for a Sundance 2008 premiere and their entry as Best Animated Short for the 2007 Oscars. (It was screened in a Los Angeles theater to meet the Academy's qualifications for nomination.) Gayeton created the movie with machinima, a technique of capturing video from a 3-D game (or in this case, Second Life) to use as the raw animated footage for a film. In the 1990s, Douglas Gayeton was a member of Propaganda Films, a legendary production company whose director roster has included Alex *Dark City* Proyas, David *Fight Club* Fincher, and Spike *Being John Malkovich* Jonze, among many others. In an interview, Gayeton told me he'd shown fellow Propaganda alumni his Second Life machinima and explained the development process behind it. This is why I think other major filmmakers will soon be playing in Second Life—if they aren't quietly doing so already.

And Then the Lawyer Avatars Arrived

Led by Benjamin Duranske, the American Bar Association announced a new Virtual Worlds and Multiuser Online Games Committee under the aegis of their Science and Technology Law section. "The VWMOG Committee's immediate work plan," runs the September 2007 announcement from the venerable and powerful law group, "includes creation of a website, an email listserv, and a facility in the virtual world of Second Life."

Mirror World: State of the Mixed Reality State

As of fall 2007, the following international cities and countries have built or are now building a presence in Second Life, most as an official presence sponsored in part by the host nation's government: Berlin, Germany; Copenhagen, Denmark; Holland; Mexico; Morocco; Providence, Rhode Island; Sweden (including an embassy); Tokyo, Japan—and Al-Andalus Caliphate, an island established and ruled according to "authentic Islamic principles." In August, *USA Today* reported that three hundred universities were using SL as a teaching platform, including Harvard, MIT, Princeton, Duke, Polytechnic, the University of Southern California, University of Edinburgh, UT-Austin, Vassar, and Virginia Tech. Major corporations with SL presence include (among a selected list of some one hundred, currently): AMD, AOL, BMW, Cisco Systems, Coca-Cola, Coldwell Banker, Dell Computer, Fox, IBM, ING, Intel, Major League

Baseball, Mercedes-Benz, Microsoft, Nissan, the NBA, NBC, Philips Design, Pontiac, Reuters, Samsung, SAP Network, Sears, Sony/ BMG, Sun Microsystems, TMP Worldwide, T-Online, and Toyota. (See "Top Ten Corporate Sites" on p. 246 for a list of the most successful real-world companies in terms of visits.)

Consumerist Paradise or Barter Utopia?

In September 2007, the *New York Times* ran an extended story on Second Life's virtual consumerism. "[A]s a petri dish for examining what makes many of us tick," wrote author Shira Boss, "Second Life reveals just how deep-seated the drive is to fit in, look good and get ahead in a material world." Since she was reflecting a common perception of Second Life culture as consumerist, it's worth some thoughts here. While SL certainly appears to be driven by the buying and selling of products, the most recent economic numbers simply don't back up that characterization. In August 2007, there were about 600,000 active Residents in-world. According to the Linden's economic stats, however, only 304,499 of them spent any Linden Dollars. So the rest of the population, 295,000, spent none. Of those who did buy goods and services, 131,000 spent L$500 or less—about USD$2. That data in hand, the question becomes: Just how "consumerist" is Second Life when 71 percent of the active population is spending less than $2 a month, and half of them are buying nothing at all?

What percent of active SL users qualify as avid consumers? Let's say those who spend more than L$10,000 a month, about USD$40. On Linden's stats, that would be about sixty thousand—some 10 percent of the active population.

It is definitely true that a *kind* of consumerism is an important part of SL. But what seems plausible is that the bulk of goods are exchanged in a barter or gift economy between friends and communities and just as often, total strangers, sharing and trading what they own (which would fit the behavior pattern of an Impression Society). This also strikes me as a reversal of consumerism as it's commonly understood, since it undermines the economic motives for doing so. Ironic consumerism, if you will. In any case, the economic activity of SL residents bears further study.

SL Becomes More Latin and Asian

By July 2007, Second Life's most active monthly users were pegged at roughly 560,000, according to Linden Lab's published stats. Within those figures was a potentially seismic shift: In May, the most active Residents by nation after the United States were from Germany and France. In July, *they were from Brazil and Japan*, with the Brazilian population jumping from 36,000 to 48,000 and the Japanese citizenry nearly doubling, leaping from 27,000 to 48,000. (Significantly, this growth happened despite SL's being localized for use in Japan only a few months earlier, while broadband usage in Brazil was far lower than in the United States or the European Union.) During the last couple of years at least, the United States and the European Union dominated the top five ranks by country; by mid-2007, nations from Asia and South America had become part of that upper handful.

The Competitors Keep Coming

By the end of 2007, there were at least seventeen systems launched, reported, or announced, all of which were positioned as user-created worlds/platforms or cited Second Life as an inspiration. A selected list would include Sony's Home for the PlayStation 3, Microsoft's Virtual Earth, Sun's Project Darkstar, Viacom's as-yet-unnamed world, and another one from Atari, along with startups Areae, Croquet, HiPiHi from China, Icarus, Immersiv, Kaneva, Multiverse, Ogoglio, OLIVE, Outback Online, Vast Park, and Whirled.

Counter-Terrorists Pursue Al Qaeda-linked Jihadists into Second Life

In August of 2007, terrorism expert Dr. Rohan Gunaratna (author of the generally acclaimed book *Inside Al Qaeda*) began reporting to the mainstream press that Al Qaeda terrorist elements were secretly using SL as a planning platform. Somewhat skeptical, I contacted him for confirmation.

"Dear James," Dr. Gunaratna e-mailed me back a few days later, "Instead of saying Al Qaeda, it may be more accurate to say Jihadists." As to how he knows they are in Second Life, he told me, "We are monitoring them." What should Second Life Residents do if they suspect another user is a real-life Jihadist?

"Inform government," was his terse reply, "so that he can be monitored."

The U.S. Government Jumps into Second Life

On September 10, GovernmentExecutive.com reported news of a multi-agency consortium put together by staffers at the Information Resources Management College at the National Defense University to create a substantial federal presence in Second Life, including the State and Transportation departments, National Institutes of Health, Library of Congress, and NASA (which already has an SL presence). Sure to be controversial in some quarters, while expanding SL's potential for national defense applications, is that the consortium included the U.S. Air Force and Navy.

Avatar Gets Venture Funding

In 2006 (as mentioned in "Avatars as Entrepreneurs"), a resident named Aimee Weber incorporated herself to do business in the state of New Jersey. In the fall of 2007, another business barrier between the virtual and the real was breached: Anshe Chung, Second Life's controversial real-estate baron—the creation of Ailin and Guntram Graef, a German couple who moved their SL development studio to Wuhan, China—secured an undisclosed cash infusion from Gladwyne Partners, a New York venture capital firm. As first reported by 3pointd.com, Gladwyne was the same company that invested in $7 million metaverse developer Electric Sheep Company, but this was the first time such a deal was formed around a known and established avatar in any world.

Top Ten Corporate Sites, September 2007

On my Second Life blog, metaverse demographics expert Tateru Nino has regularly tracked the number of unique visits to the top sites owned by real-world companies. Her "Mixed Reality Headcount" is an imperfect but valuable resource to measure how well these corporations were engaging the Second Life community. For the week ending September 10, when about 460,000 residents were in-world, here were her top company sites:

The Pond (owned by Australian telecom Telstra) weekly visits	12,252
IBM	7,032
The L Word (for the Showtime program)	5,364
Pontiac	4,524
Greenies (promotion site for UK studio Rezzables)	4,152
The Weather Channel	2,976
Nissan	2,376
Virtual Holland	2,352
Playboy	1,968
ABC Island (Australian Broadcast Co.)	1,620

Open Source Shows Results: A Child Shall Lead Us

In the summer of 2007, a fifteen-year-old-member of Teen Second Life, driven by little more than "boredom, wanting to talk to people," padded over to her Mac and changed Second Life forever. Since she couldn't access SL from her school, she began playing with SL's open source code, and very shortly launched AjaxLife, a way of accessing selected Second Life functions from the Web, including Instant Message/Chat, Map, and Teleport.

Before AjaxLife, accessing Second Life required a separate download installation and a powerful graphics card—high barriers for almost everyone on the Internet. A slew of would-be Second Life competitors were targeting this very weakness, aiming to create a Web-based user-created world without such an awkward, time-consuming impediment to entry. Using protocols from libsecondlife, an open source project, Katharine changed that assumption considerably. (Nothing like upending the entire online-world industry just for fun!) With all this in mind, it's not an exaggeration to say that Linden Lab did not take Second Life into its next generation: A kid named Katharine did.

Rosedale's Vision for an Internationalized Second Life

In early September 2007, I accompanied French filmmaking couple Alain Della Negra and Kaori Kinoshita to interview Philip Rosedale for a documentary about Second Life they were just completing. (For postmodern reasons, they liked the idea that the avatar journalist would also be the one interviewing Rosedale in physical form.) This gave me a chance to incorporate one last conversation with him into this book, and so I asked Linden Lab's CEO how he believed Second Life would function when they added connected servers in countries across the world—including in nations with wildly different laws and standards regarding sexual content and other contentious forms of expression.

Servers will probably be in all the individual countries where Residents physically lived, he suggested. Rather than entirely assent to the censorship or regulations each of these countries would demand, Rosedale had another proposal: Each user would be able to select a content restriction filter defined according to country, while the criterion of each nation's filter would be made publicly available somewhere (on the company's Web site or in the SL client itself). By making the censorship and regulation process so transparent, he argued, countries would feel market pressures to relax their standards, converging into greater general freedom.

This was all well and good, but I had to press him on the starker point: Transparency or not, what would happen if an SL server in a repressive state contained real-life information about a resident using Second Life's expression tools to express political dissent? Would they follow Yahoo's lead, and simply give the person up to the authorities? Rosedale said no, insisting that this would be against the company's corporate values.

Visionaries Versus Reality:
Some Cyberpunks Come, Some Stay Away

By 2007, a number of influential science-fiction writers who had written extensively about online worlds had mentioned or visited SL. Among them were Bruce Sterling, Vernor Vinge, and Cory Doctorow—and even cyberpunk grand master William Gibson, who described to an Amazon interviewer how he once visited as an anonymous noob, spurned by all: "I wound up being this grotesquely overweight, bright blue smurf. In a tutu. Nobody thought that was cool."

But even four years into its history, one name was conspicuously missing.

Neal Stephenson's *Snowcrash* is the most recurrent title through-out this book, and while finishing the manuscript, I suddenly real-ized it had a gaping lacuna: I hadn't asked Stephenson himself about Second Life. As Stephenson was notoriously reclusive with the press, I steeled myself and sent him an e-mail. Had he visited? What did he think of this online world that was so deeply associ-ated with this novel he had written fifteen years ago, people already used "metaverse" and "Second Life" interchangeably?

Several days later, on May 28, he sent me this reply, repro-duced here in its entirety:

James,
    I know that people are finding this hard to believe, but I have not checked Second Life out yet. Too many other things going on in my life.
Good luck,
Neal

Final bulletins from October 2007:

• IBM and Linden Lab announce an initiative to create a uni-versal interoperability standard for avatars moving between mul-tiple online worlds.

• Following young Katharine Berry's lead, at least three compa-nies launch alternate SL viewers: 3Di's web-based Movable Life, Penguin Crossing's inDuality (which runs SL within the web), and most noteworthy, the Electric Sheep Company's OnRez, which integrates browsing sites in SL with browsing sites on the web, effectively turning their viewer into an operating system.

• In the same October week, NBC's *The Office* features Sec-ond Life as a major plot point, while CBS's *CSI:NY* premiers a multipart search for a murderer in Second Life (which viewers can continue by tracking down clues revealed in the TV show in the world itself.)

• UK telecom giant Vodafone launches a service allowing residents to send and receive text messages from SL to mobile phone, and vice versa.

• In September, an international coalition of labor unions protest a paycut levied against IBM's Italian workers by converging on the company's Second Life campus, with an estimated 1800 union members in attendance as avatars. (Attendees include a giant sign-waving banana.) In October, IBM's Italy CEO steps down; the coalition acclaims this as a triumph of their virtual protest.

A Selected
Second Life Glossary

Alt—Alternative **Resident** account. Popular with users who wish to maintain more than one identity **in-world** for various purposes, such as a "public facing" Resident for conducting business, another for recreational/private purposes, and so on. The cultural and economic robustness of Second Life, in other words, has provoked a desire in many to have third or even fourth lives (or more).

Animation—A series of customizable **avatar** movements saved in a Resident's **inventory** or **poseball**.

Attachments—Avatar enhancements fixed directly to part or all of the body, including clothes, custom hair, and weapons.

Augmentationist versus Immersionist—A term coined by former Linden staffer Henrik Bennetsen in an influential essay describing the two main perspectives of Second Life held by Residents. An augmentationist sees Second Life as a 3-D complement to the Web, other media, and the real world; an immersionist sees it as a self-contained, alternate world, and generally considers outside media or reality as breaking this illusion.

In one interpretation, Augmentationists will make up the mainstream users of SL, while the Immersionists will be the smaller community of hardcore users.

Avatar—From the Sansrkit for "godly incarnation," a common virtual-world term for an onscreen alter ego or character controlled by the user. Avatar generally refers to the specific physical characteristics (gender, race, etc.) of a **Resident**. Many Residents have several avatars for different events, moods, social situations.

Bebop Reality—My description of the community's perception of Second Life: a universe in which the fundamental laws of physics and identity are open to constant improvisation by its inhabitants, who constantly modify and embellish it to a positive effect (as long as the world's underlying structure isn't harmed—see **gray goo**).

Beta—Common high-tech jargon for software in the last stages of testing, often by volunteer users, just before commercial release.

Bling—Inspired by hip-hop culture, a term for jewelry and other fashion accessories that literally cast beams of light. It's associated with **social gamers**, who are sometimes referred to pejoratively as "Blingtards."

Camping chair—Developed to boost a site's **in-world** foot traffic, a piece of furniture that, when sat upon, generally pays the user **Linden Dollars** in proportion to the duration of the sitting. Not necessarily a literal chair; other examples include **poseballs** that animate a **Resident** to dance, perform chores, or do other activities.

FIC—"Feted Inner Core," a title coined by longtime **Resident** conspiracy theorist Prokofy Neva (profiled in my blog as "the Noam Chomsky of Second Life") to describe a supposed collusion between elite Residents, Linden Lab, and **metaverse developers** at the expense of casual and inexperienced new users.

Furry—Among the most visible subculture in Second Life, anthropomorphic cartoon animal **avatars** (squirrels, raccoons, etc.). Once the object of scabrous Internet mockery, the role-playing subculture is renowned in-world for its building and scripting talents.

Gesture—Short **animation** and/or sound effects launched by a keyword or other shortcut, generally to express an immediate **avatar** reaction, such as applause or laughing.

GOM-ed—Bane of the **Resident** innovator, the process by which a user-made content or service is undermined or superseded by a subsequent official software/Web site update. From "Gaming Open Market," a Resident-run Web site that was once the leading **Linden Dollar** currency exchange outlet—until Linden Lab's new LindeX trading service effectively rendered it obsolete.

Gray goo—Nanotechnology's worst nightmare comes to the metaverse—griefer-created, self-replicating objects that overwhelm the world and crash the server(s). Linden defenses include creating "fire breaks" of disabled servers—or, more recently, reporting the perpetrators to the extra-territorial authorities (the Federal Bureau of Investigation).

Green Dot Effect—A feedback loop in which a group of **Residents** displayed as green dots on the **viewer** map attracts still more Residents.

Grid—The totality of simulators available and accessible to **Residents**—i.e., the known world. It does not include Second Life simulators that are not immediately accessible to users on the rest of the grid. (There have long been rumors of off-the-grid simulators owned by government intelligence agencies and other covert operators.) Often abbreviated as MG (Main Grid) to distinguish it from TG (Teen Grid, i.e., Teen Second Life).

Griefer—An individual dedicated to annoying or upsetting a designated user, sometimes through confusion and trickery that violates the spirit but not the letter of the online law.

Immersion—The visual, audio, and social cues that create the illusion of being in an alternate world, interacting with **avatars** who are distinct from their users.

Impression Society—My definition for Second Life's social hierarchy: **Residents** are most valued and respected to the degree they make cultural, economic, or social contributions with organic creative flair, distinction, and sustained effect.

Inventory—A **Resident** storage folder containing all owned objects, **landmarks, animations,** et cetera.

In-world—The state of being online in Second Life.

Lag—In general, network congestion that slows down communication between client and server. Specifically to Second Life, lag is typically caused when an excess of **Residents, prims,** or active **scripts** exist in a given **simulator.**

Land baron—A large landowner/property manager whose business model focuses on acquiring, owning, and hosting large blocs of land and charging **Residents** rent to use or live on designated parts of the property.

Landmark—Similar to a Web browser bookmark, only in 3-D, used to teleport to a specific x,y,z location on the **grid**.

Linden—A staffer of Linden Lab, with "Linden" as an **avatar** surname. Most commonly seen Lindens **in-world** are "Liaisons" and Community Team members, a combination of permissive Berkeley cop, social worker, and cruise director—an omnipotent, omniscient demigod.

Linden Dollar (L$)—The official currency of Second Life, released to and withdrawn from the economy in relation to the population and inflation. At publication time, its status to the outside world is still in flux; some consider it mere "play money," but others feel it deserves official status equivalent to the currency of a foreign nation.

Linden Script Language (LSL)—A Second Life–based programming code similar to C+.

Machinima—Movie file created by capturing the action in a video or computer game—or in this case, a 3-D online world.

Metaverse developer—A company creating sites, events, and experiences **in-world** on behalf of real-world companies and organizations other than Linden Lab.

Mirrored Flourishing—My term for a general community belief that positive contributions to Second Life can and should have a positive impact on **Residents** in their real lives—and vice versa.

Mixed reality—A combination of Second Life with real-world elements, such as marketing or an external input. A typical "mixed reality event" is a real party where Second Life is projected onto a screen, so partygoers and geographically removed **Residents** can interact.

MMORPG—Massively multiplayer online role-playing game, or sometimes MMO (massively multiuser online world), an acronym that includes both traditional role-playing games like World of Warcraft and open-ended platforms like Second Life.

Noob—Common gamer jargon for new user; usually a pejorative term for a foolishly inexperienced or incompetent **Resident**.

Permissions—The code-based heart of user-created content intellectual property rights, a series of checkbox designations the creator can choose in order to determine whether the object or script can be copied, sold, modified, etc.

Poseball—A small scripted object that, when sat on, launches a preset animation on your **avatar**. It's the key technology underlying nightclub dancing, sexual intercourse, and other social activities.

Prim—Short for "primitive," an essential building block with which all objects on the grid are constructed. Originally **rezzed** as a primary shape such as a cube, cylinder, or sphere, a prim can have its form altered, its surface textured, and its physical composition changed in an infinite number of ways. Most **in-world** objects are comprised of two or more prims linked together. Prims can be set to respond to the physical forces of Second Life, including gravity and wind. They can also be turned invisible, or made visible but without physical substance.

Profile —A viewer window listing **Residents**' name, creation date, and other self-selected details (interests, real-life identity, etc.).

Resident—A Second Life **avatar**, and the user account (e-mail, credit card information, etc.) associated with it. A term used by Linden Lab from inception, to suggest ownership and community status, as opposed to that of a mere paying customer. Individual users may own more than one Resident by having an alternate or **alt** account. This point has provoked some controversy over the total number of unique users in Second Life. According to a Linden Lab report published in January 2007, approximately 63 percent of total Residents were unique users, with the rest alts or incomplete registrants.

Region—A **simulator**.

Rez—To instantiate **prims** into the world, either with the Build function or by removing a preexisting object from **inventory**.

Ruthed—As in, "I've been Ruthed!" Phenomenon whereby (due to server error) an avatar loses its individual characteristics, temporarily regressing to original, default demale avatar form, colloquially known as "Ruth." Particularly disconcerting to most male users.

Sandbox—A free build area, where **Residents** can **rez** objects without having to own land. The sandboxes are consistently the most creative places in Second Life and enjoy their own subculture of inventors.

Script—A set of instructions in Linden Script Language that enable Residents to add functions and program behavior such as motion or interactivity into their creations.

Simulator—Often abbreviated as "sim," a discrete area of in-world geography, approximately sixteen acres in size, contained on a single server. (Also refers to the space directly above and the area below the simulator's perimeter.) Most simulators are physically linked together to create a single, contiguous continent.

SLURL—A Web-based link that launches the Second Life client and automatically teleports a user directly to a specific x,y,z location.

Social gamer—Common game industry jargon used in this context to denote a Resident whose Second Life activity centers around social activity, such as clubbing, partying, playing casual games, or engaging in sex. Often pejoratively referred to as "blingtards," social gamers have a stronger culture than is generally credited, with role-play involving "mafia families," nightclub rivalries, sexual drama, et cetera.

Subcultures—Numerous discrete communities in Second Life abound, most centered around preexisting subcultures. The most prominent include furries, elves, Goreans (fantasy/S&M role-playing inspired by the novels of cult pulp-fiction writer John Norman), robots, social gamers, Space Navy, and vampires. Native Second Life subcultures include sandbox denizens, scripters, and members of the fashion industry (such as designers and models).

Teleport (TP)—The automatic and near-instantaneous ability of Residents to move from one x,y,z coordinate to another.

Viewer—The Second Life client/program individuals must install and run to enter the world.

Appendix One:
Three Tips for Exploring
Second Life

Your first step, of course, is to download and install the software available at Secondlife.com, with versions for Apple, Windows, and Linux. As of this writing, basic accounts are free. However, you will need a broadband connection and a newer computer with a 3-D graphics card. (See the official site for full specs.) Here's a cheat sheet for what to do next.

Go with a purpose—or embrace purposelessness

Every day, thousands of people try Second Life with the vague aim of finding out what the fuss is about. Most of them leave, disappointed and frustrated, expecting a traditional online game experience with set goals. For this reason, I often advise the uninitiated to wait until they learn of a specific event or site they want to experience. Either that, or explore with no set goals, chatting with Residents who seem experienced, going from place to place until you find a niche.

Find a seasoned guide

With so much to learn and a world that's often overwhelming, not to mention a cantankerously difficult user interface (at this writing), it helps to begin with a friend who's already well versed in SL. Explore together on adjacent computers or while on a phone/Skype call, so the person can talk you through its many complexities.

See Seven Wonders

There's far more than that, of course, but here's a personal starter list. In Second Life, use the Search > Places function, enter the below **bold keywords,** and when the selection is displayed, click Teleport:

Svarga, an artificial ecosystem with a weather system and several species of interdependent creatures, created in 2006 by a UK programmer with the Resident name Laukosargas Svarog. Rosedale pronounced it as an example of the simulated natural world he originally intended Second Life to be.

Lost Gardens of Apollo, a dreamily romantic location of high towers and narble walkways.

Greenies, a Pixar-worthy playspace in which you beacome a thumb-size avatar in a sixteen-acre apartment from the fifties.

For gamers, the (often risqué) role-playing regions of **Midian, Norsim, City of Lost Angels, Wasteland, Midgard,** and **Samurai Island**. These are some of the new Nexus Primes mentioned in "Engines of Creation."

The four-dimensional **Crooked House** in **The Future** (difficult to reach, but worth the effort).

A **Sandbox** denotes a free-build area; these locations are teeming with improvisational talent, Bebop Reality at its purest.

The indispensable community-run site for helping Residents just starting out: **New Citizens Incorporated**.

Appendix Two: Three Tips for Real Businesses Starting Out in **Second Life**

As with the first corporate Web sites of the mid-nineties, most of the initial companies to jump in created a Second Life presence with limited interactivity or usefulness, and consequently attracted few visitors. Here's some general initial advice: If an employee at your company hasn't already stormed into SL and made himself an expert and advocate, contact a metaverse development company; these are listed on the official site under http://secondlife.com/developers/. (My own particulars as a consultant are available there, as well.)

Learn from what works

As I write this, the top five corporate sites are attracting about three thousand to ten thousand visits, meaning that at the current numbers, they're garnering a .8 percent to 2 percent click-through rate, so to speak. (By contrast, typical click-through for a traditional banner ad on the Web is an estimated .5 percent to 1 percent weekly.) These are the sites that you should explore before launching one of your own. Even more important than that, however, is to visit the grassroots places that are even more popular (at least those that succeed without the ready-made hook of free money or sex) and the in-world business owners who are making the best profits.

Respect and serve the existing community

For the near future, SL's barrier to entry is fairly high, so don't plan on drawing many new users to your presence. Instead, expect that most of your audience will be seasoned Residents. While there is little opposition to real-world corporations per se, arrogant companies are scorned. Never imply that your arrival is some heralded "first" because odds are it isn't. Instead, reach out to the community by hiring local talent and engaging them on a regular basis.

Find a killer SL app

Take the time to create a utility or service that both is unique to SL and leverages the main element that makes SL unique: dynamic user-created content in an international virtual community. Rather than giving away copies of your latest product, for example, encourage Residents to improve or riff on them—and make sure your own developers and designers are taking notes, for ideas.

Acknowledgments

A book about a user-created world has its advantages, but it also means far more people who helped make it possible—and subsequently, many more names to remember when it comes time to offer thanks. I am certain this list has inadvertently omitted many, but among those I am certain gratitude is owed:

First, Jennifer Schlegel, my beautiful partner in all words, who shepherded and supported me when the book consumed all other rational thought, and in the final hours, offered indispensable editorial insight.

My parents, Whit and Dorothy, and extended family, always encouraging if occasionally bemused, to whom I owe so much for where I am today.

My agent, David Fugate of Launch Books, fought for this project when Second Life had less than a hundred thousand active users, and helped me shape it into something far more ambitious than I originally imagined. Ethan Friedman of HarperCollins grasped the essence of the proposal before it was even written, and steered it with a light hand toward a coherent shape.

To Linden Lab's staff in general, and in particular (besides those featured throughout the book—Philip, Cory, Robin, Mitch, Andrew, and Hunter), those who worked with me closest during my Lab years and kept in touch afterward: Catherine, Lauren, Jean, Ian, Jeska, Ben, Liana, Bub, Haney, Sky, Daniel, Ginsu, Kona, Jim, Kyle, Pathfinder, Ryan, Beth, Peter, Jeff, Torley, Mark, Chadrick, Henrik, Nicole, Peter, Charity, Karen, and Babbage.

Fellow Second Life–based journalists and metaverse blogs have been a valuable resource to this book and great colleagues in both worlds, most especially Mark Wallace of 3pointD.com, Peter Ludlow of the lovably scandalous tabloid SecondLifeHerald.com, Dan Terdiman of News.com, Mitch Wagner at InformationWeek, Adam Pasick and team at Reuters SL, and the team at Virtualworldsnews.com. Moving outward into the wider technorati, there are the hipster academics of TerraNova.blogs.com, Cory Doctorow and his colleagues at Boingboing.net, along with Henry Jenkins, Robert Scoble, Lawrence Lessig, and Joi Ito. Still more assorted luminaries of high-tech culture and gaming who inspired in this book's evolution in ways large and small, in no particular order: Doug Church, Harvey Smith, Regine DeBatty, Robin Hunicke, Susan Wu, Clive Thompson, Jane Pinckard, Aleks Krotoski, Alice Taylor, Eric Rice, Jamais Cascio, Brian Yeung, Ren Reynolds, Jane McGonigal, Eddie Codel, Betsy Book, danah boyd, Jerry Paffendorf, Justin Hall, Philip Torrone, Howard Rheingold, Ralph Koster, Scott Jennings, Ethan Zuckerman, and Erik Wolpaw.

Om Malik and the team at GigaOM.com have been great supporters throughout this process. Om especially helped guide and shape my thoughts about business uses of Second Life, if only by pushing me to think more in bottom-line terms.

Reuben Steiger and his team at Millions of Us have been energetic partners for Second Life projects and a steadfast sponsor of my blog. (And before them, albeit too briefly, Rivers Run Red.) John Battelle, Bill Brazell, Chas Edwards, and their staff at Federated Media adopted my Second Life blog very soon after Linden Lab nudged it from the nest.

Dan Hunter of Terra Nova and Wharton lobbied me to write this book as far back as 2005, marshaling numerous shots of Lagavulin in one hand and the irresistible Professor Beth Noveck in the other as leverage, finally convincing me to push it forward. As the driving force behind State of Play, the premier online world academic conference, Beth's influence on this book is subterranean and essential.

In the mid-1990s, *Play Money* author Julian Dibbell had the audacity to write about an online world as if the things that happened within it mattered; he pioneered the way and made this book conceptually possible.

Neither should I forget the circle of friends outside this strange new medium, morale boosters and sounding boards: Damien Samuel, Nolan Cook, Andrew Leonard and his BBQ consortium of Ben and Cyndie, Chad and Nancy, and many more.

Above all, the book is dedicated to the community of Second Life residents, in all their lovably ingenious, inventive, geeky, resourceful, open-hearted, wildly diverse if occasionally cantankerous varieties. SL has succeeded only because of them, and this book exists only because they do. The main reason I have devoted so much of my career to this one online world is because they deserve to have their story told.

First to the regular writers on my Second Life blog: astoundingly stylish glamour columnist Iris Ophelia, great-souled demographer Tateru Nino, energetic events impresario Rik Riel, arts columnist Amalthea Blanc, and incisive game reviewer Onder Skall.

What follows is a very highly abbreviated list of Residents

who've inspired with their creativity, or been invaluable inter-
preters, guides, and friends:

Adam Zaius
Aimee Weber
Aliasi Stonebender
Angrybeth Shortbread
Artemis Fate
Baccara Rhodes
Bel Muse
Bhodi Silverman
Biscuit Carrol
Boliver Oddfellow
Catherine OmegaCe-
    lebrity Trollop
China Tracy
Chip Midnight
Cory Edo
Cubey Terra
Damien Fate
Dane Street
Dane Zander
Dave Zeeman
Derek Jones
Dominik Bauer
Eboni Khan
Eddie Escher
Eddy Stryker
Eggy Lippmann
epredator Potato
Falk Bergman

Fallingwater Cellar-
    door
Fey Brightwillow
FlipperPA and Jenny-
    fur Peregrine
Forseti Svarog
Foxy Xevious
Frances Chung
Frogg Marlowe
Gwynneth Llewellyn
In Kenzo
IrightI Shirakawa
Jade Lily
James Miller
Jeffrey Gomez
KatanaBlade Anubis
Keystone Bouchard
Lainy Voom
Laukosargas Svarog
Launa Fauna
Lyra Muse
Michi Lumen
Mistress Midnight
Moo Money
MSGiro Grosso
Nada Epoch
Nephilaine and Neil
    Protagonist

Nylon Pinkney
Oneironaut Escher
Ordinal Malaprop
Pancake Stryker
Pierce Portocarrero
Pirate Cotton
qDot Bunnyhug
Robbie Dingo
Satchmo Prototype
Seifert Suface
SignpostMarv Martin
Slade Onizuka
Snakekiss Noir
Starax Statosky
Sue Stonebender
Sukkubus Phaeton
Surina Skallagrimson
Talila Liu
Tao Takashi
Tasrill Sieyes
Timeless Prototype
Tom Bukowski
Torley Linden, née
    Torgeson
Torrid Midnight
Tripper Tapioca
Washu Zebrastripe
Yossarian Seattle

Index